P9-DEM-383

WATCHDOG

WATCHDOG

**HOW PROTECTING CONSUMERS CAN
SAVE OUR FAMILIES, OUR ECONOMY,
AND OUR DEMOCRACY**

RICHARD CORDRAY

OXFORD
UNIVERSITY PRESS

OXFORD
UNIVERSITY PRESS

Oxford University Press is a department of the University of Oxford. It furthers
the University's objective of excellence in research, scholarship, and education
by publishing worldwide. Oxford is a registered trade mark of Oxford University
Press in the UK and certain other countries.

Published in the United States of America by Oxford University Press
198 Madison Avenue, New York, NY 10016, United States of America.

© Richard Cordray 2020

All rights reserved. No part of this publication may be reproduced, stored in
a retrieval system, or transmitted, in any form or by any means, without the
prior permission in writing of Oxford University Press, or as expressly permitted
by law, by license, or under terms agreed with the appropriate reproduction
rights organization. Inquiries concerning reproduction outside the scope of the
above should be sent to the Rights Department, Oxford University Press, at the
address above.

You must not circulate this work in any other form
and you must impose this same condition on any acquirer.

Library of Congress Cataloging-in-Publication Data
Names: Cordray, Richard, author.
Title: Watchdog : how protecting consumers can save our families,
our economy, and our democracy / Richard Cordray.
Description: New York, NY : Oxford University Press, [2020] | Includes index. |
Identifiers: LCCN 2019042464 (print) | LCCN 2019042465 (ebook) |
ISBN 9780197502990 (hardback) | ISBN 9780197503003 (updf) |
ISBN 9780197503010 (epub) | ISBN 9780197508251 (online)
Subjects: LCSH: United States. Consumer Financial Protection Bureau. |
Financial services industry—Government policy—United States. |
Consumer protection—Government policy—United States.
Classification: LCC HG181 .C69 2020 (print) | LCC HG181 (ebook) |
DDC 381.3/40973—dc23
LC record available at https://lccn.loc.gov/2019042464
LC ebook record available at https://lccn.loc.gov/2019042465

1 3 5 7 9 8 6 4 2

Printed by LSC Communications, United States of America

CONTENTS

FOREWORD BY SENATOR
ELIZABETH WARREN

As the country struggled out of the Great Depression, the collapse of thousands of banks loomed large. Bank regulators were installed, and banks were given access to federal guaranties so that no family would lose money they deposited. Banks steadied out, making profits year after year by taking in those deposits and lending out that money for a little higher price—steady, not extraordinary, profits.

By the 1970s big banks and corporate executives were itchy for something bigger and more daring. They hatched a plan that was sinister, but simple: buy Washington. Shake off the regulators and federal laws that hemmed in their business model. Over time, they flooded the political system with money and deployed lobbyists across Capitol Hill. One tax loophole led to another; one rule rollback led to the next. The banks loaded up on ever more complex products that produced greater profits—and greater risks—all while hanging on to their federal guaranties. By the early 2000s, the corporate executives on Wall Street were calling the shots while bank regulators and elected representatives sat on their hands and looked the other way.

In 2008, our economy finally snapped under the weight of greed and corruption bearing down on Washington. If only the corporate executives and their investors had paid a price, that might have been the end of the story—a cautionary tale about risk. But this crash crushed millions of people, costing them their homes, their savings, their jobs. And then, as if to rub salt in the wound, they were forced to watch as our government bailed out the enormous banks and lavishly paid executives who had ruined their lives.

The Great Recession hit everyone hard, but the people with the smallest economic reserves and least political clout took a punch straight to the face. The blow was devastating for working families, seniors, communities of color, and veterans. It was the worst recession since the Great Depression.

I'd seen this disaster coming for years. I told anyone who would listen that our economy was being driven to the brink, but it felt like I was screaming into a void. I talked about the dangers of subprime loans, the rising foreclosure rates, the middle-class families struggling to make ends meet and relying more and more on debt. But the people in power would not listen.

In the wake of the financial crisis, Democrats took a stand. Never again would Wall Street trample on working families without consequence. Never again would giant financial institutions be given license to boost their profits by cheating hard-working Americans. Never again would the self-proclaimed financial wizards be allowed to run over the cops on the beat. The tool to make sure that Never Again was truly Never Again was an idea I'd developed for a real watchdog.

The concept was simple: create an entirely new agency, one whose purpose would be to rein in the financial institutions that were taking advantage of families across the country. The agency would have the power to oversee and regulate all consumer lending—credit cards, mortgages, student loans, payday lending, car loans. It would be a tough watchdog whose sole mission would be to look out for the interests of families.

The idea was bigger than a single new law or a complex regulation—it was about changing the structure of consumer credit regulation. More than a dozen federal laws already addressed issues involving consumer credit, but the laws were tangled and responsibility for enforcing these laws was spread out among seven—seven!—different federal agencies. Worse yet, each of those agencies had some other first priority, like making sure the banking system was stable or administering housing policy. Not a single one of those agencies had as its primary job protecting consumers from dangerous credit products—not one—and the big banks had already perfected the art of circumventing new laws.

We needed an agency—one agency—that would be a cop on the beat every day, watching what the big banks were up to, writing new rules when needed, and enforcing those rules. President Obama agreed, and he began fighting to create the Consumer Financial Protection Bureau (CFPB).

The big banks fought the idea of a cop on the beat. The moment the CFPB hit the airwaves, the political knives were out. Big financial institutions spent millions in a massive lobbying campaign to try to kill or weaken the bill to create the CFPB. Lobbying was nonstop. Members of Congress were overwhelmed. But we got organized, we built a grassroots movement, and, nevertheless, we persisted.

Persistence paid off. More than a year after President Obama first called for the agency, he had the chance to sign it into law. A few weeks later, he called me to help set up this new agency. I needed help, so I called Rich Cordray.

Rich was the perfect choice to help set up the new agency. He understood what was at stake for American families. First as treasurer, then as attorney general of Ohio, he'd had extensive experience going toe to toe with financial institutions. He would come to Washington to fight for working families.

And that's exactly what he did for six years as the founding director of the CFPB. Rich took on financial giants like Wells Fargo, JPMorgan Chase, Citibank, and Bank of America. He took on for-profit college chains like Corinthian and Bridgepoint. He tracked down cheaters, big and small. He was quiet, steady, and relentless.

Today, because of my friend Rich's courage and tenacity, Wall Street has been forced to return more than $12 billion back to the people they cheated.

Watchdog is the harrowing story of how the Consumer Financial Protection Bureau grew up and became a major force for fairness in the marketplace. Rich shows what a difference good government can make for millions of Americans. In my book, *A Fighting Chance*, I began to tell this story, and now Rich has picked up where I left off, describing how the bureau gained momentum and secured its future by helping out Americans every day.

Along the way, he describes in vivid detail the tough fights the Consumer Bureau took on and what it meant for every household in America.

At a deeper level, *Watchdog* is the story of how we can make government work for the people, even in the face of powerful industries and billionaires that spend huge amounts of money to wield power and influence in Washington. The story of the Consumer Bureau is proof that strength of conviction can lead to strength of action and that we can deliver the kind of big structural change that gives people a fighting chance to build more secure lives, thrive, and protect the ones they love.

PREFACE

Consumers—individual Americans and their families—spend far more every year than businesses and the government combined. Just as the people rule in a democracy, consumers form the backbone of a free market economy. But consumers are fragmented as a group, and on their own, individual consumers have little clout against large corporations, especially the big banks and financial companies. This imbalance was painfully evident during America's first century, as households bore the brunt of a boom-and-bust economy that produced widespread suffering amidst general conditions of rising prosperity. Our government did little to prevent or address these ruinous panics—with no consistent monetary or fiscal policy and no societal safety net—leaving workers, seniors, veterans, and sometimes whole communities to founder in the random cruelty of economic reversals. The Great Depression was the worst of these frequent collapses, but many sharp setbacks preceded it.

In that era, consumers had few legal protections. They were regularly cheated in the marketplace: in the weighing and measuring of goods; by the sale of adulterated foods and worthless medicines; and through the calamitous price spikes imposed by financial trusts, railroads, and monopolists that wielded oppressive market power. As our government began to devise ways to combat these problems, corporate interests denounced the new measures as radical, claiming they would suffocate businesses and economic growth. Yet the public outcry for relief sprang from a powerful principle: the economic marketplace works only if it is competitive and honest. Calls to reform the market—to stop fraud and break up monopolies—fueled the Progressive movement and paved the way for the New Deal to support and uplift the broad mass of the people.

Nonetheless, the power of the financial companies, with their unmatched capacity to strain the economic system, remained largely intact. Even as our government passed new laws and regulations to address some of the worst abuses, in the last half-century the financial industry has embarked on a remarkable period of growth, entrenching its power throughout the economy and securing enormous influence over the levers of government in Washington. Over this period, regulators and lawmakers became more permissive, allowing financial companies to create and sell products that were highly profitable, but increasingly complex and risky.

In 2008, these excesses collapsed the housing market and then the entire economy. Once again, individual Americans, their families, and their communities bore the brunt of the damage. Millions of people lost their homes, millions more lost their jobs, and entire communities sank into despair. The breadth and magnitude of the suffering drove Congress to enact strong new financial reforms, including the Consumer Financial Protection Bureau (CFPB), which has a single mission: to protect consumers and the financial marketplace from fraud and abuse. At the end of 2010, I was tapped to help build and then ultimately lead the new bureau. Over the next seven years, I saw the worst of what financial predators can do, but also the best of what government can do when it stands on the side of everyday Americans. This book tells my story of how we built the CFPB, what it accomplished, and why its work is and will continue to be vitally important.

To explain the "why," the book describes the kinds of problems people face in the financial marketplace, and how the bureau's expertise and clout could make a crucial difference in solving those problems. Some of the stories come from people who told me personally what happened to them, some from consumers who asked the bureau for help, and some from people who came to work at the bureau because of what they saw happen to their friends or families. Throughout the book, I've changed the names in many of the stories to protect people's anonymity, and I've combined the details in some of the stories for ease of presentation.

The people I worked with at the CFPB were extraordinary and dedicated public servants. The assistants and advisers in our front office were an enormous help to me personally in leading the bureau, and they know the gratitude I feel to each of them. I wish it were possible to describe more fully how much I appreciate the ability, energy, and compassion that every one of my colleagues gave to building the bureau and carrying out its mission of supporting and protecting consumers. They were indeed, as Tennyson said, made of "one equal temper of heroic hearts" and "strong in will. To strive, to seek, to find, and not to yield."

My deepest thanks go to my wife, Peggy, and our twins, Holly and Danny, who gave me their loving support throughout. And special thanks to my friend Elizabeth Warren, who conceived of the Consumer Bureau, recruited me to it, and has always been our formidable champion at every turn. Barney Frank and Chris Dodd crafted a practical statute that gave us all the authority we needed to protect consumers against fraud and abuse. Finally, I owe an enormous debt to President Barack Obama, who believed in the bureau and fought for it to be "America's consumer watchdog."

Grove City, Ohio
October 2019

PART I

THE CASE FOR A CONSUMER WATCHDOG

1

CONSUMERS AND PREDATORS

Day in and day out, across the country, we all face issues, large and small, with credit cards, mortgages, car loans, student loans, or other types of household credit. When we are cheated or mistreated, all too often we find ourselves hitting a brick wall with the big financial companies. It can happen to any of us, and we have all seen it happen to someone we know, like a sister or brother, mother or father, son or daughter, friend or colleague. People often do not know how best to manage their household finances, and too many lenders are willing to exploit them for financial gain. We are fed up with being run over by big corporations, and few among us have the resources or the expertise to fight back on our own. As we try to deal with these frustrations, we sometimes find ourselves wondering: Can anything meaningful or lasting be done about it?

That is the basic mission of the Consumer Financial Protection Bureau (CFPB), a new federal agency created in 2010 to support and protect people who have problems in the financial marketplace. The bureau represents an experiment in whether it is possible to make our government work for all the people, even against some of the most entrenched interests in our society, such as the powerful financial industry lobby. This book presents a front-row account of how a dedicated corps of people applied the powers of our government to help millions of Americans cope with their everyday problems of household finance.

Congress designed the CFPB as a buttress for the financial marketplace, not as an antagonist. The bureau's mission is to support and protect consumers in positive and empowering ways, not in paternalistic or restrictive ways. When people can make informed choices, markets provide individual opportunity, enhanced well-being, and greater freedom. But for the market to work, both companies and consumers must follow the rules. They must not lie, cheat, or steal. And consumers must take responsibility for the decisions they make and the consequences that follow. Before making a purchase or taking out a loan, they need to compare products, know what they can afford, and make sustainable choices.

Yet this equation only works if people are in position to make informed choices. Over time, this ideal has not been achieved in consumer financial markets. With products from credit cards to mortgages, companies command exclusive power to write the contracts, whose terms are not negotiated with consumers on an equal footing. These agreements are impenetrably complex, with obscure terms written in dense legalese that slant heavily in favor of the company, sometimes even giving the company the right to make unilateral changes.[1] People should not have to consult a lawyer to take out a credit card or learn its basic terms. But as many of these agreements ballooned to thirty pages of fine print, incomprehension became the norm. The markets became imbalanced, as people could no longer reliably compare products, shop for the best deal, or in some situations even recognize when they were exceeding their own limits. This imbalance also opened the door wide to predators, who were able to deceive and defraud people with less risk of being held to account. When the consumer finance markets stopped working for consumers, the stage was set for the dysfunctional mortgage market to blow up the entire economy, as it did in 2008. The bureau was put in place not to give consumers a free pass, but to rebalance the marketplace and stand up for people who are harmed by unfair, deceptive, and fraudulent tactics—practices that undermine markets to the point where they do not operate properly.[2]

The central story of the CFPB, though, is really the story not of impersonal markets, but of individual Americans. This book is about consumers—all of us. Legions of stories make clear how easy it is for good people to fall into bad situations, and how often they encounter callous indifference or even intentional predatory behavior when they try to fix the problem. The CFPB's job was to use its tools and resources to help people address these problems.

CREDIT CARD TROUBLES

Take Mary, for example. Over the years, as she accumulated several credit cards, she learned to juggle the balances and to seek out promotional offers that allowed her to transfer her balances to new cards that temporarily offered lower interest rates. But sometimes her careful arrangements were upset when the interest rate on one card or another spiked unexpectedly. She did not fully understand why that happened, but the explanation lay deep in the fine print, where the companies gave themselves the benefit of "universal default." Under this practice, the credit card companies asserted the power to increase her interest rate at any time, even on existing balances for purchases she had already made, if she was late on any payment to anyone else. Mary thought that seemed unfair, since she had made each of her credit card purchases while relying on the interest rate that she knew she was paying at the time. But the companies made it clear that there was nothing she could do about it.

Jeremy encountered a different problem after he bought a big-screen television. The cashier at the store talked him into getting a new credit card to make the purchase, which would allow him to make no down payment on the TV and to pay 0% interest for the first year. That sounded like a smart option, so Jeremy agreed. Over the course of the year, he went back to the store and used the credit card to make some other purchases. All the while, he was diligently making each of his payments on the TV so he would continue to qualify for the 0% interest rate. But at the end of the year, he was surprised and angry to learn that because he had a remaining balance—for the other purchases that had nothing to do with the TV—the contract allowed the store to charge him, retroactively, a high rate of interest on the entire cost of the TV as well.

These are situations anyone with a credit card could encounter. This product, which seems so simple on its face, has become an easy and useful payment mechanism for people all over the world. But it comes at quite a cost for many consumers. Although estimates vary, the average American household with ongoing credit card debt owes around $7,000, accumulating at a typical interest rate of over 16%, which means that they pay more than $1,100 per year just in credit card interest alone.[3] And as we can see from Mary and Jeremy, there are many situations where even credit card users who are trying hard to be careful can be caught out—by the complexity of the contract terms, by unexpected charges, or by mistakes that the companies may make in handling their accounts. When problems arise, if people take the trouble to go to the credit card companies with their complaints, they never know what to expect. With some problems, they may find a customer service representative who will help them get relief. But with many problems, people are left frustrated, unable to get any satisfactory resolution. And most of the time, they find that the unwelcome explanation lies buried somewhere in the fine print of their contract.

Student Loan Debt

Student loan debt is soaring. The cost of college has outstripped even the cost of health care as the fastest-rising expense that American families now face. Just a few years ago, the total amount of unpaid student loan debt first surpassed $1 trillion. Today, it stands at $1.6 trillion and is still mounting. We now have forty-four million borrowers who carry an average loan balance of over $35,000 apiece. Efforts to cope with the debt can involve not only the students but also their parents and even their grandparents.[4] And they encounter many problems that just make things worse.

Consider a typical student loan borrower like Joan. Over four years, she accumulated about $42,000 in student loan debt to earn her degree in education. Toward the end of college, she began to fret about how she would manage to repay her loans, which would become due after she graduated. She had taken out both federal and private student loans, which made things complicated. She would be dealing with three different loan servicers, all pushing to get paid ahead of the others and ahead of her other financial obligations. Joan felt fortunate that she had her degree and had fulfilled her childhood dream of becoming a teacher, but the strain of dealing with the loan collectors was taking its toll. The interest rates on the private student loans were high, so she was not able to pay them down very quickly. She also discovered that the loan servicer was directing some of her payments to the lower-interest loan, when she had intended first to pay down her more expensive loan, and she never did get that problem reliably straightened out.

She began receiving phone calls insisting that she pay more on the private student loans and threatening to garnish her wages. At the same time, Joan also was paying on her federal student loans. Eventually she learned about a federal income-based repayment option, which allowed her to lower her monthly payments and helped her stay afloat—an option that her loan servicer had mistakenly told her in the past she did not qualify for. But nothing could be done about the previous years, when she had been paying more and postponing other bills, which had damaged her credit score.

Or consider the case of Rodney. He served in the US Army for seven years, reaching the rank of corporal, and upon his honorable discharge he was entitled to educational benefits under the GI Bill. He suddenly found himself bombarded with offers to attend various for-profit schools. They touted their high graduation rates and job placement rates, and they were willing to let him take his classes online. Since Rodney was not certain where he wanted to settle down for the next few years, that flexibility sounded good and he signed up to pursue a health care degree at one of the schools in a large for-profit chain. The company that ran the schools seemed stable, as it operated more than a hundred campuses in the United States and Canada. It even used military seals in its advertisements. The tuition was high, but the company also offered "gap loans" to help students cover the difference between their educational costs and all other sources of financial aid.

Knowing that students who fell behind on their gap loans were barred from accessing courses until they caught up on their payments, Rodney was careful to stay current. But after he had completed eighteen months of schooling, he learned that the for-profit company had been operating illegally and committing rampant fraud. A state and federal investigation found that the company had misrepresented its graduation and job placement rates, misstated the terms of its gap loans, and misled students about whether they would qualify to be certified for certain jobs. Rodney knew nothing about any of this, but he had squandered almost two years of his GI benefits pursuing a degree that would not certify him for the job he had hoped for, and he still owed money on his gap loans. He was also told that his class credits might not transfer anywhere else. In the military, the path forward had always been straight and clear, but now he did not know what he was going to do.

The weight and anxiety of student loans not only take a huge emotional toll but also hold young people back, making them less willing to take risks, such as switching jobs or professions, moving to a new place, or starting a business rather than earning a steady paycheck. And the overall effects are substantial enough that they affect the broader economy as well. As the burden of their student loans causes people to wait longer before deciding to form a new household or buy a home, the domino effect is dragging down the housing market, one of the cornerstones of economic growth.[5] And the kinds of problems that individual consumers like Joan and Rodney face, where they cannot find ways to get reliable help, no doubt make the overall situation even worse.

Auto Lending Issues

When sales representatives see any prospective customer walk through the door of an auto dealership, they immediately begin to size him or her up. They know the customer tends to focus on two things: the vehicle itself and the price. But the sales reps are keenly aware that they can adjust multiple levers—not just the vehicle price but also the price of any trade-in, add-on products, warranties, the interest rate of any loan used to finance the transaction, and the length of the loan term—to make their targeted profit. With the customer concentrating on the vehicle price, it is all too easy to hide the true cost in the complexity of the financing, at least until the paperwork has been signed.

Ari, for example, was a young soldier training to deploy to Iraq who bought a used Dodge Ram truck. Like many young men and women who leave home for the first time when they enter the military, he had his heart set on buying his first set of wheels. Many predatory companies locate near military bases specifically to finance high-cost purchases for young people known to have a guaranteed paycheck from the US government; some companies are so bad that they end up getting "blacklisted" by the base commander. But it is hard to keep up with them all. Ari's military base was surrounded by lenders that financed electronics, cars, and other products. One of them advertised the "U.S. MILES" program to finance the sale of cars and trucks to military customers. By the time Ari walked out the door, he was saddled with a subprime auto loan costing 70% of his take-home pay, including undisclosed fees and misleading add-on services. The loan terms required repayment through the Pentagon's allotment system, meaning the lenders always got their money before it ever reached his bank account. Even if Ari wanted to prioritize some other payment that he owed that month, he had surrendered the freedom to do that. The terms of that single purchase would be enough to undermine his finances for years. When he was deployed, his father took over his financial affairs and tried to raise concerns, but he was told nothing would or could be done, since Ari had signed the contract.

Even where financing companies and auto dealerships are not targeting a specific set of consumers, the overall setup—with salespeople working on commission and having multiple levers with which to obscure the true price—still produces tremendous opportunity and incentive to take advantage of customers. For a poor or inexperienced negotiator, it can be open season. As each new customer arrives, the sales rep is assessing whether he or she is a good negotiator, sometimes based on visual clues such as race or gender or ethnic background. It is illegal under the fair lending laws to discriminate in extending credit on any of these bases, whether by refusing to make a loan or by offering it on less favorable terms.[6] In many instances, however, none of this is explicit, and the salespeople may not even consciously realize what they are doing.

The problem is that the customers have no way of knowing this is happening either. Unless they somehow come to see that they are being offered higher rates or prices than they should be—with no objective benchmark available to gauge what those charges "should be"—they may never realize that they were victims of unlawful discrimination at all. That was the case with Ramon. When he bought a new car, he was offered a loan rate that was 3% higher than he could have qualified for. He was happy with the price of the car, and he did not understand that he was being swindled on the interest rate. Instead, he assumed that he was being offered the same rate that anyone else with the same credit score would have been offered. He ended up paying the excess amount for all six years that he owned the car. But unless someone was able to analyze the statistical patterns of the loans being made, it would never become clear that Ramon and others in his ethnic group were being treated differently from other customers with a similar credit rating.

DEBT COLLECTION ABUSES

Debt collection is part of every consumer finance market. Everyone who lends money must face the possibility of not getting repaid. And it is a basic principle that people who owe money bear the responsibility to pay their debts. But even when they cannot do so, the law entitles them to be treated with dignity and respect.[7] Many debtors, however, are relentlessly harassed and mistreated.

Donna, for example, owed $900 on an overdue car repair bill. She had been laid off work for several months, leaving her strapped and unable to pay it off. Soon she was receiving twenty or more calls per day, sometimes within minutes of one another, demanding payment. The calls started early in the morning and continued until late at night and were often filled with abusive language. The debt collectors seemed to be trying to wear her down so she would pay the debt just to make the calls stop. After she got another job, they started calling her at her workplace, where she was not allowed to receive personal calls at the risk of being fired. By reviewing her social media, they located some of her friends and family members and started calling them too, leaving messages with personal information about the debt she owed on their answering machines. Obviously, they were counting on embarrassing her to get her to pay. Each of these tactics is illegal, but most people are not aware of that and do not know what they can do to protect themselves.

Sometimes debt collectors make mistakes, have bad information, or are engaged in fraud themselves. Large sets of debts are often sold by the original creditor to a debt collector, which collects what it can and then might sell off the rest of the unpaid debts to yet another collector. As debts pass from company to company, the information can become garbled, and the absence of any relationship between the collector and the supposed debtor makes any misunderstandings nearly impossible to sort out. Noelle's elderly mother began getting calls claiming that she owed more than $10,000 in condo association fees. She had owed this debt at one time, but later she had paid it off and still had the receipts to prove it. Yet when she sent copies of the papers to the debt collector, they did not respond, and the calls demanding payment kept coming.

Jeffrey was a victim of fraud. A former employer had stolen his Social Security number and used it to open a credit card in Jeffrey's name, racking up thousands of dollars in charges. Over months of tedious and repetitive phone calls, Jeffrey spoke to dozens of customer representatives at the credit card company, but they refused to erase the debt, which they continued to hold him responsible for. It also showed up on his credit report, which ruined his credit. Jeffrey later noticed that new fees were being added to the amount of the debt. When he asked about it, he was told these were standard fees to cover collection costs. Jeffrey didn't know what he could do about it—the debts were still being reported and they prevented him from being able to qualify for credit to borrow any money.[8]

In recent decades, with computerized databases, a gigantic market has grown up around the specialty of debt collection. It is estimated that seventy million people are contacted each year by a creditor or a collector seeking to collect a debt, which means debt collection likely touches just about every other household in America. The anxiety most people feel about owing money is compounded by the misery that is doled out by many collectors. Just about anyone can open a debt collection agency, so thousands of companies operate in this fragmented market. Some are careful about observing the boundaries of the law, but many others are not. The incentives for good behavior are weak because many collectors have no ongoing relationship with the people they are targeting, and they only get paid if they manage to collect.

CREDIT REPORTING PROBLEMS

Every consumer's financial history is closely tracked by companies whose entire business is devoted to collecting and sharing that sensitive data. The three biggest companies in this market—Equifax, Experian, and TransUnion—maintain credit files on approximately two hundred million Americans. Errors contained in the files can block people from accessing credit of any kind, such as a mortgage or a credit card or a car loan. Even if they can still access credit, it may cost more because their reports wrongly identify them as a greater credit risk than they truly are. People are affected in this way constantly, and most do not even know it.[9]

Take Kim, who applied for a mortgage and was denied. When she asked why, she was told that she had problems with her credit. She struggled to pursue the matter with the credit reporting companies, and eventually learned that her credit files reflected a foreclosure and a bankruptcy. That was wrong, as she had never owned a home. The credit reporting company had mixed up her financial information with another woman who had the same first and last name. After months of going back and forth and providing her financial records, she was at her wits' end, still unable to correct the problem and get her life moving forward by buying a home.

Phyllis also needed a loan and was denied based on an error, but in her case the error originated with a creditor, not the credit reporting company itself. A credit card company had reported that she still owed them about $250, even though she had stopped using the card and closed the account years earlier. When she disputed the matter, she provided the credit reporting company with all the information to prove her case. But the credit reporting company merely sent her claim back to the credit card company, which continued to insist that its original information was correct. The credit reporting company refused to overrule the credit card company, which was one of its regular customers for buying and selling consumer data, so Phyllis was unable to get her file corrected.

Like forty-three million other Americans, Stan had some unpaid medical debt. Health insurance coverage, co-payments, and office visits often leave patients uncertain what they are supposed to pay and what their health insurance is paying. Sometimes they are caught in a dispute between health insurers over who will pay which parts of a bill. Many doctors' offices send unpaid debts out for collection before the insurance companies have even decided which claims to pay and which claims to deny. Stan had three unpaid medical debts on his credit report, two of which he had expected his insurance company to pay; the third was a co-pay that he thought his doctor's office had waived.[10] But rather than continue to dispute the charges in a hassle-filled process that was already taking months, Stan gave in and paid them off just to clear up his credit report and qualify for the auto loan he urgently needed.

Payday Loan Debt Traps

Short-term consumer loans of one form or another have been around for over a century. But in the last twenty years, a new type of market has developed in over thirty states, where lenders are permitted to offer high-cost payday loans with annualized interest rates of 390% or more (the other states do not allow loans at such high rates). Many consumers take out such loans intending to cover a shortfall for just a brief period, and then find that they are unable to pay them off right away and get stuck with them for a much longer time.

Consider Ellen's predicament. Lacking any savings, she had lost her job and needed help paying her rent. It was easy to borrow money from one of the payday loan outlets in her neighborhood, but when it came due two weeks later, she was unable to pay back the entire loan along with the high fees. A clerk at the payday loan store told her she could simply pay the fees and roll over the balance for another two weeks. She was relieved that they seemed to be so understanding, and she ended up doing that six times. She later took out a second loan to help manage the costs of the first loan. All in all, she borrowed $1,000, but even after she had paid back $1,700, she still was carrying a growing balance on the second loan.

Bart was also desperate for cash, so he decided to go online and search for a loan. He found many offerings available, including some from Indian tribal lenders and others from sources outside the United States. He agreed to take out a $500 loan and a $300 loan, each of which carried a 575% annual interest rate. Both loans also required Bart to authorize the lenders to debit the payments directly from his bank account. Over the next several months, he could not keep up with the amounts due and the extra fees, so he kept rolling over the growing balance. In time, he had repaid the full amount of each loan, but he still owed more than he had borrowed to begin with. After agonizing discussions with a lawyer, he concluded that his only recourse was to close his bank account and declare bankruptcy, which forced him into a supervised sale of the family's few remaining assets, left him unable to qualify for a bank account, and blocked his access to credit for ten years. He later learned that because these online loans were prohibited in his home state (which capped the interest rate he could be charged), he had been under no legal obligation to repay them.

Defenders of payday loans often justify them as providing consumers with needed access to credit. But this kind of high-cost credit, which often ensnares consumers in a persistent "debt trap," leaves many people worse off. The loans are marketed as short-term credit, and some people manage to get in and out of them without lasting damage, but the average borrower winds up in debt for five months each year. Payday lenders make millions of loans every year, and well over half of those loans are rollovers that go to existing customers who are using them to make payments they already owe on their previous payday loans. As one former executive reportedly said, "The model is designed to print money"—and much of it is extracted from consumers living at the margin.[11]

The Importance of Consumer Finance

Stories like these can be found everywhere. The financial crisis of 2008 brought things to a head, but consumers routinely get hurt or exploited. That was true before the crisis and it remains true today, as these problems are an everyday part of people's lives. Yet consumers who are cheated or treated unfairly often are helpless to address these problems with large financial companies. Big companies deal with problems in high volume and at great scale; they are less concerned with, and less effective at, taking the time and making the effort to work through discrete problems for dissatisfied individuals. Consumers often find that they are ignored and frustrated, knowing through bitter experience that they generally get the runaround if they try to raise their concerns. For those who do take the initiative to speak up, after they are stymied once or twice, they usually give up, leaving them with no recourse but to absorb the unexpected charges, fraud, or other abuses.

These concerns are made worse by the hard reality that financial problems often have a snowball effect. Rodney, who used his GI benefits and took out gap loans at a for-profit college that defrauded him, no longer had the money to get his degree, which could restrict his job opportunities and upward mobility throughout his career. Kim, who was denied a mortgage because the credit reporting company mixed up her financial information with someone else, was unable to buy a house, which locked her into paying rent rather than building equity in a home, setting back her plans to move her children into a better school district and build momentum toward saving for retirement. As Donna was hounded by debt collectors, she had to deal with their constant unpleasantness, her fear of losing her new job, and all the other embarrassment they caused her. Bart, whose payday loan ultimately led him to file bankruptcy, struggled with feelings of failure and the crippling effects of depression. And inevitably each of their families was deeply affected as well.

One of the root causes of these problems is that people receive very little instruction about financial matters, leaving most consumers ill-equipped to handle their affairs.[12] Consumer finance is vital to almost every American, and our market economy is built around personal responsibility. Yet this gap in consumer education remains, and it hinders people from leading satisfying and productive lives. People who are constantly in financial trouble or who go through the tribulations of filing bankruptcy cannot function at their best and find it much harder to attain a sense of well-being.

This starts with our young people. As they face the transition from being a dependent to going out "on their own," they are expected to assume complete responsibility for their finances. Yet many young people are not well prepared to do that. Parents are often uncomfortable talking about finances, giving their children little if any guidance at home, and surprisingly few students receive any meaningful training in household finance in school. As they become adults, this lack of direction causes them to make mistakes that could easily be avoided. Running up debts on a credit card, borrowing at the teaser rate to buy a new car, or getting in the habit of falling behind in paying bills can dig a hole that is hard to escape, and it may set patterns that last a lifetime. Even those who are focused on improving their financial future through higher education or vocational training may be piling up substantial debts that take decades to pay off.

And the troubles that young adults face do not get any easier with the passage of time. Left to bounce around in the so-called school of hard knocks, older consumers have more experience but rarely more know-how in handling their financial issues. Alarmingly, more than half of Americans live from paycheck to paycheck, with little or no cushion to handle the shock of either an unexpected shortfall or an unexpected expense.[13] As they face their regular bills, many find that they have more "month than money," and their slim margin for error exerts constant daily pressure to handle everything just right. In a time of rampant income inequality and growing wealth inequality, the squeeze felt by most consumers is becoming more and more intense.

In addition, lack of financial savvy makes consumers highly vulnerable to predators. Many financial scams take advantage of people's inexperience with major transactions and their willingness to believe that the person on the other side of the counter (or the computer screen) has their best interests at heart. All too often, this misplaced trust leads to lasting regrets. An ever-changing variety of predatory schemes home in on the elderly, many of whom live alone and in isolation but may have access to funds that scammers aggressively target by phone, by mail, and on the internet. And the financial companies—some honest, some crooked—are creating more complicated loan products, with more onerous provisions, such as the "universal default" term that caused Mary's interest rate to spike on all her credit cards, for purchases past and future, when she missed a payment on any single one of her accounts.

These tragic events permeate every community in America. The bottom line in our free-market economy is that each of us is on our own, and nobody is truly responsible for looking out for you other than yourself. So what, if anything, can be done to address these concerns? With individual consumers ranged against the big financial companies or financial predators, it usually turns out not to be a fair fight. Consumers need a more level playing field, which means they need to have someone looking out for their interests. The challenge lies in figuring out how to make that happen.

THE RISE OF THE
FINANCIAL CONSUMER

Big changes in our economy magnify the challenges facing consumers. Our grandparents generally had less credit available to them—some basic mortgage products, a few in-store cards with very limited credit, and perhaps an auto loan. Many who grew up during the Depression were very reluctant to borrow money at all. Credit reporting and debt collection were mostly local, which made lenders uncomfortable about extending themselves too far beyond nearby communities. The few choices offered to consumers were safer and more straightforward. People lacked the opportunities that credit can provide, but they were much less likely to get into serious financial trouble by racking up consumer debt. And the kind of trouble we are talking about is not simply personal—the total accumulation of consumer debt can have consequences not only for our own fortunes but also for others in the community and for our economy as a whole.

THE EXPANDING REALM OF CONSUMER FINANCE

In 1962, President Kennedy gave a notable speech to Congress, calling for a Consumer Bill of Rights. Mostly he talked about buying physical items, like food or appliances or other things that improve our quality of life. But he also made a passing observation about the growing importance of consumer finance, pointing out that US consumer debt had tripled in the past decade, to over $200 billion. In the flash of a moment, he touched on something that was only at its threshold—the growing availability of consumer credit on a mass scale. In the years since, US consumer debt has exploded to more than $13.8 trillion.[1] On average, each American carried consumer debt of about $500 in the era just after World War II; today, that figure is over $40,000 per person. Even when corrected for inflation, that expansion represents a transformative change in people's lives. Virtually every purchase we make—every product we buy, every service we choose—now carries with it the need to consider the ramifications of credit issues and methods of financing.

Over the last fifty years, this change in the economy has proceeded rapidly. The huge expansion in household credit was still negligible at the time President Kennedy spoke, but it rose to 68% of disposable income by 1980 and all the way to 128% of disposable income by 2007, on the eve of the financial crash.[2] And the nature of the credit available to consumers has become considerably more elaborate. Mortgage loans have developed complex and unusual features. Credit cards have been extended to more people using computer algorithms based on records of individual credit history that affect pricing and other terms and conditions. Other types of consumer loans, including auto loans and leases and new forms of payday loans, have become accessible to virtually all consumers. Credit reporting and debt collection are now computerized, and they increasingly have been nationalized in highly sophisticated operations.

The onslaught of available credit has not been matched by greater comprehension on the part of consumers, however, which spells trouble for many Americans. The details often are unfamiliar, and making comparisons among financial products may not be easy, exposing people to new hazards. The fact that credit is now a central part of consumer life also makes things harder in another way. With any purchase that involves credit—and many more now do—the consumer must consider two things simultaneously. One is the physical purchase, which requires attention to what product to buy, its price, and its quality. The other is the choice of what financial product to use, which requires attention to the nature of the credit instrument, its interest rate, payments over time, and many terms that make up the *financial* deal. Consider buying a car, for example. Survey research shows that people are distracted and often exhausted with the simultaneous process of shopping for a car while also shopping for an auto loan. They may take great care in selecting the type of car they want, then fall well short in securing the best loan to finance it—sometimes because of their own limitations and sometimes because they are victims of predatory behavior.

Mortgages and Consumers

Nowhere are these trends more evident than in the mortgage market. People go to great lengths to find the exact home that they want—closely considering its location in a desirable neighborhood and school district, its size and amenities, and its cost. Yet they often fail to secure the best deal on the mortgage loan that is essential to purchase their new home, and often they do not even understand all its terms or the risks they may pose.

That remains true today, though the problem was especially severe in the years leading up to the financial crisis. Some mortgage products became fantastically complicated in that era—teaser-rate mortgages, variable-rate mortgages, and negative-amortizing mortgages, to name a few. The lenders had so much confidence in the stability of housing values that they often did not review the income or assets of borrowers, counting on their ability to sell the home and recoup the value of the loan if the borrower later defaulted. A revealing nickname for these so-called NINJA loans—No Income, No Job, No Assets—shows the casual approach many lenders were taking to evaluating the largest financial transaction most consumers ever make. Not only did the exotic terms of these loans exceed the grasp of many consumers but also they outstripped the understanding of many Wall Street analysts and investors, who failed to see the growing perils and far-reaching consequences of rising defaults.

Countless consumers found themselves colliding with greedy lenders, with no help available to soften the blow. One such case involved Rafael, an immigrant from Lebanon. His wife was expecting a child, and they decided to buy a house. They found a real estate agent and signed a contract with a mortgage company. The contract was long and dense, but one of its terms required them to put up a contingency fee of $8,000 while they sought to qualify for a home loan. They did not realize that if they failed to qualify for the loan, they would end up losing their money, which is precisely what happened. They made many calls and sent many emails; their calls were all ignored, and their emails got no response. The money was gone, and they were simply the latest victims forced to learn an expensive lesson about sharp practices in the marketplace.

Susan had better luck, at least at first. She found a house she liked and was able to qualify for a mortgage to cover the remaining cost after making her down payment. The mortgage didn't come easily, given her finances, but by signing up for a low teaser rate over the first year, she could afford to make the initial monthly payments. For a year, everything was fine, but then the interest rate jumped from 2% to 12% and she could no longer make the payments on her income. Contrary to what she had been told, the value of her house did not appreciate over that time. When she fell behind, she reached out for help in seeking a loan modification, but her efforts to deal with the customer representatives were frustrating and ultimately fruitless, as they claimed to have lost her paperwork on several occasions. With no alternative to avoid going into default, she could see no way to save her home from foreclosure.

Russell had bad luck, though he never knew it. When he bought his first home, he applied for a mortgage through a broker. What he did not realize was that the lender could have qualified him for a mortgage at a 6% interest rate, but instead he was offered a 10% interest rate. He assumed this was the right amount, given his income and assets and level of risk, but in fact the broker and the lender were splitting the proceeds of the extra 4% between them, through a financial device known as a "yield spread premium."[3] For his entire work life, Russell paid the extra amount year in and year out, missing out on the savings that the lower rate would have provided for his family.

Helen and Nick had a joint income of about $60,000 per year. They decided to shop for a house, and the mortgage broker told them he could qualify them for a $400,000 loan. That seemed like a stretch, but the broker assured them that the real issue was just the value of the house. Because home values in that neighborhood were rising steadily, he advised them that they could always sell the house if they had trouble making the payments. The broker didn't even bother to verify their income or ask about any other assets they had. They struggled with the mortgage for several years, falling behind and then catching up again, until they simply could not manage it anymore. At that point, however, home values in their neighborhood had declined, and selling the house would not cover the remaining cost of the mortgage. They finally had to move out of their home, which went into fore-closure. But they still owed tens of thousands of dollars and were forced to declare bankruptcy, which ruined their credit for years and forced Nick to the verge of a nervous breakdown.

Paul and Beth were in a much better situation. They had bought a house three years earlier in a new subdivision, with an affordable mortgage that was within their means. The developer suffered some financial setbacks, had trouble finishing the subdivision, and had to extend more exotic variable-rate loans to the last few dozen homebuyers. Over the next two years, there was a flurry of foreclosures in the neighborhood. When Paul wanted to move to take a better-paying and more interesting job, he and Beth found that their home now was underwater, worth $80,000 less than they had paid for it. If they sold it, they would sustain a big loss on their mortgage. They could not afford to do that, so Paul had to forgo the new job and stay put.

Deborah was another homeowner who fell behind on her mortgage payments. She spent several months working with the customer represent-atives at her mortgage servicer, and they verbally agreed to work out a new payment schedule for her at a lower interest rate she could manage. When she received the paperwork, however, the loan modification they offered to save her home included more than $11,000 in additional fees, which she could not afford to pay. She called them again and again, trying to get some explanation of the extra fees, but nobody could provide one. They just told her she would have to pay it or lose her home.

Stories like these, and others just as poignant, could be heard in every community prior to the financial crisis. As we will see, new regulations put in place by the Consumer Financial Protection Bureau have cleaned up many of these damaging practices, but people still encounter stumbling blocks. The market for residential mortgages remains the biggest consumer finance market of them all, worth around $10 trillion. The process of qual-ifying for a home loan is hard to navigate, and the huge stack of paper that accompanies any real estate closing attests to the complexity. Even aside from some of the atrocious lending practices just described, many con-sumers have trouble grasping all the nuances of the transaction. They dread the kinds of surprises they might find at the closing table, where abrupt changes in fees and terms can leave them little leeway to reverse course. When things go wrong, some are lucky enough to find someone who can help them straighten out a problem, whether that happens to be the right person at the lending company or perhaps a real estate agent, an attorney, or a housing counselor. But during the financial crisis and since, many people are just stuck making the best of bad situations. They often fail, though, as they are regularly nicked for hundreds or even thousands of dollars in unexpected fees, and over the years so many have lost their homes to foreclosure.

MORTGAGE FAILURES AND THE FINANCIAL CRISIS

In some of these instances, poor decision making by consumers themselves is fully or partially to blame for what happened to them. As a result, some declare that nothing should be done to address these problems and people should be left to suffer the consequences of their own actions. "Live and learn" is the philosophy of rugged individualism. But the overall effects of these situations can go far beyond the circumstances of specific consumers. The problems people have, while serious enough at the individual level, are not solely their own. The aggregate effect of many loan failures becomes a systemic default, and at that point many other innocent bystanders wind up getting hurt. What we need is systemic *reform* to prevent and to treat these systemic problems. America has confronted such huge economic collapses twice in the past century.

In the 1930s, the Great Depression showed jagged cracks in the free-market economy, leading to what was known in the country as a "panic" but what economists refer to in more sterile terms as a "disequilibrium." More tangibly, it produced millions of people out of work, driven into poverty and ruin, experiencing searing hardships that would dominate their outlooks for their rest of their lives, with little or no safety net. Unlike in the economists' blackboard models, where such dislocations are the stuff of abstract equations that quickly self-correct, this one lasted almost a decade and stifled the economic prospects of a generation of Americans. In fact, it only ended after the ailing US economy was sharply disrupted by government intervention that placed it on a rigid war footing, with price controls and rationing of many consumer items for several years. Throughout those hard times, we held steadfastly to our capitalist system. Our leaders patched together responses to improve the workings of our market economy to preserve it rather than to discard it.[4] As the glaring deficiencies of Communist and Socialist systems around the world showed us over the rest of the century, they were right to do so.

The financial crisis of 2008, and the Great Recession that followed, created another watershed moment in the history of America's political economy. The massive disruption in people's lives began with irresponsible and predatory lending in the housing and mortgage markets. Eventually, it spread to the broader economy through fancy investment instruments on Wall Street. The inherent complexity of those instruments helped obscure how badly the terms and risks involved in underwriting home loans were deteriorating. A simple story illustrates the point. I met a woman in Washington who cleaned houses. She worked hard and had a deep pride in her ability to pay her own way. After years of living modestly, she decided to buy a new home, and she was offered a mortgage worth almost a half-million dollars. Not knowing any better, she made the natural but misguided assumption that the *lenders* knew what they were doing. She believed they would not have offered her a loan that she could not manage on her income, so she agreed to take out the mortgage. But a short time later, she had to face foreclosure and suffer the tragedy of declaring bankruptcy when the value of her home declined. That this could have happened seems absurd on its face, but it was repeated all over the country. Wall Street either missed or did not wish to see the red flags, blinded by the huge profits from deal fees on investment securities that were based on bundling together many of the bad mortgages being made. The result was the financial crisis.[5]

At the time of the crisis, the toxic effects of irresponsible and predatory loans in the mortgage market so infected our communities that the cumulative blow to US housing values upended our entire economy. That came as a surprise to many policymakers, including those in charge of setting financial and economic policy at the Federal Reserve. They did not have good enough data to diagnose or address these problems in the mortgage market, and they did not recognize that the disproportionate growth of the financial sector and its relationship to consumer finance had created new risks to the economy. The mortgage meltdown brought on the crisis through the web of relationships created by leveraged investments in household credit.[6]

Nobody had imagined that the day-to-day problems of individual consumers could loom large enough to bring about the downfall of America's mighty economic engine, with broad effects that rippled around the globe. In the summer of 2008, Republican Senator Johnny Isakson from Georgia, a long-time real estate expert before he entered politics, was on a trip with Senator Harry Reid to visit our troops in Afghanistan. On the way there, he and his group had a layover in Kazakhstan, where he saw extensive new construction underway in the new capital, though all the projects were idled. When he asked whether it was a holiday, they said no, that the reason for the inactivity was the US subprime mortgage crisis. The answer startled him, as did the fuller explanation that the Bank of Kazakhstan had purchased a slew of subprime US mortgages from Lehman Brothers Holdings. When the housing market began to falter and the portfolio had to be written down, the bank was forced to stop all construction funding as a result.[7]

What happened halfway around the world also happened here at home, when the credit markets froze up and suffocated commercial lending. This in turn led to millions of people losing their jobs, millions losing their homes, and virtually everyone losing much of their retirement savings either in the financial markets or in declining home values. Many of these people were entirely blameless, like Paul and Beth, who were not themselves involved in any of the bad lending but still had to suffer its consequences.

This failure raised important questions about what could or should have been done to prevent all this harm if we had understood more before it happened. Many responsible lenders, such as community banks and credit unions, had seen the problems for what they were. In fact, they lost market share because they refused to adopt the unsound practices that they saw going on around them. A community bank leader told about seeing a new Lamborghini in his parking lot one day during the runup to the financial crisis. When he asked about the car, which typically sells for $200,000 or more, one of his mortgage lenders said it was his. Asked how he could afford it, he explained: "You don't have to qualify anybody for mortgages. We can sell these mortgages to all these people. They don't even care what's in them. The real estate market's always going to go up." This complacency sounded alarm bells, leading the bank to shut down its mortgage banking operation. But many loan officers who were enjoying the party left and went down the street to some other lender, where they kept doing the same thing. And neither the investment bankers in New York nor the policymakers in Washington saw what was coming.[8]

Even with the safety nets that we have in place today, such as unemployment insurance, public assistance, and Social Security and Medicaid programs that did not exist during the Great Depression, people suffered tremendous pain as a result of the crisis. Employment did not fully recover for almost a decade; nor did housing values, which still have not bounced back in some areas of the country. During the prolonged trough, the Federal Reserve followed an extraordinary policy of zero interest rates for seven full years, which hurt many retirees who were trying and failing to live off their savings. These extreme dysfunctions were set against the ominous backdrop of a sharp increase in economic inequality over the past generation. Wages largely stagnated for the middle class, while most income gains were absorbed by the top sliver of the wealthiest Americans.[9]

What is less often noted, however, is that inequality of *wealth* also spiked after the financial crisis. That opened a gaping wound within the economy that continues to narrow the pathways to opportunity for many people who lost much of their hard-earned savings. In communities of color, most of all, as well as for other groups whose net worth was tied to the value of their homes, millions of people saw their accumulated wealth shrink when housing prices plummeted. Existing wealth evaporated altogether for those who went into foreclosure. Not only did they lose everything they had but also then they were blocked from re-entering the housing market for seven years while that blot remained on their credit report. Over the past decade, therefore, many Americans who were not invested in the stock or bond markets have seen whatever wealth they once had suddenly disappear, and the passage of time has not restored it. Their ability to make investments in the future, such as moving into a secure retirement or financing higher education for their children, is gone as well.[10]

There also is an important dignitary element to how people are treated in the financial marketplace. As Justice Oliver Wendell Holmes once noted, "Even a dog distinguishes between being stumbled over and being kicked." Each of us likewise knows how it feels to be cheated or mistreated, and to have our concerns be ignored or relegated to faceless bureaucratic processes that never seem to produce any meaningful responses. And credit obligations, unlike most physical transactions that occur all at once, extend over longer periods and thus become more visible and persistent parts of our lives. If you have ready money, you can manage to avoid most of these indignities; if you don't, you are made to feel them and the utter indifference with which you may be regarded. The greater financialization of American life means that consumers feel the weight of disrespect more frequently. And it imposes heavy psychological costs on people and their families.[11]

The Challenge Ahead

The lasting scar on the American psyche from the 2008 crisis is still felt deeply in many areas, and it will continue to shape people's outlook for many years to come, just as the Great Depression did for those who lived through it. Our youngest generation has been set back severely on their path to the American dream, especially those who sought to enter the workforce during the bust. Many young people have lost faith in economic markets altogether. Both lenders and consumers pulled back and became more cautious as they picked their way through the economic wreckage. Some consumers and communities have not yet recovered from their financial setbacks, which has deepened their feelings of alienation. The resulting hopelessness has fueled further societal ills, such as the opioid epidemic that has afflicted many areas of the country. These broader consequences of consumer financial problems have helped make the case for a new approach to protecting not only consumers and their families but also the US economy.

In response to these events, some argued that people who created their own problems by making bad decisions should have to bear their own economic losses. But for most Americans, that formulaic answer now seemed sadly inadequate. Many who lost their jobs or their homes or their savings had not made *any* of the same mistakes that others made, yet they and their families had gotten hurt as well. To them, the problem lay within the economic *system*, and they were looking for better solutions. As Congress found it necessary to bail out the biggest players in the financial industry to salvage the economy, many people grew angry about how little was being done for main-street Americans. And the banks that were infused with additional capital were not required to pass on this funding in the form of loans that supported ailing businesses and homeowners in local communities. The people who needed help the most were not getting it, and they developed a deep and lasting resentment for those who did.[12]

On a broad scale, the situation called for changes that would link the plight of individual consumers to the preservation of our strong economy. If we could find ways to support and protect consumers so they can cope better with the challenges of the consumer finance markets, then we could avert these threats to our prosperity. We needed to develop a more informed perspective on consumer welfare, and we needed more effective safeguards to improve the functioning of these markets. These financial reforms came to be regarded as essential, to protect not just those among us who are economically vulnerable, but *all* of us.

AN OMINOUS MISMATCH

Our financial system was badly broken in 2008, and reforms clearly had to be made. It was not the first public outcry for tough new restrictions on the moneyed elite. The frequent devastation caused by a boom-and-bust economy plagued America from the Founding to the Great Depression, and the excesses of financial speculation often intensified the depth of the cycles. Over time, people developed a deep mistrust of economic power concentrated in the banks or the trusts or the syndicates, which frequently misused it but usually seemed to land on their feet.[1]

The 2008 crisis was the country's first full-blown financial panic in seventy-five years, and many people were calling out for help. Our leaders needed to make a case for refocusing our government on the financial issues faced by individual Americans. The bill to bail out the banks took a crucial step away from the precipice by injecting more capital into the banks to stabilize them but did not require them to lend the money in turn to businesses or mortgage holders who were being wiped out. The fact that the bailout stopped with the banks and did not reach the millions of people who were hurt by the crisis was an enduring source of strain. The stimulus package passed during President Obama's first month in office provided $800 billion for projects to rebuild our communities. These investments would make a difference as the work progressed over time, but they did not touch people's everyday financial lives directly and immediately. Something more was needed.

To address the root causes of the crisis, President Obama proposed major financial reforms. Much as it had done during the Great Depression, Congress fashioned a vast legislative package to save capitalism from its excesses, through new mechanisms of oversight and regulation. These measures were intended to improve the workings of the financial markets but not to supplant them. Nonetheless, many were aghast at the scope of the proposed changes, which covered dozens of major issues, all bundled together in an unwieldy bill of more than 2,300 pages.

The financial industry flatly opposed most of these reforms. Just as it had battled what it perceived as the "radicalism" of Franklin D. Roosevelt's New Deal, once again it sought to block efforts to make far-reaching changes in the regulatory landscape. Its adamant resistance to most of these proposals intensified a bitter political struggle over how much change was called for to protect the public interest. The array of new regulations would impose expensive costs on the financial companies, and overhauling their existing compliance systems would be burdensome. At the same time, however, the ongoing devastation wrought by the financial crisis loomed over everything, reinforcing the undeniable point that too much self-policing in the financial markets had not worked. A coalition of consumer groups known as "Americans for Financial Reform" effectively pressed the case for the new law.

At a deadly serious time for those hurt by the crisis, Americans expected bipartisan reform efforts from our leaders in the public and private sectors. Instead, the legislative fight deteriorated into a fierce squabble along partisan lines. Much the same thing was happening with health care reform during the same period, with entrenched interests mustering their forces to defend the status quo. Most Democrats pushed for financial reform, while almost every Republican opposed it as a blatant expansion of government that would intervene too heavily in the marketplace. In the end, the new law was handily passed in the House, but on the final roll call it attracted just three votes from the 178 Republican members. It then passed by the barest margin in the Senate, where again it attracted only three Republican votes, every one of which was needed to ensure that it became law.

The Consumer Financial Protection Bureau

Most of the issues treated in the financial reform bill—known as the Dodd-Frank Act after its chief sponsors, Senator Chris Dodd and Representative Barney Frank, who fought relentlessly to secure its passage—dealt with arcane subjects like bank capital requirements and the trading of complex investments. Reforms of this kind, though important, are highly technical and not readily comprehensible. But tucked away in the new law was one provision that focused directly on the common problems of consumers and their exposure to predators. It also forged a new link between consumer finance issues and the broader economy. That provision created a new government agency, the Consumer Financial Protection Bureau, popularly known as the Consumer Bureau or CFPB. Representative Frank cared deeply about this provision, and he passionately defended it against substantial opposition.

The Consumer Bureau was based on an idea that Elizabeth Warren formulated when she was teaching bankruptcy law at Harvard Law School. Her research showed that most individual bankruptcies are caused not by irresponsible spending, but by misfortune and adversity, such as job loss and health care problems. I had seen the same pattern with delinquent taxpayers when I worked in local government. People who live near the margin are often in crisis because a single surprise or mistake can tip them over the edge. And people who are constantly struggling to keep their heads above water are especially vulnerable to being exploited by others, which only magnifies their problems. The idea was to create a government agency with a singular mission: to stand on the side of consumers and ensure they are treated fairly in the financial marketplace. That idea sparked an intense partisan battle over the new agency, which carries a broad mandate to oversee banks and other lenders to protect people from fraud and abuse in financial transactions, such as managing credit card debt, paying for college, or buying a home. The financial companies wanted nothing to do with this new source of scrutiny that would impinge on their decision making and their operations. And they strenuously resisted the prospect of an agency with the authority and resources to level the playing field, rather than leaving individual consumers to fend for themselves.

Elizabeth had published her idea in a 2007 article, well ahead of the mortgage meltdown.[2] In the article, she drew a powerful contrast between how we approach consumer products and consumer finance. She noted that we take great care to regulate the safety of physical products sold to consumers but fail to regulate the safety of many financial products. Government oversight has made it unlawful to sell people a toaster known to have some real likelihood of bursting into flames and burning down their house, yet it remained perfectly legal to sell people a mortgage with a similar chance of producing a foreclosure and putting them out on the street. Her point made a lot of sense, but the concept had not yet borne fruit.

A tenacious and creative team of people in President Obama's Treasury Department were intent on making this idea a reality. They crafted the authority for this new agency, fleshed out its workings, and inserted it in their initial drafts of the financial reform bill. The financial industry was dead set against the idea from the beginning and sought to kill it, with the US Chamber of Commerce flatly announcing that it would "spend whatever it takes" to defeat the agency. The industry was especially concerned about how far the legislation went to protect the agency with a high degree of independence. This was not unusual—it simply made the Consumer Bureau much like the other banking regulators, such as the Federal Reserve Board of Governors, which has its own dedicated sources of funding and whose leaders, with fixed terms, are safe from being fired by the president for mere policy disagreements.

Banking lobbyists did not want the new agency at all, and they certainly did not want it to have this kind of independence, which insulates it from the pressures they can exert with their considerable influence over legislative and executive oversight. As the bill progressed in the House, Representative Frank was ingenious in finding ways to ensure that the agency would have robust authority and a secure source of funding. Even with the skillful leadership that he and Senator Dodd exerted, and with fervent support from consumer groups and the Obama administration, the Consumer Bureau barely managed to survive the hazards of the lawmaking process. Ultimately, the new law located the bureau squarely within the Federal Reserve system, where it would be funded with a fixed budget cap and its decision making would be independent of direct control not only by Congress but also by the board of governors and the president.

As enacted, the Consumer Bureau was designed to be both independent and strong enough to take on the financial industry on behalf of individual customers. This was in sharp contrast to the Office of Thrift Supervision

(OTS), a financial agency that was eliminated by the new law. It had advertised itself to the public as a "deregulatory" agency friendly to the industry. In 2003, the leading regulators appointed by President George W. Bush held a press briefing to show their commitment to cut back on regulations. With the financial rules heaped on a table before them, the others held garden shears but the head of OTS brandished a chainsaw. The OTS was viewed as a classic instance of "agency capture," where some key officials had cozied up so closely to the companies they were supposed to regulate that they came to share and support their perspective on the world.

Those companies included some of the most bloated mortgage lenders that drove the downward spiral in bad home loans—Washington Mutual, IndyMac, Countrywide, and the mortgage-lending arm of the insurance giant AIG. Together they overpowered the OTS with their size and clout, and it made little effort to stop them from doing anything they wanted. During the crisis, Washington Mutual, which was on a spree to become the second-largest mortgage lender in the country, instead became the biggest bank ever to fail. IndyMac was the bank failure that cost the most. Countrywide aggressively sold subprime mortgages to those with credit problems, tripled in size over three years, and became a poster child for bad lending; after Bank of America bought it for $4 billion, its mortgage operations went on to lose more than $100 billion over the next six years in investor claims, legal settlements, fines, and expenses. No doubt the OTS had the worst record of the regulators charged with protecting the public, but it was hardly alone. The chumminess of government officials who were known to refer familiarly to "our banks" was widespread at the time. The very existence of a new and different kind of regulator stood as an undeniable reproach for their failures to look out for consumers.

The Consumer Bureau would have to be a very different place to succeed at reining in misconduct by the big banks and powerful financial companies. Under the law, it had a one-year transition period, starting in July 2010, to build its structure and operations from scratch, before opening its doors in July 2011.[3] That timeframe was utterly unrealistic, but it did create a sense of urgency. President Obama decided to tap Elizabeth Warren to lead the transition, while also advising the president on nominating someone to serve as a permanent director for the agency. She was a magnetic leader who exuded the can-do spirit of someone seeing an idea she had first conceived being validated and brought to life.

The work began with a tiny group of colleagues housed at the Treasury Department—fewer than a dozen people—who began moving quickly to fill key spots and build a bigger team. Those early days were filled with an electric excitement, as a steady flow of new arrivals joined in to shape the action. They were engaged in constant debates over how to fulfill the vision of an agency that would oversee a rebalancing of consumer finance, take on the financial industry to look out for individuals, and help the country ward off future catastrophes like the one we had just been through. Yet their adversaries watched the growth of the new entity with alarm, and they had not given up the fight.

The Powerful Financial Lobby

The Consumer Bureau's mission to protect individual Americans posed a direct challenge to the financial industry. It was plainly a mismatch. In the past half century, the dramatic growth in consumer credit has fueled the financialization of our economy. The steady shift away from manufacturing to services upended employment patterns in much of the country. But this general trend has obscured the even more dramatic expansion of financial services, where greater access and use of household financial products has transformed life for American families and reshaped the economy. Recent economic analysis indicates that the disproportionate growth of the financial sector has itself contributed to greater volatility of economic growth cycles.[4]

Indeed, the surge has been remarkable. Levels of employment in financial services grew enormously over time, and the industry's sales have doubled as a share of total gross domestic product from 10% in 1947 to 20% in 2010. More than six million people now work in the industry. Each of the four US mega-banks has over $1 trillion in assets and employs hundreds of thousands of people. As a group, they have continued to grow even larger in the wake of the financial crisis. And the full reach of the industry is vast; because the banks command the levers of finance and investment capital, they are naturally allied with every other segment of the business community.[5]

The industry is also a tremendous force in Washington, never more so than today. It is now the single biggest source of lobbying expenditures and campaign contributions to federal candidates and parties, spending about $1 billion annually, based on the figures that are publicly reported, which is far more than any other business sector. During the fight over the Dodd-Frank Act, reasonable estimates pegged the financial industry as deploying five lobbyists for each member of Congress. This flood of money begets wide influence over legislation and executive action. And this strategic work is carried out by many of the top lawyers in the country, augmented by the revolving door of former officials who can effectively leverage their valuable contacts and special expertise.[6]

These assets have not failed to produce results. Starting in the Reagan administration, but continuing through the Clinton and Bush administrations as well, major deregulatory measures were adopted that loosened restrictions on national banking practices. For decades, the financial industry seemed to win almost every important fight over policies that encouraged its growing might, such as allowing bank branches to cross state lines, the convergence of investment banking and depository banking, and bankruptcy law changes that favor credit card companies and student lenders over consumers. This triumphal progress included major court victories as well, such as the crucial Supreme Court decision that allowed national banks to export higher interest rates from one state to another, without regard to state interest rate caps.[7]

The clout of the financial companies is also visible in the massive size of the House Financial Services Committee, which is the second-largest committee in Congress. It is known as a "fundraising" committee, where lobbyists can be expected to target campaign contributions to secure favorable treatment on issues affecting the financial industry—whether this means pushing for legislation, shaping it, or blocking it altogether. For over forty years, the US Chamber of Commerce has wielded its "How They Voted" scorecard to punish or reward members for their votes on key legislation, which it regards as a critical component of its work to advance probusiness policies. The larger financial companies have also shrewdly managed their relative unpopularity by maintaining a coalition with small business leaders who are influential in every congressional district—community bankers, real estate agents, housing developers, and auto dealers—which helps them greatly in pushing their agenda.

The Dodd-Frank Act, which made big changes over the financial industry's objections, was a surprising setback for their interests. The altered regime was likely to cost them substantial revenues they could no longer extract from consumers. New reforms in the credit card market alone were projected to cost the industry $4 billion per year.[8] Even beyond the money the financial companies would forgo in a cleaned-up marketplace, they objected to the rebalancing of power itself, which left them no longer quite so much in charge. But the financial lobby is relentless, and there was no chance they would meekly accept this new order of things. On the contrary, they were already pursuing their next line of attack.

Just four months after the Dodd-Frank Act was passed, the financial industry was an integral part of a campaign coalition that engineered a political earthquake. In reaction to what were viewed and portrayed as "big government" measures on economic recovery, health care, and financial reform, a new grassroots movement had caught fire. The Tea Party movement galvanized millions of voters in the 2010 election with its calls for fiscal conservatism, tax cuts, less government spending, and a reduced budget deficit. With a generous amount of "Astroturf" help in the form of extensive financial assistance from wealthy donors, including the larger financial companies, Republicans engineered a wipeout, gaining 63 seats to take over control of the US House and winning 680 seats in the state legislatures, the largest swing since the Great Depression.[9] The Tea Party activists did not want more government, regardless of whether it claimed to be working for the people, and they did not trust anyone who made such claims. This new political force now entered directly into the halls of Congress, and it would influence these policy areas for some time to come.

A Champion for the People

The early days of the CFPB focused primarily on recruiting and hiring the people who would form the backbone of this new enterprise. They came from all over, motivated by the chance to do something about the financial crisis that had blindsided America and affected their lives.[10] One stream of people had their own personal stories about how the crisis had hurt their families and communities, or those they worked with as consumer advocates—people who had lost their jobs and homes. Another group came from the financial industry itself, people with first-hand insights about what had gone wrong and what should be done to fix it. Young people were seeing their generation saddled with crushing student loan debt and entering the economy at the exact wrong time, blocked by the recession from finding the kinds of jobs they had trained for, and they came to us eager to make a difference. Many officials moved over to us from other parts of the government, including the other federal regulators, and from the states. They had seen what had happened, felt a responsibility to help fix it, and wanted to see things done right.

I was one of those who came out of state government. My journey to the CFPB was unexpected; during and after the crisis, I had been serving in elective office in Ohio—first as the state treasurer and then as the attorney general. Like many others, I was ousted in the political sweep produced by the 2010 election. Shortly afterward, I got a call from Elizabeth Warren, whom I had never met. She said she was eager to have me come to work at the Consumer Bureau as the head of its law enforcement team. She was aware of my record for aggressively pursuing major cases against Wall Street firms that abused Ohio's pension systems, through which we brought back over $2 billion for our taxpayers and retirees. And she knew that I had worked closely with the other state attorneys general, which would be important at the Consumer Bureau as well.

I was dimly aware that the CFPB had been created by the new financial reform law, but it seemed utterly fantastical to me that I would go to work in Washington, DC, when my family was living in Ohio. Elizabeth was undeterred, telling me that she and her husband had coped with long-distance commutes and emphasizing that this was a once-in-a-lifetime opportunity to do on a national scale what I had been doing within my state—cleaning up bad practices by vigorously enforcing the law. She was very persuasive, and the case she made was intriguing to me, in part because as a state attorney general I had often been blocked from pursuing the national banks when federal law preempted our authority under state law. Before I knew it, and with my family's blessing, I agreed to try it out for a year or two. Once I arrived at the CFPB, I found that I was not alone in making this kind of effort; many others were also flying home every weekend and footing the cost like I was. At least I was in the same time zone—one of my colleagues, Edwin Chow, was so dedicated that for about a year he flew back and forth to San Francisco almost every week!

The unifying force among the diverse people who made up the CFPB was their deep dedication to the mission of protecting consumers. I had never seen so much and such distinct talent together in one place. As the members of the team gained more sense of how to work with one another, the dynamics of our meetings could be dazzling and I had to work hard to keep up, especially with the experts who came to us from the financial industry. Our fundamental text was Title X of the Dodd-Frank Act, which authorized our existence, fixed our powers, and set our limits.[11] We all had our own bound copy of the statute on our desks and referred to it often. It said some things about the structure of the bureau—for instance, that we must have an Office of Research, an Office of Financial Education, an Office of Servicemember Affairs, and several others. The statute also laid out the bureau's "functions" and "objectives," which guided us in the most important duties we were expected to perform. But we had to make our own choices about the rest of the structure and develop the strategies and tactics for carrying out our functions and achieving our objectives. The work was exciting and deeply absorbing.

But the truth was that we did not see it as "work." We were doing something that we believed would have great meaning for the future of the country. We matched that zeal with the brash vigor of a startup organization, with its seemingly endless stream of possibilities. In our early days, we were often crammed three or four to an office, yet we felt lucky just to be part of the club. We would have "All Hands" meetings while sitting or standing in the elevator lobby—the only place we could fit that did not have an official human capacity set by the fire marshal—and listen to pep talks by Elizabeth that never failed to rouse our spirits even when dulled by lack of sleep. But in all this early enthusiasm, I think the heart and soul of what we felt we were supposed to do was captured best by former senator Max Cleland, the decorated veteran who lost three limbs in the Vietnam War. He told me we needed to be "a champion for the people." He urged us to see ourselves much like Franklin D. Roosevelt's corps of innovative New Deal reformers, who found ways to address the economic plight of those who were suffering through the misery and anxiety of the Great Depression. It was a sobering aspiration.

Muzzling the Watchdog

Even as we were marshaling our forces and planning our strategies, the financial industry was doing the same. They had not spent millions of dollars on the 2010 elections just to accept an unwelcome reality of ramped-up oversight. Instead, they flexed their enhanced clout in the House and Senate to reopen issues that had already been resolved in the Dodd-Frank Act.

From the outset, the new Consumer Bureau ignited a political fight about its leadership. The first public evidence came when President Obama tapped Elizabeth Warren in September 2010 to lead the efforts to build the agency during its one-year transition period. That move pleased consumer groups, who were strongly behind her, but it worried the business groups that were gearing up for a tough confirmation fight. More hostility erupted the next spring in congressional oversight hearings, with House Republicans and their allies accusing the bureau—which was not yet even open for business—of behaving like "a bureaucratic rogue" that was unaccountable for its actions and indifferent to the financial soundness of the banks.

As time slipped away with no nomination for the role of director, a bigger problem emerged. In May, forty-four Republican senators, enough to sustain a filibuster that would prevent any nominee from coming to a vote, sent a joint letter to the president. They pledged to block *anyone* who was nominated to be the first director, regardless of the nominee's political affiliation, unless broad structural changes were made to the bureau. Most notably, they wanted more leverage over its budget, and they wanted to convert its leadership to a commission structure or impose other controls that would reduce its independence and slow down its work. Their audacious plan was to hold the leadership position hostage while seeking to renegotiate the fundamental legislative settlement of the bureau's independence without even commanding a majority in the Senate. And though the letter did not mention Elizabeth Warren or anyone else by name, it sent a menacing signal of serious trouble ahead. Around the same time, several House members formed a plan to take turns staying in Washington when the other members went home. By going through the motions of conducting "pro forma" legislative sessions, they could avoid having the House ever adjourn. These efforts were plainly designed to prevent President Obama from taking advantage of any recess in congressional activity, which could allow him to install a director for a further temporary period.

The financial industry and its allies hoped that blocking a director would cripple our efforts and lead to further legislative compromise. Elizabeth was having none of it, frequently commenting that though her first choice was a strong consumer agency, her second choice was "no agency at all and plenty of blood and teeth left on the floor." We all assumed that, one way or another, she would ultimately be named as the director. But once the staunch opposition to her became clear, she regrouped and in June 2011 she recommended that President Obama nominate me instead. He knew me from campaigning together in Ohio in 2008, and we had mutual contacts at the University of Chicago Law School, where I had been a student and he later was a professor. He was also aware of my record for taking on Wall Street financial abuses during my term as attorney general, which he saw as the right experience for the job. In a memorable job interview in the Oval Office, the president forecast that his legacy would consist primarily of health care reform and consumer protection, then entrusted me with carrying out the latter task. I was worried about the prospects for a nasty confirmation fight and the pressures on my family of prolonging my long-distance commute, but they were fully supportive, so we decided to go ahead.

The vetting of my background was a rapid affair, given how quickly the White House now intended to move on my nomination. Because I had a long history in electoral politics, there may have been less concern about so-called skeletons in my closet, since any such issues likely would have been dug up and aired out in those campaigns. As that process unfolded, I had the chance to sit down with Elizabeth for a longer conversation over lunch. In discussing plans for the bureau's future, we agreed on the main points. We both wanted to position it as a sensible regulator, driven by data analysis and cutting-edge research while supporting consumers; we were committed to simplifying disclosures that would help people better understand their financial choices; we knew we needed a strong enforcement arm, supported by our authority to supervise compliance by financial institutions; and we sought to educate and empower consumers in various ways that were not yet very well defined.

We also discussed what would happen during the further interim period when I would be nominated but not yet confirmed. However long that might last, I would remain as the head of enforcement and her deputy, Raj Date, a veteran of the financial industry who had joined the movement for consumer financial reform, would step into her role as special advisor to the Treasury secretary. He thus would be the one making recommendations about the daily running of the bureau, reflecting our limited independence in the meantime without a director in place.[12] She also told me that she had made the definite decision that she would be leaving the bureau as soon as I was nominated. Her subsequent announcement of that decision was a profoundly emotional moment for everyone at the bureau, and we all felt a bit lost, despite her confident assurances about the course that lay ahead of us.[13]

A ceremony in the Rose Garden followed shortly thereafter. It was a hot, muggy day typical of Washington in July. The event included President Obama, Secretary Geithner, Elizabeth, and me. My wife, Peggy, came to Washington for the occasion and we all gathered beforehand in the Roosevelt Room, then spent some brief moments in the Oval Office before heading outside. While we sweltered, the president spoke about the critical importance of the work we were doing. He urged that politics should not stand in the way of doing the right thing to achieve the goals of financial reform, including the strongest consumer protections in history. He described how the financial crisis had hurt so many people, and he emphasized that he would fight any attempts to repeal or undermine this new agency. He lauded Elizabeth for championing the idea of the agency and for all the work she and Secretary Geithner had done to make it a reality. And he warmly described me as "the best possible choice" to head the new watchdog agency.

I hoped he was right. It had been a surprising journey already. Yet the road ahead was murky, and I knew that as well as anyone. The financial industry would continue to fight hard and was buoyed by winning a partial victory in this round. They had formulated a creative strategy to hinder us and it seemed to be working. Now the bureau was due to open its doors in just three days, facing high expectations and a demanding mandate to overcome this resistance and deliver results for consumers.

THE MAKING OF A WATCHDOG

On July 21, 2011, the Consumer Bureau was supposed to become an independent agency with full authority to protect consumers. But the impasse over the nomination put a crimp in this schedule, as our opponents intended. Without a confirmed director, the situation was cloudy at best, falling outside anything Congress had considered. The laws governing the bureau suggested that we were still subject to oversight by the Treasury secretary, and some of our new powers likely could not be invoked yet. These included certain powers to enforce the law and secure a complete range of remedies for harmed consumers and our ability to supervise large financial companies other than the banks. Everyone was passing around memos seeking better insight, but we all knew in our hearts that we were just guessing at possible solutions for unforeseen problems. We also knew that whatever decisions we made would be challenged by the finest banking lawyers in the country. Yet we had to find a way forward with our mission to support and protect consumers.

Pushing Through the Politics

In those early days, we decided on a strategy that never wavered—to push through the politics by aggressively pursuing our work on behalf of the public. We sensed that holding back or being tentative would only embolden our critics and make it harder to get things done. Throughout the fall, the Senate Republicans remained united in using the filibuster to hold up my confirmation and block the Democratic majority from putting it to a vote. During the same period, the bureau pressed on our early theme of "Know Before You Owe." Under Raj's leadership, we held public sessions in Philadelphia, Minneapolis, and Cleveland, where we presented streamlined mortgage forms, a financial aid shopping sheet on paying for college, and a simpler model credit card agreement. One of the overwhelming problems facing consumers is the tricks and traps buried in the fine print of their contracts. The contracts often contain page after page of unreadable legalese, usually leading up to a take-it-or-leave-it signature line or an online link to simply click "I agree." Financial companies and their lawyers lard the text with long and complicated discussions that they claim are needed to treat the issues accurately. Our new models aimed to show that the same topics could be covered in plain language that highlights the key points and is more understandable to the average person. We weren't trying to make anyone's decisions for them, but if people could be clearer about what they are deciding, they would make fewer mistakes and have fewer regrets.

In this way, we were working to address the kinds of hidden problems that people run into all the time. Mary, for instance, had been surprised about changes in the interest rates on her credit cards because the explanation of their dense processes was squirreled away in the fine print. She was trying to manage her finances by juggling different cards, which depended crucially on her knowing which purchases were being made at which interest rates. But the long and confusing contracts made it almost impossible for her to be clear about that. In the same way, Jeremy had been tripped up by the deferred-interest offer he got on his new credit card to buy a big-screen TV. Things were more complicated than they seemed if you dug deep down into the explanatory pamphlet, but Jeremy, like many others, never made it that far. Similarly, Joan suffered a major financial setback by missing out for years on the benefits of income-based repayment on federal student loans, after being misinformed about her eligibility. And Rafael and his wife lost the $8,000 contingency fee they put up to apply for a mortgage because that consequence was buried somewhere in the mind-numbing pages of their contract. Too often, people paid a steep price because companies erected obstacles to obscure the basic principle of "Know Before You Owe." We sought to clear the path forward.

We also made some progress on another front. Although our enforcement authority was hampered by our political situation, we were building relationships with other federal and state officials that allowed us to play a constructive role on important issues. One of those was the infamous "robo-signing" scandal in the mortgage market. The servicing companies that receive and process people's mortgage payments had engaged in widespread misconduct, including the mass signing of documents by employees who attested to the validity of "facts" they knew nothing about. These documents were used to paper over gaps in the case files to justify putting people in foreclosure and taking away their homes. It was, as I had observed when I served as the Ohio attorney general, "a business model based on fraud."[1] The companies also misrepresented the terms of loan modifications, causing many people to end up in foreclosure, and thwarted those trying to save their homes by routinely losing documents or giving them the wrong information. The ravages of their illegal and inept conduct were lasting, and they brought extreme misery to homeowners and communities all over the country.

The attention given to these matters brought together a broad law enforcement coalition, not only of state attorneys general and state mortgage regulators but also of the Justice Department, Department of Housing and Urban Development (HUD), Treasury, and federal banking agencies. As that coalition assessed the issues, the CFPB was invited to take part in discussions over a prospective settlement, since it was clear that eventually we would be writing new mortgage rules and supervising compliance with them. The timing of these events, which unfolded before we gained our full authorities, prevented us from playing a lead role or conducting our own investigation. From the sidelines, however, we influenced the discussions by providing a financial analysis that justified a much larger settlement than originally contemplated. We also helped shape some of the terms to create more effective oversight of how the banks and mortgage companies would have to comply. We signed on to the final agreement, which sought to force the largest banks and mortgage companies to act more in line with the interests of their customers. The settlement was initially estimated to cost the companies $25 billion in consumer relief and penalties, but the total price tag grew to almost twice that much over the next several years.[2]

Although these joint efforts produced a wide-ranging resolution that helped clean up some of the worst practices, much of the damage was already done and for many families it would never be rectified. We would have many more frustrations with mortgage servicers in the years ahead, and the terms of the settlement only partially addressed their manifest shortcomings. Through the adoption of new mortgage servicing rules, constant battles with the companies we examined, and further investigations and enforcement actions, we learned how hard it is to achieve comprehensive and lasting reforms of a deeply flawed industry that had thrived by cutting corners. The frequent blunders and lapses of the mortgage servicing companies continued to affect homeowners like Susan, who could not get her loan modified because the customer representatives repeatedly misplaced her paperwork, and Deborah, whose loan modification was approved but then held hostage for unexplained fees that added up to more than $11,000. Through our interventions, and those of the national monitor who was put in place under the mortgage servicing settlement, at least some of these infuriating situations were being resolved successfully, and we could feel ourselves beginning to make a difference for consumers. But at the same time, the depth and complexity of these problems, combined with the breathtaking scale of the fraud that had taken root in this market, pointed the way to the many challenges ahead.

RECESS APPOINTMENT

While we tried to focus on our mission, the political impasse seemed to be hardening. In December 2011, Senate Majority Leader Harry Reid put my nomination to a procedural vote, which "failed" by a count of fifty-three in favor to forty-five opposed—short of the sixty votes needed to break the Republican filibuster. Yet there was a noticeable absence of vitriol. Republican senators made the point that there was nothing personal about their opposition to me, and many praised my qualifications for the job. But the numbers were still the numbers, and almost every member of their caucus continued to back Senator Shelby, who vowed that without structural reforms to the agency, there would be no confirmation of any director.[3]

President Obama was holding firm as well, and two days before the Senate vote he traveled to Osawatomie, Kansas, to deliver a political speech that set up key economic themes for his re-election campaign, which was increasingly underway with the election less than a year away. His theme echoed a speech given in the same town a century ago, when Teddy

Roosevelt proclaimed his program of federal trustbusting against the greed and recklessness of big business and special interests. Among other things, President Obama stressed the importance of a strong consumer watchdog agency. He was applauded as he said, "The fact is that financial institutions have plenty of lobbyists looking out for their interests. Consumers deserve to have someone whose job it is to look out for them. And I intend to make sure they do." His arguments seemed promising for our prospects, but they were not yet enough to carry the day in the Senate.

After the Senate vote, President Obama denounced the stalemate as making no sense for the American people. He insisted on the need for a consumer watchdog that was working at full strength to protect consumers against "unscrupulous operators." He pointedly noted that no options were off the table, including a possible recess appointment over the holidays. But as the end of the year loomed, no further word came from the White House.

In looking at the calendar, we thought any recess appointment might occur on the day designated as the formal "break" between the two sessions of the 112th Congress. Apparently, President Teddy Roosevelt made well over a hundred recess appointments in December 1903 in the moment between the two sessions of that Congress, which seemed like a good precedent. On the modern legislative calendar, that day fell on January 3, but our hopes were dashed as noon came and went with no word from anyone.[4]

Later in the afternoon, I was sitting in my office rather dejectedly when I received a call from Bill Daley, the president's chief of staff. He was, as always, brusque and to the point. "Where are you going to be tomorrow?" Brightening up, I asked, "Where do you want me to be?" He told me they wanted me to travel with President Obama to Ohio so he could announce his decision to make a recess appointment for me to serve as the first director of the Consumer Bureau. That was a thunderbolt, and after the strain of the past six months, we were overjoyed. It was also significant because a recess appointment allows the person to serve for the rest of that session of Congress plus the following session. Because this would be the first day of the second session of the current Congress, the extra day would mean that I could serve as the temporary director for two full years rather than just one.

The day ahead was magical. There were just four of us on Air Force One—President Obama, Senior Adviser Valerie Jarrett, Press Secretary Jay Carney, and me. As we winged our way to Cleveland, Senior Adviser Jarrett encouraged me to make a few phone calls. "It's not every day you can say to someone you are calling from Air Force One," she said with a smile. I made the judicious decision to place two phone calls—one to my father and the other to my father-in-law. Thankfully, both calls connected.

When I was making the call to my father, the president happened to walk by. "Who are you talking to?" he asked. I told him it was my dad. "Let me talk to him," he said, so I handed him the phone. "Mr. Cordray? It's Barack Obama. I'll bet you're very proud of your son." As I learned later, my dad responded by saying that he was proud of all his boys, then added, "And I'm proud of you too." At the time, I was curious to see the president seem to choke up a bit. The moment passed, but it stuck with me.

We made two stops in Cleveland. First, we visited with a family who had been threatened with the loss of their home at the height of the fore-closure crisis. Nonprofit groups and others had intervened and managed to save their home, but the situation was emblematic of the need for the new Consumer Bureau to prevent and rectify the kind of damage done to people during the financial crisis.[5] Then we went to Shaker Heights High School, where a large crowd had gathered to hear the president's announcement. As he put it, echoing the speech he gave earlier in Kansas, "Richard's job will be to protect families like yours from the abuses of the financial industry. His job will be to make sure you've got all the information you need to make important financial decisions." The president also explained why he was having to make a recess appointment, noting that though everyone seemed to agree that I was well qualified and I had majority support in the Senate, the Republicans had refused to allow an up-or-down vote. He called it "inexcusable" and "wrong" that "millions of Americans remain unprotected" and said he refused to take "no" for an answer. "Not when so much is at stake. Not at this make-or-break moment for the middle class."

The Ohio crowd was boisterous and supportive. The president had broken the political gridlock on an issue that mattered deeply to him and, as he explained, to the country. Back in Washington, however, the Republican congressional leaders were fuming about the move, calling his actions "crazy" and "outrageous." It rubbed salt in the wound that he made three other recess appointments on the same day, to key posts at the National Labor Relations Board. Those too would be challenged in court, but for now the legal battles lay somewhere in the future. We headed back to the White House on Air Force One.

Once we arrived, and my carriage turned back into a pumpkin, I began to settle down to the new realities of the situation. Over the course of that trip, everything had changed: the CFPB finally had a director, at least for now. All in all, it was a scintillating and joyful day.

Standing Up for Consumers

Under the Constitution and long-standing tradition, a presidential recess appointment is just as legally effective as a Senate confirmation to place the person in the designated role on a temporary basis. But under the specific terms of the statute governing the CFPB, that was not so clear, and some of our powers perhaps could not be used until I was confirmed by the Senate. The lawyers were split on the subject, so we had to determine how to move ahead. We decided to assume on every debatable point that we had full powers to act and we should do so, unless or until we were blocked in court from carrying out our duties. This posed some risk of getting slapped down publicly, but we preferred that to the risk of not taking needed actions when we might otherwise have been able to do so.

We were being tested, however, which came as no surprise.[6] One tense area was our authority to send supervisory teams in to monitor and evaluate the operations of large financial companies other than banks. The credit reporting companies, for example, keep credit files on virtually every American and would be a major subject of attention for us. For the most part, they had never been subject to direct oversight from either state or federal authorities. We had mixed reports on how frequently errors occur in people's credit files and how careful the companies are in gathering and maintaining this sensitive information. These were the kinds of problems that kept Kim from getting approved when she applied for a mortgage and caused Phyllis no end of aggravation when she tried and failed to get erroneous information corrected on her credit report about a closed credit card account.

In the first week after the recess appointment, as we prepared to send in our first team to examine one of the credit reporting companies, the company resisted. We did not know if we would be turned away or exactly what would happen. But when we pushed ahead, their lawyers gave way and we were given access to all the people and information we needed. It was a major victory that settled the point for good. We would use our examination process over the next several years to prod these companies to improve their frustrating processes and become more effective in responding to people like Kim and Phyllis.

Around the same time, we learned that employees at a payday lender we were scheduled to examine were shredding papers prior to our arrival, even though they had been told to secure all documents for our review. We levied a hefty fine, and we never faced that challenge again from them or anyone else. Our examinations of payday lenders over the next several years would bear considerable fruit: we cleaned up erroneous disclosures, improper efforts to pressure consumers into cycles of debt, and debt collection abuses, all while gaining a better perspective on how the industry operated.

The most important blow we struck for consumers during this uncertain period was to take our first major enforcement actions. These cases involved people who were harmed by the deceptive and misleading marketing of credit card add-on products. For many years, when consumers took out a new credit card or renewed an existing card, the bank would require them to activate the card over the phone. During that call, telemarketers would try to get them to sign up for related products that would supposedly benefit them, such as credit insurance or payment protection. But most of these "benefits" were basically worthless. The conditions imposed on when people could actually use the insurance or payment protection were so restrictive that people almost never qualified. That reality, combined with the fact that many consumers could be pushed to buy them, made the products incredibly lucrative for the banks. People at the bureau with experience in the credit card industry told us that some bank executives derisively referred to fleecing consumers in this way as "selling air." It was happening at virtually every bank that offered credit cards, costing consumers billions of dollars.[7]

Take Bill, for example. After he had been working for about a year, he applied for his first credit card. Although he was glad to be approved, when he called the company to activate the card, he was told that he really should sign up for several forms of credit protection insurance as well. He didn't fully understand what it would do for him, but the person on the phone insisted that he was supposed to sign up for the add-on products because they went along with the card. These products ended up costing him hundreds of dollars and became the first unpaid balance on his new card. A few years later, when Bill was unemployed for several months, he recalled that his credit insurance was supposed to help him cover this kind of shortfall. But when he spoke to the company, he was told that for various reasons specified in the fine print of the contract, he did not qualify after all.

Most banks hired out the selling of these products to telemarketers, who were paid according to whether they succeeded in making the sale. If they were not monitored carefully, they had few scruples about how they did so. We had the approved scripts of their sales pitches, but also audiotapes of actual calls so we could identify how they were deviating from the scripts. The temptation in selling a product that is worth very little is to misrepresent its value to persuade the customer to buy it, and that happened routinely. In addition, even when the customers tried to decline the add-on products or responded in ways that were unclear at best, the tapes showed that the telemarketers often overrode their wishes and completed the sale. The tapes made it very clear that credit card add-ons were being marketed in deceptive and misleading ways, and these violations were widespread across the industry.

Our first two actions were against Capital One Bank and Discover Bank. Based on the compelling evidence we had on the audiotapes, many customers were being misled into buying the products. Both matters were resolved by consent orders with total compensation of about $200 million each, including money that was paid back to customers and penalties. In time, we brought similar actions against every credit card issuer, with the monetary amounts ranging much higher, exceeding $700 million for both Citibank and Bank of America.

These actions were notable for several reasons. They highlighted bad marketing practices where the banks were taking advantage of people. They also demonstrated how a profit of a few hundred dollars per customer could add up to billions of dollars across the entire marketplace. By refusing to allow the banks to skirt their own responsibility for violations by blaming their vendors, we held them accountable. Maybe most important, these actions showed that we were willing to take on the banks and stand up for millions of people just like Bill. Exposing this type of deceptive behavior and getting people their money back sent a powerful signal that the bureau was needed and could be effective.

Another early issue arose over the Credit Card Accountability Responsibility and Disclosure (CARD) Act, in which Congress had adopted "ability to repay" requirements for consumers in the credit card market. The new law required an individual to demonstrate that his or her *own* income, rather than available household income, was sufficient to meet this test. But this limitation prevented stay-at-home spouses with little or no distinct income from qualifying for credit in their own name. It also meant they could not build their own credit history in the event they later became divorced or widowed, and it felt demeaning, as it disrespected the important contributions they make in their households. This technical legal problem soon became a broader consumer issue, as an online group called "Moms Rising" presented a petition with thousands of signatures, demanding that we adopt a new rule to fix the problem. If my own mother were alive, I know she would have joined them. Our team was stretched thin by our small numbers and heavy workload, but the problem was significant. Under the new law, the process for underwriting credit cards is more painstaking, and the question of how to handle accessible income from members of the same household is complex. We carved out time to complete a rule that fixed the problem, showing we could be responsive to input and find ways to help consumers who were hurt needlessly by prior regulatory actions.[8]

We were hearing stories like these all the time. People need someone to help make sure they are treated fairly, including strong action against those who violate the law. And our broader goal was to help create a more resilient economy and a stronger country. Amid the continued political struggles, we tried to stay focused on these concerns.

A Proper Confirmation

In the aftermath of the president's controversial recess appointments, the Republicans in Congress and their allies in the financial industry pushed back hard, including filing lawsuits to challenge the appointments as unconstitutional. The senators felt the president's action had squarely infringed on their prerogative to advise and consent on executive appointments. In the House, the level of anger was even higher. Some of the representatives weren't sure what to call me when they addressed me in press releases or when I came to testify. They didn't want to call me "director," because they viewed me as a usurper in that role. But it was undeniable that I was no longer just the enforcement chief either, since I now was running the bureau. Eventually, some settled on calling me "Citizen Cordray"—which was ironic, since they usually cast me instead as an all-powerful czar.

During this early period, my colleagues and I started making what became a familiar trip up to Capitol Hill to testify in front of the legislative committees with oversight over the CFPB. The law called for me to testify at a minimum of four hearings per year, two each before both the House and the Senate. Yet they could also request our testimony on any subject at any time, and nobody saw these invitations as voluntary. We ended up testifying almost monthly—more than sixty times over the course of my tenure—and the time we spent preparing for the hearings took precious time away from helping consumers. In my first House hearing, the experience was harder than I had anticipated. One fellow regulator likened it to stepping into the French Revolution. Because the questioning alternated between Democratic and Republican members, it was a yo-yo back and forth between tough questions on one side, followed by friendly questions on the other, with the two sides inflaming one another. A major theme from Republicans was that the CFPB did not have enough oversight and I was an unaccountable dictator. They refused to concede that any of our other oversight mechanisms, such as compulsory reports, regular audits, and scrutiny from our inspector general, amounted to anything. On one occasion, Representative Frank observed that here we were at yet another oversight hearing while the Republicans complained about lack of oversight. "Which raises the question," he commented dryly, "are we really here?" His delivery was so deadpan that it took me about a minute to get the joke, and I chuckled about it for the rest of that hearing.[9]

The recess appointment created a conundrum around the issue of our independence. On the one hand, we were now supposed to be operating as an independent agency, distinct from the Obama administration, as part of the Federal Reserve. On the other hand, I was still mired in the very political process of seeking Senate confirmation, with the White House quarterbacking the legislative strategy. We had first encountered the awkwardness of this dual posture on the return flight from Cleveland on Air Force One. Press Secretary Jay Carney was considering more White House events to push consumer finance issues, and I expressed reluctance, noting that we were now an independent agency. President Obama grasped the point immediately and suggested we take time to think further about it. In the end, the president simply paid a visit to the bureau to rally the troops and celebrate the appointment, which was a very special event. Later that month, First Lady Michelle Obama invited me to sit in her box for the State of the

Union speech. We debated how to respond until we learned that Federal Reserve Chair Alan Greenspan had accepted a similar invitation from First Lady Hillary Clinton in 1993, and with that as precedent, we accepted the invitation. Partway through his speech, President Obama singled out the CFPB by saying, "If you're a mortgage lender or a payday lender or a credit card company, the days of signing people up for products they can't afford with confusing forms and deceptive practices—those days are over. Today, American consumers finally have a watchdog in Richard Cordray with one job: To look out for them."

As the year wore on and we went about our work, the political season geared up. Despite our independence, we knew our fate still hinged precariously on the outcome of the elections. When President Obama was renominated at the convention in Charlotte, I kept a safe distance. Because my position was covered by the Hatch Act, I had to avoid politics and I took pains to do so. On election night, after a few nervous moments, it became clear that the president was going to win again and Democrats would keep their majority in the Senate, though still without the numbers to overcome a filibuster. The overall political landscape for us was essentially unchanged, except that Elizabeth Warren won her race in Massachusetts and would come to the Senate as a strong supporter of our work.

As the end of 2012 approached, we were grateful that the recess appointment had occurred a day later than we had expected, and I could continue to serve for the next year as well. A broad constitutional challenge to the CFPB was pending in a district court, but it was not making much headway. The recess appointments for the labor officials, made on the same day as mine, had been challenged in the US Court of Appeals. Although I was not part of that case, its outcome plainly would set a precedent that would cover my situation as well. When the court issued a ruling striking down the recess appointments, a menacing shadow hovered over us for a few days, but the case was quickly appealed to the Supreme Court and everything remained on hold until it could be conclusively decided, which would take at least another year.[10]

Early in 2013, I began nudging the White House to renominate me so I could try again to get confirmed in regular order. They had seemed satisfied to let things be for the past year in the runup to the election, but time was passing, and they decided to wait no longer. Thus, we started the process all over again, with a new application, a new round of vetting, and a new round of Hill visits. During the vetting process, the White House attorneys told me they had never seen so much visible activity as they were seeing from the CFPB. We were taking enforcement actions, issuing regulations, producing research and reports, creating new tools for consumers, and handling large numbers of consumer complaints. My meetings with Republican senators were at least neutral and often positive. More of our Hill visits and committee hearings were focusing on the substance of what we were doing for consumers rather than fights over structure or ideology. Our work was being noticed, and it was helping our cause.

Congressional Democrats continued to resist any efforts by the Republicans to weaken or restructure the agency, and though the House had pushed forward with legislation to do that, it was clearly going nowhere in the Senate. Yet even though we were making progress and the Democrats still controlled the Senate, no Republican had made a public break with their caucus, so the filibuster was holding. As the summer approached and the second anniversary of my original nomination was nearing, we started to hear chatter that Senator Reid was tired of how the Republicans were blocking or slow-walking President Obama's nominees. The rumors indicated that he intended to wield the so-called nuclear option to change the rules to confirm nominees by a simple majority vote, which would not be subject to a filibuster. When we heard that, our hopes rose, yet everyone could see that it would be a wrenching shift for a body deeply steeped in its traditions, so it was unclear how much stock to put in the rumors.

Finally, the day came when we were told that Senator Reid had committed to push several nominations to a vote, including mine, and that he would insist on confirming us on a simple majority vote. This spurred a long evening caucus of the Republican senators. Many of them were deeply committed to the ways of the Senate, and now Senator Reid was threatening to upend one of those cherished ways. We strained for any news about what they were saying, and after they emerged from a prolonged private session, several senators told the press that they thought a group of their colleagues would vote to confirm several nominees rather than see the filibuster damaged. Suddenly we seemed to be on the verge of a long-awaited triumph.

The next morning, as we anticipated confirmation votes in the Senate, there was a flurry of phone calls from several Senate offices. Before they voted, some Republican senators wanted to know if we would agree to certain concessions. I was willing to consider any reasonable item that would not undermine the bureau, so I agreed voluntarily to appear before the House and Senate appropriations committees on an annual basis to review our budgets and our spending. None of this was binding legislation, but it stood as my personal commitment, and the favorable news was that it was being accepted as valid currency by the senators engaged with us. The final tally was almost an anticlimax. In the end, seventy-two senators voted to end the filibuster. On the floor vote, sixty-six senators voted to confirm my appointment—a thumping bipartisan majority.[11] And in the chair presiding over the Senate for the vote was Senator Elizabeth Warren, pleased to see that her fledgling agency would now have more time to grow up.

The White House was in a hurry to arrange my swearing-in. Vice President Biden did the honors, with Health and Human Services Secretary Kathleen Sebelius holding the Bible during the ceremony. For a few minutes beforehand, the vice president spoke with us about the initiative he was heading to address concerns that would help the middle class, and we all recognized again how integral both health care and consumer protection are to those efforts. This discussion echoed the observations President Obama had made during my initial interview in the Oval Office. Two years had passed since then, but the essential foundations of middle-class life in America remained the same, and no doubt they will for a very long time.[12]

In retrospect, the White House's recess appointment had worked out, and the two-year horizon created by their choice of timing had been the key to success. Almost a year after I was confirmed, the Supreme Court finally ruled that the original recess appointments of the labor officials were invalid, as the three-day Senate recess was too short to permit such appointments to be made. That necessarily meant my initial appointment was improper as well. But because I had been validly confirmed in the meantime, our legal team led by Meredith Fuchs determined that we could minimize any disruption by issuing a simple order ratifying the actions we had already taken. This order too would be challenged in due course by a company that was subject to one of our enforcement actions, but the ratification was upheld.[13]

In tough, hand-to-hand combat, we were beginning to realign our government to put it on the side of consumers. After a two-year battle, we had finally defeated the financial industry lobby and fought off this crucial initial assault on the bureau. The win was made possible in large part because people could already see that we were doing things to improve their lives. Nothing would come easily, but the ability to carry out our mission was squarely in our hands.

PART II
LEVELING THE PLAYING FIELD

GIVING PEOPLE A VOICE THAT MATTERS

Most government financial agencies focus on regulating the operations of the banks to preserve their safety and soundness. That is important, as having dependable banks is itself a form of consumer protection, yet attending to how consumers themselves are treated is a lower priority. We intended to make a 180-degree turn and focus on the *customers* rather than the companies themselves. There were many ways we could help ordinary people deal with big financial companies. One of the most important would be getting someone to pay attention to their problems.

An unexpected fee on our bank account, a charge we don't recognize on our credit card, negative information that doesn't belong on our credit report—we've all had experiences like these. Sometimes the company, once prompted, will fix the issue, but often it is unresponsive. People feel frustrated and alienated when they are ignored or they get the all-too-familiar runaround, with no results. Recall Kim, for example, who was denied a mortgage because her credit report reflected a foreclosure and a bankruptcy. That information was wrong, as she was being mixed up with another woman who had the same name. After months of going back and forth, she still could not get the problem fixed and didn't know where to turn. Or consider Donna, harassed by debt collectors who called at all hours of the day and night, pestered her at her job, and even bothered her friends and family members. These tactics are illegal, and they made her life miserable, but she did not know how to stop them. Kim and Donna are typical of millions of Americans, and giving them a voice that matters would go far to improve their lives.

High Anxiety

In our early stages, we were still thinly staffed and just starting to get a handle on many issues in the complicated world of consumer finance. This was particularly true of consumer complaints. Congress required us to create a system of responding to complaints, and though the law was skimpy on the details, it did say several things. First, we must establish a unit to collect, monitor, and respond to complaints about consumer financial products or services. Second, to support these functions, we must have a toll-free telephone number, a website, and a database. Third, we should coordinate and share information with other agencies and officials that accept consumer complaints. Fourth, we had to keep personal information confidential and safeguard the security and integrity of all this data, as required by federal law.[1] Each of these provisions was sensible. But taken together, as a road map to handling potentially huge numbers of complaints each year, the combined responsibilities were downright terrifying.

How were we going to manage all this and make it a success? An incredibly dedicated team was brainstorming all this, day in and day out, but it seemed impossible. Among other things, it was hard to know just what the volume and kinds of complaints would be. Would their sheer numbers overwhelm us and make it impossible to respond effectively? And would the complexity of certain complaints—such as mortgage complaints—bog us down and gum up the works?

Agencies have very different views about what it means to "handle" a consumer complaint. At some level, of course, every component of our government must have some way to respond to the public. And any entity that engages the public must be able to provide information and answer questions so that people can successfully engage with it. Take the Internal Revenue Service (IRS), for example. It has the job of collecting taxes, which involves providing people with appropriate forms, guiding them in filling out the forms, processing the forms, and implementing the results (including refunds, penalties, audits, and adjudications). Over time, those basic functions have spawned a cottage industry of accountants and tax preparers in the private sector, just to help the government manage this process. The IRS's ability to respond to questions and concerns has been a persistent issue, and the amount of work needed to deal effectively with the public often overtaxes its corps of employees, especially if they are short-changed in their funding.

Many government agencies limit the burdens of responding to the public by treating public complaints merely as informational data to be collected and monitored, but nothing more. The Federal Trade Commission, for example, makes clear that complaints will be entered into its database for law enforcement to access and evaluate, but the agency does not otherwise seek to resolve them. To each consumer, this approach frankly says: thank you for letting us know your concerns, which we might or might not ever address, and we appreciate you submitting this information as an altruistic public service. But it provides little hope to people that their own individual problem will be resolved, which gives them much less incentive to file a complaint in the first place. This method dramatically reduces the agency's total workload, but it does so at the cost of declining to help people solve their own specific problems.[2]

Within the Consumer Bureau, we wanted to address and actually resolve individual complaints wherever possible, using a "constituent service" model that reflects the approach taken by the offices of most elected officials. People deserve answers to their problems and a just result if they are cheated or mistreated. But this would be burdensome and more time-consuming, and it could be messy if it required the bureau to weigh and evaluate facts, in a quasi-judicial role. It might necessitate further fact gathering, in a quasi-prosecutorial role. Any appreciable volume of complaints could swamp and discredit our new agency from the outset. Even before we opened our doors, as various inquiries began to pile up, we tried to provide this maximum level of involvement by assigning members of the enforcement team to help investigate and evaluate them. The team often found the experience informative and valuable, and it helped them identify some systemic practices calling for a broader investigation and potential enforcement action. But this more extensive involvement with each individual consumer complaint did not look feasible with our resources.

I had my own experience with complaints from my time as Ohio attorney general. There we also followed the constituent service model.[3] But when I arrived, the office was employing a screening process to keep the volume manageable by putting obstacles in place that deterred consumers from using the service. Anyone who submitted a complaint by any means was sent a paper form to fill out and return before it would be processed, causing many to drop out, while also slowing things down. When we abandoned that perverse requirement and allowed people to file directly online or by phone, the volume of complaints rose accordingly. Another way we handled certain complaints was to direct them to the complained-about company to handle in the first instance, to see if they could reach a satisfactory solution before deciding whether our office should take any further action. We did this most notably with auto dealers. They were motivated to fix the problems, since the attorney general's office was looking over their shoulders, and they often managed to do so.[4] These experiences taught me good lessons about how our government can be more effective in responding to the public.

As the bureau approached the July 2011 date to start dealing with consumer complaints, this area of our operations aroused more concerns than any other. An alarming indicator of the difficulties involved was an enormous white board that the consumer response team had constructed. It was covered with yellow Post-it notes, each indicating some issue that had yet to be worked through. There were dozens, if not hundreds, of Post-it notes on that board, which would move around as the team worked meticulously to solve the challenges. But it seemed like all that work could not possibly get done in time.

HANDLING COMPLAINTS

As the deadline neared, the consumer response team had done its homework on systems from both the public and private sectors, and they made several crucial judgments that were both brilliant and inspired. First, they decided to implement the mandate to respond to complaints in stages rather than all at once, beginning with complaints about credit cards, with others to follow over time. This was a canny choice, because many credit card problems are uncomplicated and have smaller amounts of money at stake. The number of credit card providers is relatively limited, so it was more feasible to deal with them. It also helped that the first head of our team, Sartaj Alag, had run a major credit card operation earlier in his career.[5]

We also adapted the approach that had worked well with the auto dealers in Ohio. When we received a complaint, we first transmitted it to the complained-about bank or company to let them address it in the first instance. Our statute did not specify this approach. It did require us to establish reasonable procedures to provide timely responses to complaints, and it required the companies to provide both us and consumers with timely information needed to work through the issues. But by making the companies the first line of response, we gave them a chance to solve many problems before devoting our own resources to them. Sometimes all customers wanted was to know that they had been heard or even simply an apology.

The real question was whether companies would take complaints seriously and address them effectively. We told them that the complaints made against them, and their handling of those complaints, would be key data points for us in deciding which companies and problems to prioritize for further oversight and investigation. By integrating our tools and our authority in this manner, we created incentives for companies to do the right thing for their customers. The adage "the customer is always right" is a venerable ideal that is literally untrue, yet it represents an attitude or state of mind that gives the customer the benefit of the doubt. And that mindset often produces more satisfying results for customers who are unhappy about something.

We found that this approach worked surprisingly well, especially with credit card complaints. Because of the smaller amounts at stake, companies often were willing to make things right for the customer. This was so even though many consumers who filed complaints with us had already raised the same issue directly with the company many times without satisfaction. It seemed that the leverage created by our direct involvement pushed companies to look harder at the situation and to be more accommodating to the customer than when the companies were acting purely on their own.

What also made this system work was the tremendous technology our team developed to process complaints more efficiently. They created a "portal" system that largely automated the intake and processing through the entire first round of the company's response. Once a company was onboarded, our system would transmit the entire complaint immediately to the people whose job it was to handle it. Corporations, like government, have lots of bureaucracy, and this approach cut through much of it, allowing us to access the right people and insist on a timely response within a matter of days. Again, we made clear that a pattern of failing to respond to complaints in a reasonable and timely manner would prompt us to consider using our other compulsory tools to deal with the problem. It worked like a charm: the companies got the message and for the most part they took the complaint process seriously, providing timely responses to approximately 97% of the complaints we received and meaningful relief in many situations.

The other financial regulatory agencies also had been taking complaints over the years—from bank customers, in particular—but with varying degrees of enthusiasm. Some were quite willing, even eager, to retreat from this business by shipping those complaints over to us or by directing people to us in the first place. Over time, their average volume of complaints declined, reflecting both that our system was becoming better known and that satisfied consumers were advertising us by word of mouth. This too represented a new efficiency in government, by directing these types of problems to where they could and would be handled most effectively.

We also regularly received referrals from elected officials, including the president, who themselves get complaints from constituents and need help resolving the problems. Increasingly, they could see that the best place to go for help was us. Since these complaints often concern large national companies and issues of federal law, many are submitted to congressional offices, leading some legislators to quietly transmit their constituent complaints to us while continuing to loudly criticize us when the cameras were present.

A Moment of Truth

Over the first few months, the consumer response work went surprisingly smoothly. But a moment of truth was approaching, for we had committed to begin taking complaints about mortgages in December 2011. This was another scary prospect, because we were still in the middle of a housing market crisis and these matters often involve extensive paperwork and situations that are confusing for all concerned. They also put larger amounts of money at stake, as well as related issues that go beyond money but are extremely significant for people, such as home titles, mortgage assignments, foreclosures, ouster from the home, and servicing problems that plagued the industry. On top of all that, the legal and factual issues in many cases can be quite complex and tough to solve.

As the Ohio attorney general, I had come face to face with this complexity in dealing with the "robo-signing" scandal. The old direct link between mortgage lender and mortgage borrower had been severed irretrievably by more sophisticated arrangements peddled on Wall Street, where mortgages were sold and resold and packaged together into financial securities that were sold and resold in turn. Many people who paid their mortgages for years, then later ran into trouble, did not know where to turn if they needed help. If they tried to go back to the original lender, that company often was no longer able to address their problems. Nor, in many cases, could anyone else. It could be hard to communicate with the companies that were responsible, and the industry's sloppiness in keeping all the documents in order often was egregious. As a result, when companies with financial rights in the original mortgage wanted to foreclose on a delinquent borrower, they sometimes simply fabricated documents to "validate" their claims, "robo-signed" by a designated corporate representative. Much of this fraudulent work to fill gaps in the loan file was legally invalid, if anyone knew to challenge it and could get the attention of a court, but that was not easy to do.

So how were we going to manage these types of complaints? For regular mortgage lending complaints, we could begin by handling them the same way we handled credit card complaints—by sending them through the portal to the banks and mortgage companies. In some cases, though not predictably, that worked to get a solution. Knowing exactly whom to contact, we cut through the confusing and burdensome phone trees. And because we had the leverage of exerting oversight or opening investigations against companies that violated the law or showed a pattern of treating customers unfairly, our efforts prompted more responsiveness.

But for mortgage servicing complaints where people need a loan modification, we never quite found a way to get consistent customer service to solve the problems. Largely this was due to the difficulty of the problems and the rampant dysfunctionality of many servicers. In many instances, of course, delinquency does not lead to happy endings and those complaining were not entitled to any relief. But the servicers often were simply ineffective in solving hard problems and could not manage to do so even under the pressure of having to deal with us. In fact, we found that some of the worst mortgage servicer operations were highly random; sometimes they provided oddly satisfying solutions, other times nothing at all. Of course, some servicers did operate effectively, and then our complaint process could provide an efficient way to accomplish whatever could and should get done.

One success involved Roxanne from Iowa. After her husband died of cancer, Roxanne became responsible for the mortgage and was able to resolve a foreclosure threat by successfully negotiating a loan modification. Every month, after she got her Social Security check, she would make her payment during the grace period. Nonetheless, she still got constant phone calls asking for her deceased husband, sometimes three to six times per day, harassing her to pay more promptly. Although she asked them repeatedly to stop calling, they did not stop until she filed a complaint with us. Less than a week later, her mortgage servicer sent her a letter of apology and stopped calling her for good.

But though we got some individual results, we were no substitute for a strong and dedicated housing counselor who could sit down and spend hours with individuals, sort through their situation, and give them the personal service they needed, or for an attorney who could go to court to defend them in a foreclosure action. Those people were the real heroes of the mortgage crisis, and we were only a next-best mechanism that occasionally managed to cut through the dense haze of delinquency, foreclosure, and confusing corporate processes that often didn't work. Where we were more effective was in diagnosing the kinds of systemic problems that we could address through our enforcement and supervision authorities.

In dealing with mortgage complaints, we decided to allow other parties to file complaints on the individual's behalf, such as someone more expert in such matters or more experienced with our process. This led to situations like that of an African American minister in Atlanta who filed dozens of complaints on behalf of her congregants and told us she had been well pleased with the results we got for them. After she told us her story, we began to urge other ministers, and faith leaders of all kinds, to "make us their outbox" for these kinds of consumer finance issues, and some happily took us up on that offer. We also decided to take complaints from people who were represented by an attorney, unlike many government entities that decline to do so. If they were already embroiled in a lawsuit, our intervention was limited accordingly. But many attorneys began to see that one powerful way to get results was to help their clients file complaints with us and see what happened. And taking the larger view, if people could resolve their problems short of pursuing litigation, that often seemed best for all concerned.

As we worked through the addition of mortgage complaints, which were the hardest of all, we also learned to handle situations involving voluminous documents through our powerful computer database and electronic document scanning. This led to greater accountability by helping cut through a common problem with the worst mortgage servicers, who consistently lost, or claimed to have lost, documents sent to them. As we gradually expanded the categories of complaints that we covered, we found that the same problem of thick-file controversies arose in other areas, most notably debt collection and credit reporting. There too, our involvement imposed more consistency and orderliness on the complaint-handling process at these companies, which people often found terribly frustrating.

Eventually, we began taking complaints about all our issues—auto loans, student loans, debt collection, credit reporting, payday loans, international remittances, bank account services, prepaid cards, money transfers, consumer loans, and more. In just a few years, we built out a complaint response function for the entire universe of consumer finance. And it was not limited to the portal experience. From the day we opened our doors, we had two call centers up and running, in Iowa and New Mexico, where the staff were trained to help people file complaints over the phone and to answer questions about consumer finance issues objectively and honestly. It was a full-service shop, available 24/7, for 320 million American consumers. Anyone can file a complaint at consumerfinance.gov.

And for many consumers, it worked. When Kim complained to us about the erroneous information on her credit report that had been dogging her for months, the problem was fixed in less than a week, which surprised and delighted her after she had spent so much time getting nowhere. When Donna filed a complaint with us about how she was exhausted and tormented by harassing debt collectors, we intervened and stopped the illegal calls. With our government now standing on their side, these individual Americans found themselves suddenly on a more level playing field with the big financial institutions.

THE CROWN JEWEL

It was an extraordinary achievement by an energetic team with vision and a profound commitment to our mission. It did not come without cost. The engine was running very hot to get all this done, and inevitably it took its toll.

When consumer demand threatened to exceed our capacity, the team executed a very difficult pivot they called Project Mosaic, to overhaul the whole machine and put it on a stronger platform to deal with the huge volumes of complaints we were now handling—more than twenty-five thousand per month. Under the weight of these immense challenges, it bent but never broke.[6]

Indeed, we increasingly realized that the consumer response function had become the crown jewel of the Consumer Bureau. It was a remarkable means of putting the voice of the consumer right at the heart of the agency, in real time, and we all recognized it as such. To me, it was the key to keeping sight of our real agenda, which was to understand and address the problems people were confronting in their lives. It helped us avoid both an ivory tower mentality and the problem of agency capture, where agencies get so comfortable dealing with the companies in their realm that they begin to identify with those companies rather than the broader public.[7] The hours that people worked, and the ground they covered, were consistently amazing. During one major system upgrade, I noticed people walking from room to room carrying their laptops with their arms crooked between the two pieces—so the machine wouldn't close and require them to waste any time restarting it. I had my daughter create an inspiring image of that picture as I had seen it, showing Rosie the Riveter posed with a CFPB laptop just so, and the caption "We Can Do It!"

In our early days, when we were only taking consumer complaints in a few areas, we developed a catch-all function on our website, called "Tell Your Story," which at least gave people an outlet to inform us about other matters we were not yet covering. Once we built out our whole process, we maintained that outlet, and some consumers who had their complaints resolved would use it to thank us for helping them. Many explained how pleased (and surprised) they were to see how we had successfully resolved issues, sometimes in days or weeks, that had stymied them for months or even years.[8] We mounted some of these first-hand accounts on the walls in our hallways. We often met with industry leaders on site, and we wanted them to take in our keen focus on the personal experiences of consumers and how serious we were about getting individual complaints resolved. It conveyed the blunt message that we expected the same of them—to focus on the need to be highly responsive to their customers.

Public Database with Broad Benefits

The consumer response team also showed courage in the face of another significant challenge. Early on, we had committed to making our database of consumer complaints public. Most agencies shroud their complaint handling from public view, requiring people to file public information requests to learn more about it (even about the handling of their own complaints). But we wanted people to know what we were doing, and to know what kinds of complaints were being made, which might encourage them to file their own similar complaints. The team captured this aspiration in a phrase they often repeated: "attach a bullhorn to the complaint!" We estimated that between general lack of awareness of us and skepticism that filing a complaint would do any good, the number of consumers with a valid complaint was at least one hundred times greater than the number who ever actually filed complaints.

We believed that if companies could be called to account publicly for the complaints they generate and how they handle them, it would stimulate better performance on their part. And making this information public would allow others to dig into it and analyze it in ways that would yield further insights. The Public Interest Research Group, for example, began publishing informative reports that broke down the data and drew conclusions about the nature, scope, and intensity of customer service problems across the entire spectrum of consumer finance.[9]

The complaint database also helped us prioritize issues for attention at the bureau and elsewhere. We had recently opened our secure government portal, to allow federal and state law enforcement officials to view our complaint data in greater detail and improve their own work. This mechanism provided more perspective to state attorneys general and others on how best to enforce the law and improve the workings of the financial marketplace. Even if an individual complaint was not resolved successfully, it still could inform our work in useful ways. Students who told us about taking on unsustainable debts helped us understand the effects on their lives. Older Americans hurt by a reverse mortgage sensitized us to how the products could be misused and how their marketing could be improved. In this way, people were helping us think about how to help others even if they could not be helped themselves.

Our expanding complaint database was achieving yet another major result by taking thousands of individual stories and turning them into more objective data. As with the macroeconomy, it is very hard to comprehend the aggregate effects of millions of different actors. Even economic data that has been examined and refined for years is often wrong and needs to be revised after the fact, sometimes many times until it is accurate.[10] Each consumer complaint is like a pixel on a television screen. Each pixel on its own is just a dot of color, significant by itself, yet insignificant to form a broader perspective. But as the pixels fill in and begin to blend together, they yield a sharper and clearer view of the whole picture. In this way, individual anecdotes pile up to become actual data—accumulating many individual experiences into a broader mosaic of the consumer marketplace.

This aspect of the database, however, went well beyond research. Other tangible things can be done with the information. As we frequently noted, not all, or even most, consumer protection comes from government agencies. Instead, the first two places to look for consumer protection are out in the marketplace itself: in how a business decides to treat its customers, and in how those customers can stand up for themselves. Good businesses, of course, routinely mine their own customer complaints for insights into where they are falling short, where their best intentions are not being fulfilled, or where members of their organization are subverting the company's plans.[11] But each company typically only has insight into its own customers. Our public database was more robust; it gave them access to information about what was happening at other companies industry-wide, enabling them to learn about and take steps to avert potential problems.

In addition, consumers and consumer advocates working on their behalf could learn more about experiences others were having with specific financial companies. They could use the information to decide whether to file their own complaints or to select one company over another. With more and better information, they would be in a stronger position to pressure companies to change practices and be more responsive.

As expected, industry lobbyists and trade associations felt the sting of our public database and saw very little benefit from it. They criticized us for using "unverified" complaints, which was a criticism they never adequately explained. Unless they meant a complaint that had been reviewed and upheld by a court, "verified" was a pretty vague concept. Our process began by having the company verify the existence of a customer relationship, which largely ruled out the possibility of entirely fictitious complaints. And our research showed that the average person who filed a complaint had already tried to resolve the issue directly with the institution at least three times. Of course, there always could be a big gap in perception between the company and the customer, but that is true of any complaint process. By giving companies a chance to work things through, under the shadow cast by our further scrutiny, consumers were getting good results. And we kept a close eye on the patterns, looking for evidence of companies that were systematically rejecting complaints at an unusual rate, which would trigger further investigation and potentially an enforcement action with penalties.

Over time, many companies caught the spirit of what we were trying to accomplish. Some showed us how their compliance officers were using our public database to supplement their own customer service efforts. Others acknowledged that consumer complaints should be viewed as opportunities to improve their relationships with those customers who chose to engage with them rather than simply taking their business elsewhere. This was one of our main goals: to encourage and push companies to compete harder over improved customer service, which would benefit not only consumers but also businesses and the marketplace by producing fairer treatment and greater consumer confidence.

At a field hearing in Iowa in March 2013, we unveiled the public complaint database. At that point, its scope was still relatively modest. The complaints we were then adding to it only expanded it from nineteen thousand credit card complaints to ninety thousand complaints about mortgages, bank loans, student loans, consumer loans, and credit cards. But we gave indications of much more to come as we described how people could see the who, what, where, when, and why of each consumer complaint. In the years ahead, the level of sophistication would increase dramatically. We began giving people the option to share the narrative details of their complaint with the public, scrubbed of any sensitive personal information. These narrative stories helped others better understand what had happened, and more than half of all complaint filers chose to share them publicly. As we filled out the range of consumer products about which people could complain—including debt collection and credit reporting complaints, which were abundant—we held a contest to pinpoint the date on which we would receive our millionth complaint. As usual, my prediction was too optimistic: my projected date was July 4, 2016, but the actual moment turned out to be at 10:52 a.m. on

September 22, 2016. One place I was never wrong, though, was my view about what our team could accomplish—they always overachieved.

ADDING VALUE FOR CONSUMERS

With this much data, we began issuing our own monthly reports to lay out the numbers and our analysis about what to make of them. That created even more concern from the big financial companies.[12] They argued that it was unfair for us not to "normalize" complaints for size of the company. Here they had a point, for certainly credit reporting companies, with approximately two hundred million consumer files apiece, were inevitably going to have the most total complaints. We added some language in our reports to mitigate the issue and we also urged them to do that themselves by contextualizing their own complaint numbers.

Our consumer response team found yet another way to make its work central to the entire bureau. By developing and refining their analytical tools (including tagging key words and natural language processing), they could identify "spikes and trends" in the data, both generally and in response to queries about specific companies. This information was incredibly valuable to our supervisory personnel and our enforcement lawyers. It became a first step toward assessing risks and deciding how to scope a supervisory exam of a company, or whether to open an investigation that could lead to an enforcement action. And the consumer response team also began turning up interesting results of their own, sometimes identifying customer problems even before the company executives knew about them.[13] In addition to alerting company leaders about such problems, we also broadcast this capability to the rest of the industry (without revealing company names), to impress on them the futility of trying to hide things from us.

While I led the bureau, we received over 1.3 million consumer complaints and resolved a huge number of problems for people across the entire range of issues we covered. All of that was deeply satisfying, not just in general, but every single day. We were making our government work for people who need it and deserve it—not just those at the top, but ordinary people who often do not get or even expect a fair shake. This achievement was captured beautifully in an article published in *Time* magazine in August 2015. The article was entitled "The Agency That's Got Your Back," and it described the work we were doing, which it said was "striking fear into the lending industry." As an example, it featured a woman named Deborah Jacobs, a retired teacher from Michigan.[14] She described herself as "definitely a Republican," and recalled thinking when she first heard about the bureau, "Well, that's a waste of taxpayer dollars." But four years later, she found herself behind on her mortgage and desperately seeking help from any state or federal official she could find. The bank had agreed to modify her mortgage and let her keep her home but also insisted on an unexplained fee of $11,599.32 that she could not pay. The day after she filed her complaint with us, we emailed her to say we were looking into it. Four days later, she received an overnight package from the bank with a new set of papers, minus the hefty fee. At the end of the article, it noted that she was still worried that maybe we would become too powerful, but for now, "they're my saviors."

A while later, the leaders of our consumer response team brought me a blown-up version of the entire three-page *Time* magazine article, signed by every member of the team. It hung on my wall ever after, as a testament to their great work.

A POWERFUL FORCE FOR GOOD

My original role at the Consumer Bureau was to lead and build the enforcement team. As Elizabeth Warren stressed, America needed "a cop on the beat" for consumer finance. We had to carry a big stick if we were going to produce more balance in the marketplace. After all, we would be standing between some of the biggest banks and financial companies in the history of the world, on the one side, and the average consumer household, on the other. Up to this point, that had been a pretty one-sided affair.

Many enforcement actions take either of two distinct forms. One class of cases involves corporate practices that may not be predatory but are matters of indifference or inattention to details that, if scrutinized more closely, would absorb time and attention that detract from the bottom line. Our action against Citizens Bank, for example, fell into this category. The bank was failing to credit customers with the full amount of their deposited funds. Customers were told that deposits were subject to verification. But if there was a discrepancy where the receipt did not match the actual money transferred into the bank, regardless of the source of the error, the bank only bothered to correct the mistake if it exceeded a certain threshold, initially set at $50. Over several years, the bank shorted consumers millions of dollars, and though its policy may have benefited some customers, that did not justify depriving others of money that was rightfully theirs. The federal banking regulators joined us in finding that this unfair and deceptive conduct violated the law. In response to our action, the bank agreed to revise its policy and pay $11 million in consumer refunds plus $20.5 million in penalties. We then worked with all the other financial regulators to issue joint guidance about how banks and credit unions would handle discrepancies in the future.

The other class of cases involves intentional cheating of customers. Some online lenders engage in rampant fraud. Our case against the Hydra group unearthed a brazen cash-grab scam involving almost $100 million in unauthorized loans. Companies known as lead generators offer to match potential borrowers with lenders. If you go online to get a loan, lead generators often serve as middlemen to secure your information and facilitate the transaction. But when Hydra bought this information, they used it to access people's accounts, deposit loans, and begin withdrawing automated payments, all without consent. They falsified documents to claim that consumers had agreed to the loans. We found that in a little over a year Hydra made $97 million in loans, most of them involuntary, and collected $115 million in return. Many consumers were not even aware they had been targeted until they noticed money moving around in their accounts. Although Hydra was based in Kansas City, their dealings were hidden in a maze of offshore corporate entities in the Caribbean or the Pacific that evaded regulatory oversight. We shut down their criminal activities by getting a court to freeze all their assets, impose a receiver to oversee their operations, and return money to consumers. We referred the case for criminal prosecution and a jury found the ringleader guilty of multiple charges, including identity theft; eventually, he and his colleagues were banned from the industry and had to forfeit their assets to compensate victims of their fraud.

Although these two classes of cases are very different from a moral standpoint, both have serious effects on consumers. Money out of your pocket is gone either way, whether by an uncorrected error or an intentional act of theft. In either instance, consumers often face great obstacles to protecting themselves against harm, and public law enforcement is an essential bulwark against such conduct, which distorts and undermines the market.

Growing Pains

On my first day at the bureau, the enforcement team had just grown to a grand total of six people. And though many high-quality resumes were piling up, the initial budget projected that fewer than fifty people would be devoted to this task, a number that seemed woefully inadequate when compared to the banks with their squadrons of lawyers. As a new agency, we would be starting from scratch, with no existing pipeline of cases to build on. The Federal Trade Commission was the only federal agency that had ever pursued any significant litigation in the area of consumer finance, and though it was effective in some areas, it was not even allowed to investigate or sue the banks. The three banking agencies did have this power, but they rarely used it to engage in public fights with the banks they regulated, preferring to maintain supervisory relationships with the companies and use a more confidential approach to achieve their goals.[1]

We needed to devise a structure that would allow the bureau to optimize the use of both its enforcement and its supervisory powers. As the Ohio attorney general, I was familiar with enforcement, which starts with investigations and can lead to public lawsuits or regulatory actions to halt legal violations. It is a blunt instrument, but it can yield considerable results. In Ohio, for example, we filed lawsuits to enforce the securities and antitrust laws, ultimately recovering over $2 billion for Ohio taxpayers and pension systems that had been exploited by Wall Street during the financial crisis. But aggressive public enforcement was not the norm in the banking industry.

Supervision authority, however, is quite different. It evolved historically from the power of the British monarchs to grant corporate charters to royal trading or banking companies, such as the Hudson Bay Company or the Bank of England. Along with this grant of special privileges came the power to supervise the companies to determine whether they were acting properly within the limits of their charters. This power crossed the Atlantic to the colonies, where it found new form in the government's power to license companies and modify or revoke a license that was abused. Through long-standing tradition, licensed companies must open their books to their regulators for thorough examination. They generally must modify their behavior as directed, as a condition of maintaining their license to continue operations. These interactions typically are confidential, and the details are not made public. If a licensed company thinks it is being mistreated, it always has the option to file a lawsuit against its regulator, but this carries the significant risk of poisoning the relationship. This arrangement gives the regulator great power; it has been said that the governor of the Bank of England can correct irresponsible behavior just by raising an eyebrow.[2]

Combining robust supervisory and enforcement authority was largely a new approach, and we had to figure it out as we went along.[3] The banking agencies rely almost exclusively on supervision to achieve results, whereas "litigating agencies" like the Department of Justice can only bring lawsuits or enforcement actions in the courts, with all the formalities and process that entails. The puzzle is that any given problem with a company can potentially be resolved either by supervisory pressure or by bringing a lawsuit. Both mechanisms can secure changes in future corporate behavior, and both can produce compensation for people harmed by violations. The key differences are that supervision operates through confidential processes where the resolutions are often private, whereas enforcement actions are taken in public; and in enforcement actions the agency or a court can impose penalties as a deterrent (to that company and others), which the bureau could not impose in the supervisory process.

That "tool choice" decision became a feature of every matter we pursued. It was difficult to manage effectively, and over the next few years, we developed careful processes to address it. The traditional chartered banks were used to supervision almost exclusively, and they sharply opposed our use of the enforcement power. But Congress had set a goal of bringing all financial companies up to the same standard, rather than treating the banks differently. So early on, when we identified the credit card add-on problems through our supervisory process, we used our enforcement powers to resolve them by public actions. That caused the banks to take seriously our willingness to punish deceptive practices. For many nonbank financial companies, on the other hand, our supervisory power was a novelty and it came as a shock. The credit reporting companies, for example, had never faced such intrusive oversight, at either the state or federal level. They were unprepared for the new compliance management requirements we were imposing to improve their treatment of consumers. Once again, however, the aim was a level playing field for all companies, regardless of formal corporate structure, that compete with one another in the financial marketplace.[4]

In addition, the bureau was given authority over the fair lending laws. The Equal Credit Opportunity Act (ECOA) bars discrimination in any extension of credit to consumers—covering mortgages, auto loans, credit cards, and other loans. The Justice Department is empowered to enforce this law, but its crowded agenda limits its capacity to deal with these issues. As a result, Congress authorized the CFPB and other federal regulators to enforce the ECOA also. These issues are highly sensitive, involving claims of discrimination based on race, ethnicity, or sex, among other factors prohibited by law. Over decades, the difficulty of proving discriminatory intent shaped the law to encompass cases of discrimination based on statistical data—comparing, say, the treatment of male borrowers versus female borrowers or of white borrowers versus black or Hispanic borrowers. Although this approach is now established law, it remains controversial. Lenders complain that they cannot even know whether they are complying with the law until somebody runs the numbers after the fact, with bad results leading them to be tagged as "racist" or "sexist." These complaints, however, are overstated. Lenders have tried-and-true methods to evaluate their own data and check the numbers for themselves, as part of their compliance program, and they bear responsibility if they fail to do so. That said, it was no surprise that financial companies and their political allies fiercely opposed our involvement in these cases.[5]

This area posed a further complication. Although the CFPB is authorized to file its own cases, our statute required us to cooperate with the Justice Department in finding violations of the fair lending laws. Thus, we had to coordinate closely with their attorneys, jointly strategizing how to proceed in both bringing and resolving cases. It even could affect our supervisory authority in matters where we did not intend to file a lawsuit at all, since the Justice Department might disagree with us and decide to file a case of its own. But our team forged a strong alliance with their counterparts, and the added resources and diagnostic tools that we brought to the task meant that many more fair lending matters were being addressed than ever before.[6] Together, this partnership yielded significant cases against Hudson City Bank and Bancorp South for "redlining," which is defined as discouraging loan applicants in minority communities. In addition, we brought novel cases of "reverse redlining," which covers lending in minority communities on worse terms than are available elsewhere. Our work with the Justice Department also produced the largest cases of credit card discrimination in history, against American Express and GE Capital Retail Bank, for settling credit card debts on less favorable terms for Puerto Rican customers than for US customers.[7]

In addition, we brought public enforcement actions against several banks and auto finance companies for discrimination in auto lending. People should not be denied credit, or get it only on less favorable terms, simply because of their race or ethnicity or gender. This had happened over the years to many unwitting consumers, which is why Congress outlawed it. Attorney General Holder joined me to announce the resolution of our first such action, an especially contentious matter with Ally Bank, one of the largest auto lenders at the time. Based on a CFPB examination of the company, our analysis showed that they had allowed dealers to charge higher interest rate markups on auto loans made to African Americans, Hispanics, and Asian and Pacific Islanders. Ally agreed to pay $80 million to a settlement fund to go to harmed borrowers, along with an $18 million penalty, and to implement a compliance program to prevent future discrimination, including making payments to harmed consumers if lending disparities were found during annual reviews.[8]

FACING OUR CHALLENGES

The other banking regulators—the Office of the Comptroller of the Currency (OCC), the Federal Deposit Insurance Corporation (FDIC), and the Federal Reserve—regulate bank operations for safety and soundness, but the Consumer Bureau is invested with authority that has an entirely different focus: to address violations of consumer financial law by examining the banks with an eye not to their own well-being, but rather to how they treat consumers. In some ways, the two perspectives tend to converge over the long run, as no company can survive if it systematically mistreats its customers. But in the short run, a company often can profit at the expense of its customers, such as with back-end pricing and hidden fees—and much corporate behavior seems increasingly focused on the short run.

Given the dramatic differences in our aims, we needed to figure out how we could work together productively with the other regulators to oversee these different aspects of the banking business. In some respects, the bureau's mere existence represented a reproach to the banking agencies, whose work on consumer compliance was now infringed by our new and robust authority. Over time, as we got used to one another, we began to conduct joint trainings and to coordinate our banking examinations. At the start, however, the OCC sought to crimp our powers by telling "their" banks that they should not share information with us before discussing it with the OCC first. Their attitude was increasingly intolerable until Tom Curry became the new OCC leader in March 2012, bringing a welcome pro-consumer outlook. As the CFPB director, I also served on the FDIC board, which fostered close communication with Marty Gruenberg, the pro-consumer FDIC chair. All the banking regulators were members of a body known as the Federal Financial Institutions Examination Council (FFIEC), where we coordinated our approach to examining financial institutions. And, of course, the CFPB was formally part of the Federal Reserve, from which we received our operating funds.

The US Chamber of Commerce had a special concern about our supervisory practices. They made numerous recommendations about how we should operate and sought clarification about the kind of information we were seeking and whether we would share it with other law enforcement officials. They also objected to our practice of bringing enforcement attorneys to initial examination meetings, which they saw as heavy-handed and intimidating. We met every few months for further discussions and adopted several of their suggestions. We also made some concessions. For example, we stopped sending enforcement attorneys to new exam meetings and found other ways to coordinate internally, though enforcement always remained on the table and was pursued in appropriate cases. The growing strength of our corps of field managers was a crucial impetus for the progress we were making. They served as the primary points of contact with the companies being examined, coordinated with their state and federal counterparts, shepherded the exam teams from start to finish, and oversaw training and commissioning programs. Eventually, the chamber acknowledged that we had satisfied their concerns, especially as our program developed more consistency and clarity. The way our team handled this challenge showed we would make good-faith efforts to learn from our critics.

Forging Alliances

State attorneys general have long been on the front lines of consumer finance, and this was especially true during the mortgage crisis. It made eminent sense for the CFPB to forge a powerful alliance with the more activist pro-consumer attorneys general, which was about a third of them. We began to join their strategy calls and work with them on investigations that led to numerous joint actions. We brought to the table our strategic tools, our market analysis, and a willingness to devote resources, share the load, and share the credit. We also brought the obvious passion of our team. In my second month at the bureau, our whole enforcement team of six people attended the annual meeting of the attorneys general in Washington. Later that day I ran into Jim Tierney, a former Maine attorney general who is now the leading authority on attorney general offices. I mentioned that we all had come to the meeting that day. "Oh yeah, I saw them there sitting in the front row," he said, "and I knew exactly who they were because they had that look on their face." "What look is that?" I inquired. "They had that look I used to see," he said, "like they just know they are going to change the world. I hadn't seen that look in a long time."

We had many successes in our work with state attorneys general. Among the actions we brought, either together or in parallel, were dozens of cases against for-profit colleges, student loan servicers, debt collectors, credit reporting companies, mortgage lenders, and mortgage servicers, which secured far-reaching changes in industry behavior and considerable money back for consumers. Some cases were especially interesting. We joined the New York attorney general, for example, to sue companies that we alleged were scamming 9/11 first responders and former NFL players out of millions of dollars they were due from victim compensation funds and legal settlements.[9] We also consulted closely with the attorneys general on the case we filed against CashCall, an online tribal lender. In that case, we argued that loans made in violation of state licensing laws or state interest rate caps also violate federal law, at least where the company is seeking to collect money that it is not legally owed. This argument allowed us to reinforce the efforts of states that had sought to bring enforcement cases against online tribal lenders like CashCall but found themselves blocked by claims of tribal immunity that do not apply to the bureau.[10]

A second key group of state officials is the Conference of State Bank Supervisors, which is the coordinating body for the state financial regulators. They oversee state-chartered banks, though most of the biggest banks hold a federal charter and thus elude their authority. Yet the scope of the work they do is much broader, because most of them also oversee licensure of many other financial companies, including mortgage lenders, debt collectors, payday lenders, and check cashers. Like the bureau, they possess the supervisory power to examine companies that hold state licenses, and at times they would undertake public enforcement actions.[11]

Although these state banking officials could have harbored many reasons to dislike our intrusion into their territory, both sides worked hard to develop relationships and build goodwill. We soon became close allies, and many highly regarded state regulators came to work at the bureau in leadership positions. We communicated extensively, coordinated on training sessions, strategized and conducted joint supervisory exams, and took actions together to hold companies accountable. We found willing partners in this work all over the country. The Utah banking regulator teamed up with us frequently, helping us address deceptive credit card practices by American Express, including charging unlawful late fees. The top Texas regulator helped us combat mortgage fraud by companies that misled people about the benefits of paying down their mortgage more frequently and then diverted some of the money to self-dealing schemes. He had seen similar frauds hopping around from state to state to defeat prosecution and so was eager to co-ordinate with us. We also met regularly with the powerful New York banking regulator and found various ways to collaborate. We brought a joint action against companies that we believed deceive customers about the price and risks of high-cost pension advance loans. And we filed a brief supporting New York's efforts to curb predatory practices by tribal lenders. Our work together showed that close teamwork is possible even across the difficult spaces created by different agencies and levels of our government.

We also found that the Dodd-Frank Act is an unusual federal statute. The ordinary rule is that state officials enforce state law and federal officials enforce federal law. But this statute expressly blesses the states to enforce many aspects of federal law, providing a backstop in the event the federal officials are failing to do the job.[12] So that was another reason our strategic partnership was beneficial: working closely together kept us on the same page and avoided dysfunctional disagreements. Some state officials were more enthusiastically pro-consumer than others, of course, but when problems arose that clearly affected consumers in their own states, any of them might join up with us. That made sense to me—after all, a key part of these jobs is law enforcement, and some of the things we took on were violations not only of civil law but also of criminal law. But viewing consumer protection as a law-and-order issue is not a consistent theme, especially for those officials who are more partial to favoring business interests.

Points on the Board

In our first year, we opened dozens of investigations, but they took time to progress. We conducted our first examinations, but they too unfolded slowly, due to our short staffing and the need to take extreme care in producing exam reports. Every draft exam report from the field came to headquarters for review, to ensure a baseline of consistency in measuring the facts against the law and determining appropriate remedies for violations. That caused delays, but our team began to gel as we got more used to the work and to one another.

Our relationships with fellow federal regulators turned out to be crucial in the early going. Our precarious leadership situation—both before and after my recess appointment—left us vulnerable to legal challenges over our authority. But joining with other agencies in taking an enforcement or supervisory action helped insulate us against such challenges, because it was not worthwhile to try to knock us out if the action would continue regardless. The OCC and the FDIC joined us in our first major enforcement actions against Capital One Bank and Discover Bank for the deceptive marketing of credit card add-on products discussed earlier. They each issued their own companion orders to the banks, which reinforced the gravity of the issues and the need to clean up the problems.[13]

Those early cases also helped us establish the broader principle that we would hold companies responsible for harm done by those they hired to act on their behalf. In the credit card add-on cases, for example, some of the banks argued that the telemarketers they hired to sell the worthless add-on products should be solely responsible for the misleading statements their employees made to consumers, letting the bank itself off the hook. This point was important because companies often farm out various functions to other parties, known as service providers, both for specialization and in a bid to limit their own liability. In many instances, the service providers are less well financed than the larger companies that hire them, making it less likely they would be able to compensate consumers for any harm done, leaving their victims high and dry. We issued a bulletin stressing that as a legal matter no company could shift liability in this way: it was their legal responsibility to monitor companies acting in their name. Any third-party service provider would remain answerable for its own misconduct, but so would the bank or company that hired it. This principle was important in every consumer finance market.

Our major early enforcement actions were crucial for our fledgling agency. They showed we had power, were willing to exercise it, and could do so effectively. They also helped establish stronger working relationships with the other banking agencies. In the future, we would resolve the bulk of our matters with banks (and with other financial companies as well) through the confidential supervision process, often in collaboration with other federal and state officials, which typically enabled us to rectify violations and compensate consumers more quickly. But we now had made clear that in large or significant matters we would not hesitate to use the public enforcement process as well. And when we had the goods in terms of clear evidence of legal violations, we found that the banks rarely engaged in pointless fighting. Instead, they generally accepted a reasonable resolution that modified their behavior and made their customers whole—even orders that imposed penalties where the facts justified that outcome.[14] This enabled us to avoid getting bogged down in scorched-earth litigation. Good precedents were being set as we cleaned up an industry-wide bad practice and returned billions of dollars to consumers.

Much of the work to scale up our efforts—especially follow-up work to implement the principles set in public enforcement actions—was being carried out by our supervision teams. We had hundreds of examiners who were constantly on the road to scrutinize operations at the largest financial companies, which in combination provided a potent force. As we assessed the individual companies, our lodestar was practices that pose risks for consumers. If our exams identified larger issues of consumer harm, we often referred those matters for public enforcement actions, along with penalties where they were justified. Although the processes would always remain difficult to manage, the concept of a CFPB that would emphasize *both* supervision and enforcement was working out even better than we had hoped.[15]

SETTING PRIORITIES

One of the hardest tasks for any organization with limited resources is prioritization. From the outset, we cast a wide net to determine what issues should be put on our agenda or moved to the front of the line for more immediate action. We conducted our own research from all available sources and mined our growing database of consumer complaints. We sought input from our fellow agencies; from federal, state, and local officials; from the nonprofits and consumer groups; and even from industry itself. And indeed, some of our best tips came from companies struggling against the unfair competition of rivals who were breaking the law to get an improper advantage.[16] In the leadup to the mortgage crisis, many community banks had faced the awful choice of either losing market share or lowering their underwriting standards to match the bad loans that were being given out elsewhere. Some community bankers told me personally about having to deny loans to current or prospective customers and then see them go down the street and get the same loan from someone else—loans that were destined to fail eventually, just as they had predicted, though not right away.

In setting our priorities, we drew on our full array of supervision, enforcement, and fair lending authorities to cover the entire marketplace. We were determined to touch all industries under our purview and not be perceived as giving anybody a free pass. We wanted every company in the realm of consumer finance to feel our presence and worry that we might be looking over their shoulder. We analyzed the different markets and looked for priority exams to conduct, investigations to open, and cases to bring. In 2014, we attempted to summarize some of our thinking by focusing on four categories of problems in the consumer marketplace, which some referred to as "the four Ds": (1) deceptive practices, including situations where the costs and risks of financial decisions are obscured or opaque; (2) debt traps, where consumers pile up substantial costs through a cycle of debt; (3) dead ends, where consumers cannot make a choice to change providers when they are treated unfairly; and (4) discrimination and unequal treatment based on race, gender, ethnicity, or other factors prohibited by law. We engaged the entire bureau in continuing to refine and elaborate these priorities over the next several years.

Whenever we could pursue matters with partners, it helped us broaden our reach. In some areas, private attorneys had filed cases that led to orders and behavioral changes to benefit consumers, and we consulted with them about what they were seeing and hearing, including regular calls with legal aid groups, consumer attorneys, and law school clinics around the country. So, what was once a largely empty pipeline was now being filled from many sources. Our enforcement agenda touched a wide range of products and companies, and eventually we would generate a steady stream of about four or five public enforcement actions per month.[17]

Public Deterrence

To influence the marketplace, our work needed to be visible to demonstrate that we had to be taken seriously. We achieved that in three ways. First, we publicized our enforcement actions. Each one was broadcast via a press release or a press call. Our press releases were comprehensive and detailed, as were our enforcement orders, so that everyone in the industry could see what problem we had addressed at the specific company and how to avoid such problems themselves. Where we alleged violations, we laid out the facts we uncovered in our investigations and explained why the conduct was illegal. We specified how those violations had harmed consumers. The companies we charged worried about the public exposure, and though we never negotiated the language of our press releases, some were more concerned about the wording of the release than about the specific requirements of the orders and the amounts they would have to pay. We also tried to be fair to the companies. In a couple of cases, for example, where a predecessor company committed the illegal acts, we took pains to identify it as the source of the problems and expressly distinguished it from its successor. Or if a company was especially cooperative in remedying problems, we would take that into account in fashioning the terms of our orders, and we would publicly say so as well.

Second, we raised our visibility by publishing information about the work we were doing. In supervision, the long-standing tradition was to handle such matters confidentially, and in line with the other banking agencies, we respected that tradition. But it limited the speed and reach of our supervision program, by relegating it to addressing issues sequentially, company by company, rather than across the entire industry at once. To square this circle, we created a new publication we called "Supervisory Highlights," which described the kinds of problems we were identifying and resolving without breaching the anonymity of any given institution. Every few months, we would describe the nature of illegal practices that our supervision program had found at one or more companies and detail what steps we took to halt those practices and compensate consumers for the harm done, without identifying any specific company by name. This allowed us to put the entire industry more quickly on notice of problems they should be addressing without undermining the confidentiality of our supervisory process.[18] We also published "compliance bulletins" to offer guidance on various topics, such as to supplement the guidance conveyed by enforcement actions. Compliance officers at the companies told us these publications helped them get the attention of their corporate leadership to make needed changes, which in turn protected consumers while helping the companies reduce the costs of regulatory actions, lawsuits, and reputational damage with their customers.

A third way we got the industry's attention was through the bully pulpit. The leaders at the bureau regularly spoke to business leaders and the trade associations, and we used those occasions to put our concerns on the companies' radar screens. Because we were developing a reputation for taking actions to address problems that harmed consumers, the companies now had to weigh our comments and adjust to our agenda. Steve Antonakes, who became the deputy director after Raj left the bureau, gave a speech on mortgage servicing in Florida early in 2014, which sent shockwaves through the industry. He told them that we remained "deeply disappointed by the lack of progress that the mortgage servicing industry has made." He described the way many servicers kept people in the dark and gave them the runaround, and he noted that it had felt like "Groundhog Day," with mortgage servicing problems repeating themselves for far too long. His tough message continued right to the end: "Ultimately, these profound changes will be good for all Americans, including industry. But please understand, business as usual has ended in mortgage servicing. Groundhog Day is over. Thank you."[19]

The speech was especially effective coming from Steve, who was known as a top-flight career bank regulator, and we continued to hear feedback about it for months afterward. Yet mortgage servicing vexed us throughout my tenure. The business model is deeply flawed, with a revenue structure that is designed for when things are going well and not for when servicing matters most, which is when people fall on tough times. Servicers lack adequate financial incentives to save consumers from foreclosure, and we tried to strengthen those incentives through new regulations and our supervisory and enforcement work, but it was a constant struggle to produce lasting change.

Unfortunately, many consumers continued to be hurt by poor processes, faulty execution, dysfunctional technology, and seeming indifference to the scale of the problems. Later that year, we brought an action against Flagstar Bank, which largely stemmed from gross understaffing of its mortgage servicing work. We cited the bank for its heavy backlogs of applications for loan modifications, which took up to nine months to review, and average call wait times of 25 minutes (with average call abandonment rates of almost 50%). We fined the bank $10 million, required it to reimburse consumers, and barred it from accepting new servicing rights on distressed loans until the issues were addressed. Earlier, we had teamed up with fifty state attorneys general to bring our biggest enforcement action ever against Ocwen, the largest nonbank mortgage servicer, which generated $2 billion in reduced principal as relief for mortgage borrowers who were hurt by systemic misconduct at every stage of the servicing process. Even so, less than four years later, the Florida Attorney General and more than twenty state financial regulators joined us in taking further actions against Ocwen for persistent lapses. Despite repeatedly calling out the mortgage servicers for their failings, we still had trouble putting Groundhog Day behind us.[20]

Badge of Honor

Although our tough stance on enforcement and oversight served consumers well, it did carry a real cost for the bureau. The criticism and resistance to us from industry and their supporters on Capitol Hill was the badge of honor we earned through the work we were doing. We became the target of constant investigations, burdensome and repetitive demands for documents, and subpoena threats. One frequent criticism was that we were improperly "regulating by enforcement." Companies argued that we were not sufficiently clarifying our legal standards, so they felt ambushed when we brought enforcement actions against them. Most of these objections stemmed from our use of the authority Congress granted us to find companies that were violating the law by committing "unfair, deceptive, or abusive acts or practices." These well-settled standards had existed in state and federal law for over a century, but at times their application still could be controversial. Businesses would prefer that government specify every aspect of conduct that is illegal, to be sure, but it is impossible to define all the inventive ways people can dream up to cheat others out of their money.[21] The "abusive" standard was a special lightning rod for the industry. It did not have a century of history behind it, and though Congress had defined the term in the law, the industry viewed it as vague and perplexing. We were cautious in applying it, recognizing that almost all instances of "abusive" behavior likely are also either "unfair" or "deceptive," if not both.

This line of criticism had two aspects. To begin with, no company wanted to be held up as a public example when we zeroed in on some harmful practice, which other companies might be perpetrating as well. They would prefer that we identify the practice, write a rule on the subject, and give them time to comply with the rule before coming down hard on any company. But no effective regulator does that, and it would allow much harmful conduct to go unredressed. A careful survey of our enforcement actions showed that they rested on solid ground, and almost anyone looking at the facts would agree that the conduct was out of bounds and something had to be done about it. Indeed, over 90% of our enforcement actions involved some form of fraudulent or deceptive conduct.[22] The rule-writing process was far too slow to deal with all the creative damage being done to consumers. To be effective in protecting consumers and deterring new forms of fraud, it was essential to enforce the law in this manner.

The industry also objected to having the bureau announce an enforcement action against one company and then expect every other company to comply with its specifications, even though the others had not yet been adjudged to have done something wrong themselves. This was regarded as imposing an industry-wide regulation through an enforcement action. But this criticism seemed wrong. The evenhanded rule of law rests on the principle that if Company A did such a thing, and it was found to have violated the law, then Company B and Company C would likewise be in violation of the law if they were doing the same thing. At a minimum, therefore, all companies needed to review their operations and make sure they were not committing the very same offenses.[23]

In other words, the core principle of equal justice under the law means that each enforcement or supervisory action that identifies the underlying facts of a violation should be just as binding on the whole industry as any regulation we formally adopted. To give fair notice to other companies, we spelled out the details of our public enforcement actions comprehensively, and we presented our "Supervisory Highlights" to be more transparent about what we were doing in our confidential examinations. This approach is simply good government.

As we grew and we refined our supervision process, it became a well-honed engine for improving consumer finance. Our examination schedule was more strategic and comprehensive. Our time from scoping to completing an exam and issuing a final report shortened considerably. Our consistency improved. We built in constant communication between our supervision and enforcement teams about our findings and what should be done about them, so the tool choice decision did not become a source of erratic unpredictability. We developed enough findings for the teams to generate "roll-up" exam reports for the larger institutions, with a numerical rating as a gauge of their overall performance. They were used to such ratings from the banking agencies, and we gave their board members and executives detailed explanations of what the issues were, what we had concluded, and why. Even in the difficult area of fair lending, the companies were learning to work with us as we were better able to clarify our approach.

Making Headway

We began issuing a public scorecard each year on how much relief we had provided to American consumers, and the total amount was adding up. Eventually it grew to over $12 billion for thirty million Americans—far more than the money we spent over those same years to operate the bureau. That total did not even include all the relief we obtained through our non-public supervisory work.[24] And, as Senator Warren liked to remind us, every dollar we got back for consumers who had been cheated was joined by more dollars saved in the future by all the consumers who would not be cheated in the same way.

The bureau also had the authority to collect penalties in appropriate enforcement actions that would accumulate in our civil penalty fund. This money could then be used to reimburse consumers in other enforcement actions who had been harmed but had not gotten the relief they deserved. Usually this happened when the perpetrator went out of business or was driven out by our enforcement action because illegal activities were the core of its business model. Over time, we restored hundreds of millions of dollars to consumers who had been wronged, usually by deception or fraud, but had received no compensation. On receiving their checks, a surprising number of these people, unfamiliar with any entity called the "CFPB," would inquire whether it was some sort of scam. We were always glad to reassure them that indeed this was one check they could and should cash.

PLAYING BY THE RULES

The two flashpoints for any government agency that oversees private industry are enforcement and regulation. In both areas, the agency has the power to make companies do things, or stop doing things, against their will by force of law. At first glance, this seems at odds with a free market where economic actors decide for themselves what to do and how to do it. Yet free markets necessarily rest on the underpinnings of law and its enforcement: upholding property rights, enforcing contracts, pursuing justice for wrongdoers who harm others by violating the law. Both individuals and companies have rights of their own, and they need law to be enforced to plan and function along predictable lines. But beyond these accepted principles, the rub comes in how much law and enforcement we should have. The more detailed the law is, and the more onerous its enforcement, the more private decision making feels hemmed in.

We found ourselves right in the middle of these perpetual conflicts. Banks and other financial companies always want to preserve as much discretion as possible to maximize their profits. Yet the scandal of the financial crisis was that Wall Street investors—and the predatory lenders they financed and encouraged—brought down the economy through their irresponsible behavior, and much of it was entirely legal. Strong enforcement is inadequate if the laws themselves do not constrain dysfunctional and damaging conduct.

To achieve effective reform, then, the laws had to be changed. The public demanded it and Congress now required it, giving the CFPB broad powers to rein in the types of practices that had collapsed the economy, but also placing us on a collision course with the financial titans.

Data Driven

A federal agency's rulemaking authority is essentially power delegated by Congress to make law. In our statute, the Dodd-Frank Act, Congress authorized the bureau to write rules in virtually every area of consumer financial law, but also imposed specific constraints that defined and limited the boundaries of our authority to act. In addition, the Administrative Procedure Act (APA), which governs a broad range of agency actions, also lays out procedures for adopting rules, which can take years to navigate.

Even so, this framework gave us considerable latitude to write rules to govern the behavior of the financial industry. Industry's worst nightmare is an agency composed of people with their own axes to grind who simply write their personal prejudices into law. This worry was already evident, and it was important that we quell some of the concern by setting standards for careful and responsible use of our powers.

To do so, we made a commitment to be data driven in approaching our work, especially in crafting new rules and modifying old ones. "Data driven" was a bureau mantra that originated with Elizabeth Warren and Raj Date. As a law professor, Elizabeth had examined how the bankruptcy laws affect ordinary families and households. Her research involved extensive surveys, interviews, and review of court records. Her strongly pro-consumer views rested on real-world experience and data about people's financial struggles. Raj, likewise, had a strong background in financial analytics and research, with a deep understanding of how big data was changing the financial industry. He also recognized the importance of data to the bureau's ability to understand and influence the industry's future.[1]

My own background was different from theirs. I was a lawyer and a political figure, used to operating on intuition and cogent facts, and often relying on the impressions made by narratives and stories. I was not used to relying on extensive data or financial analysis, and this was a reason for industry to be skeptical of me. But Elizabeth and Raj had imprinted their vision on the bureau by bringing in many impressive people who were committed to that vision as well, including economists, analysts, and industry veterans, who worked in close quarters with the rule-writing team. Their division, which was known as "RMR" (for Research, Markets, and Regulations), was dedicated to ensuring that we had objective factual justification for every move we made in the regulatory space. It also reassured industry representatives that they could argue with us over data and evidence, not simply butt heads over competing values.

For the lobbyists, this platform was not nearly as good as the one they have in dealing with Congress to shape legislation. There they have levers such as financial contributions and political pressures on individual members. But with our data-driven focus, they would have to address issues more directly by bringing information to persuade us, rather than tactics to intimidate us. And as an independent agency, we were more insulated from political pressures, such as threats to cut our budget or fire employees. Politics were constantly swirling around us, yet most of the conversations in our meetings were substantive and on the merits. If people could not convince us of the facts, they were unlikely to get their way.

Making Rules Work

To write a binding rule, an agency needs authority from Congress, which in the bureau's case was found in the Dodd-Frank Act. The authority could come from a statutory directive requiring us to write a rule or it could be a more general authorization that allowed us to decide whether to do so. In either case, Congress could also specify many of the details and the timing. The general procedures we followed were dictated by the APA. First, we would issue a notice of proposed rulemaking, laying out what we intended to do, what authority we had to do it, and what our justification was for doing it. Next came the "notice and comment" process, where the public has a chance to review the proposal and submit comments on it. The law required us to consider the comments and any supporting data or evidence and then explain, in reasonable detail, what we decided to do in our final rule and why. The final rule would state its effective date, which typically included a transition period for everyone to make the adjustment from the old status quo to the new status quo. Anyone affected by our rule could challenge it in court on several grounds: that we lacked substantial evidence for the rule, that we had exceeded the scope of our authority, or that we had acted arbitrarily and capriciously. To survive a legal challenge, the agency must be careful in doing its work, so our rule-writing team consulted closely with our legal division on all procedural and substantive aspects of its work.

If this seems like a long road to travel, it was meant to be. But the bureau was slowed by one more procedural stage: if we determined that a rule might have a significant economic impact on a substantial number of small entities, then we could not issue a proposed rule until we convened a panel of small providers and invited the Small Business Administration and the Office of Management and Budget to join us in reporting on how the rule would affect small entities.[2] Aside from all this mandated process, our pledge to be "data driven" meant we had to get the rulemaking process underway even earlier by gathering data, conducting surveys, or issuing requests for information to learn more about whether and how to move forward.

For our team, the job of writing rules would typically take years of work and pose immense challenges. As with all the early work at the bureau, much depended on our staffing up quickly with dedicated, high-quality people. Because the Federal Reserve's main rulemaking authority for consumer finance had been transferred over to us, most of their team joined us as well, bringing their experience and expertise to continue this work.

I had my own experience with the Fed's rulemaking team. For years under Alan Greenspan, a noted libertarian, the Fed was reluctant to take aggressive action by writing rules to govern the credit card industry. Instead, it took a laissez-faire approach that largely relied on the free market to self-police issues. But in 2006, Greenspan gave way to Ben Bernanke, and by then credit card abuses were widespread and increasingly notorious. I was the Ohio treasurer, and we were holding "Women and Money" seminars on financial management around the state. When we surveyed people about their financial challenges, we heard about many problems with credit cards: interest rates spiking unexpectedly, late fees charged unpredictably, and surprise back-end fees tacked on that raised costs to consumers and profits for companies. Parents also complained about aggressive marketing of credit cards to students on college campuses. Amid prodding from Congress, the Fed crafted new measures to address these issues. Their proposed rule was solidly pro-consumer. It addressed problems with late fees and marketing to college students. It also fixed the universal default issue that tripped up so many consumers, like Mary, by causing their interest rates to spike unexpectedly, even on purchases they had already made, simply because they had been late on an unrelated payment to someone else. From now on, such rate increases would be limited to new purchases and would not apply to old debt.

But as the notice-and-comment process unfolded, we were concerned that the financial industry would pressure the Fed to water down the rule. Accordingly, we organized a "Speak Out" campaign, encouraging Ohioans to advocate in favor of tough protections. We solicited input at our public events and collected over twenty thousand comments supporting the rule. To its credit, the Fed stood firm and finalized a strong rule in December 2008 but decided that it would not take effect for more than eighteen months. As I would learn later at the CFPB, companies need time to revise computer processes for millions of customers and retrain their workforce to comply with new requirements. At the time, though, all we saw was that the credit card companies were being granted license to continue abusing consumers for a substantial period. Soon thereafter, Congress passed the Credit Card Accountability Responsibility and Disclosure Act, known as the CARD Act, which codified much of the new rule in statutory law. It also moved up the effective date for many provisions by about four months. The result was an odd tag team of congressional and agency action that together made dramatic improvements for consumers.[3]

Sending Money Overseas

In the Dodd-Frank Act, Congress directed us to write a rule governing remittance transfers, which are international money transfers into and out of the country. This topic presents exactly the kind of technical, nitty-gritty issues that do not make sense for Congress to delve into itself; instead, it often paints the broad outlines of its goals and then assigns the task to an agency—the CFPB, in this case—to work out the specifics and fill in the details.

Millions of people all over the world send money internationally, some very regularly, and in some developing countries remittances can amount to one-third or more of total gross domestic product. Money is often sent to family members and friends, but it can be sent to meet all kinds of financial obligations. In 2012, the World Bank estimated that global remittances would reach $534 billion, with $53 billion sent from the United States, though our data suggest the numbers are much higher.[4] Yet there is also a sizable black market for sending money outside the country, either because of cost or because people lack confidence in the formal market. This is an area where people—often immigrants—are easily exploited, and in the United States these transactions had no federal consumer protections at all. Eva, for example, saved $300 each month to send to her elderly parents in Slovenia. But how to get the money to them? The local banks required her to maintain an account before they would deal with her, but when she applied, they rejected her based on their screening process for financial risk. A few established companies were available in her area, but after a couple of bad experiences where she felt mistreated and her complaints were ignored, she did not trust them. Some check-cashing outlets offered the service, but they charged huge fees and she worried that they might not actually send the money. Her other alternative was to save the money until she, or someone she knew, next visited Slovenia. But holding large amounts of cash while traveling carries significant risks. Besides, she could not afford to go very often, and her parents could not wait that long for the money. The remittance market wasn't working for her.

Congress tasked us with providing new safeguards for these transactions. Our proposed rule would confer three vital consumer protections: enhanced disclosures, cancellation and refund rights, and error correction and dispute resolution requirements. But the area is complex—covering a vast range of businesses in every part of the globe—and the rule itself had to deal with these complexities.

After the president recess-appointed me, we were less than a month away from the deadline Congress had set for finalizing the remittance rule. As it was our first rule, all parts of the bureau were invited to offer input. There were internal disagreements about whether the draft of the final rule was sufficiently pro-consumer, and I faced a dilemma: either leave it as is or insist on last-minute edits to respond to the criticisms. I chose the latter course, which jumbled the process and fostered acrimony within the bureau. We issued the rule on February 7, 2012, with an implementation period of twelve months. But in July and August, we issued further modifications to the rule, and in January, just before the rule was to take effect, we delayed it to reconsider two thorny issues that the industry had persuaded us were creating impracticalities: unreasonable requirements in the statute that US remittance providers must pinpoint exactly the taxes and fees charged in other countries, and how to handle failed transactions when senders provide insufficient or incorrect information. We addressed those issues quickly, and the rule finally took effect on October 28, 2013, which was twenty-one months after it was first issued.

This herky-jerky path could be traced back to my clumsy intervention at the eleventh hour, which no doubt undermined the care that the rulemaking team had devoted to the job. It caused them much extra trouble and aggravation through the multiple stages of finalizing the rule. But in our handling of the situation, we did establish an important principle that mattered a lot: we showed that we would take seriously the concerns and criticisms of those affected by a new rule, and when people could persuade us that we needed to rethink issues to get them right, we were willing to do so. We kept all the remittance providers apprised of our approach, and we worked hard to get them ready to implement the rule, which they did reasonably well. Five years later, the bureau rendered its look-back assessment of the rule and found that in this market, volumes had increased and prices continued to decrease, compliance costs were relatively low, consumers seemed to be receiving disclosures in a uniform manner, and disputes over errors were being processed. As is often the case, the quality of the data counseled caution in drawing broad conclusions, but the rule seemed to be working as intended.[5]

A Heavy List of Chores

Even as we struggled with the remittance rule, Congress had imposed a punishing schedule for us to address the severe problems in the mortgage market. Irresponsible and predatory behavior in this market had broken the economy, and Congress required us to write *seven* mortgage rules—three of them major—over a span of only eighteen months after opening our doors. Even for a fully functioning agency, this was a backbreaking workload. Given that we were still staffing up, it seemed almost superhuman. Not only did we need people with expertise on the new law and existing mortgage regulations, but also we needed economists to perform the background analysis. And it would take mortgage market professionals to understand how our decisions could affect the workings of about $10 trillion in mortgage loan inventory. Congress had given us some guidance, but we still would have to work out many details for ourselves.[6]

Ordinarily we would expect to face heavy resistance to our efforts to make changes on such a vast scale. Yet Congress had done something extremely clever to smooth our way. The norm with rule-writing is a binary choice between the old status quo and a new regime, which leaves the industry with every incentive to dig in against change. But here Congress enacted its own far-reaching reforms to the mortgage market in Title XIV of the Dodd-Frank Act, which would take effect as written unless we adopted our new mortgage rules by January 2013. In doing so, Congress nullified the old status quo and instead reframed the binary choice between its drastic hypothetical regime and a new set of rules that the CFPB could craft to meet the same objectives in a more balanced manner. By flipping the default mode in this manner, Congress forced the industry to root for us to finish our rules on time, making it far more willing to provide invaluable information, feedback, and practical help.

The three most important mortgage rules had to do with underwriting requirements, the servicing of mortgage payments, and loan originator compensation. Each was situated very differently. The rule on underwriting requirements, which was known as the "ability to repay" or "qualified mortgage" rule, was by far the most important. The lowering of standards in making loans was a precipitating cause of the financial crisis. Bad loans, often offered on misleading or predatory terms, were bundled up and marketed on Wall Street as lucrative investments, with all the fee income that entailed for many parties, even as they and the ratings agencies ignored the deterioration of lending standards. Community bankers had seen it; many were horrified by the lax underwriting and irresponsible loans being made by their competitors. But based on the widespread confidence that any loan, no matter how bad its terms, would succeed because property values could always be counted on to hold steady or increase over time, the market kept churning—right up until it didn't, when the bottom fell out on housing values in 2008.

To me, the most astonishing feature of this lax period was the prevalence of the "no doc" loan, where lenders lent hundreds of thousands of dollars without even requiring borrowers to document their incomes. And many loans included teaser rates that lasted only a year or two before the rate jumped much higher, yet lenders and brokers were treating these loans as if the initial rate was permanent. Even worse, some loans were negatively amortizing, causing borrowers to owe even more on the loan over time, which often surprised consumers.

Our job was to clean up this mess by setting basic standards for lenders to assess whether an applicant would be able to repay a mortgage loan, as well as defining what constitutes a "qualified mortgage." If we got things right, we would put an end to the kinds of problems that Susan had suffered when the lender sold her a loan that had an artificially low rate for the first year, leaving her unable to cope with the much higher rate later on. And we would address Helen and Nick's situation where they "qualified" for a no-doc loan they could not afford based on the erroneous assumption that their home value would continue to rise over time. But we had hard questions to consider in deciding what constitutes a "responsible" loan. Should we require a minimum down payment? A loan-to-income ratio? If so, what level should we set? And what kind of documentation should lenders use to verify that borrowers can meet the "ability to repay" requirements for a loan? We went around and around on these issues, knowing that our decisions would help shape the future of the US housing market for some time to come, because the markets would likely be cautious about financing any loan that did not meet the all-important "qualified mortgage" standard.

The rule on mortgage servicing was set against a legal backdrop that had changed a great deal since 2010, when Congress passed Title XIV of the Dodd-Frank Act. Foreclosures had finally peaked and begun to crest, though they remained at historically elevated levels. And the national mortgage servicing settlement reached by state and federal officials imposed far-reaching terms that more closely aligned the interests of mortgage servicers and their customers. These terms dictated changes in almost every function the servicers performed. With the servicing settlement already in place for the largest banks, it made sense for our rule to conform to most of its provisions while blending them with the requirements Congress had imposed. And doing so would level the playing field by requiring all servicers (not just those joining the nationwide settlement) to improve their operations and abide by the same standards. Raising servicing standards, and enforcing them effectively, would help address problems like those Deborah and Susan had suffered when they tried to avoid foreclosure by seeking loan modifications but eventually faced a breaking point as either incompetence or indifference on the part of their mortgage servicers jeopardized their ability to remain in their homes.

The rule on loan originator compensation barred lenders from structuring payments to mortgage brokers and loan officers in ways that gave them an incentive to steer borrowers into loans with certain features or higher rates than they qualified for. The Federal Reserve had been working on a similar rule before Congress intervened with the Dodd-Frank Act and finalized its rule shortly after the law was passed. We now had to reconcile the different approaches. The work was technical and complicated, but it was important to address the conflicts of interest that had led to people like Russell being steered into paying higher mortgage rates than they actually qualified for—in Russell's case, a 4% higher rate that he was steered into and paid unknowingly over the entire thirty-year life of his mortgage.

In addition, we had four more mortgage rules to complete within the same eighteen-month period: two rules relating to appraisals (one jointly with the Fed), one rule on escrowing money for taxes and insurance, and one rule on mortgage counseling and protections for certain high-cost loans. Although these other rules were more technical, we learned that there is no such thing as a "simple" federal regulation. Each had to be justified and supported with evidence and legal analysis, and each had to fit with the broader corpus of consumer finance regulations.

Burnout on the Mortgage Treadmill

It was a heroic achievement for our RMR team to complete this entire set of rules in the time frame that Congress set, but they managed it somehow. Their achievement won the bureau a great deal of respect. We had been asked to shape reforms for the largest consumer finance market in the history of the world in a very short time, and we did it. Moreover, as people began to digest our new rules, they failed to see the heavy hand they expected. Rather than impose a "one size fits all" approach to defining qualified mortgages, we developed multiple definitions for different market segments to protect consumers without unduly constraining what had become a tight market for mortgage lending in the wake of the housing crash. In general, we defined a "qualified mortgage" as one that met certain product restrictions and did not exceed a debt-to-income ratio of 43%. But we also created an additional category of qualified mortgage that allowed more flexibility to smaller lenders. In addition, we created a temporary category of qualified mortgage to include mortgage loans that met the underwriting standards set by the huge quasi-governmental agencies Fannie Mae and Freddie Mac (and a few similar entities), which further ensured that our new protections for the mortgage market would not stifle lending to consumers.[7]

Five years later, the bureau performed its look-back review, which examined the data and found that our rules did not lead to higher costs or less credit. That was not yet evident at the time, however, and many hastened to criticize us. But sober heads like Senator Isakson from Georgia and some key industry leaders saw that we had listened and learned and made what they thought were surprisingly reasonable judgments.[8] And with the new protections in place, the mortgage market continued to recover and expand as the lending climate improved, with very low defaults.

We never really had time to catch our breath, however, as mortgage issues would continue to dominate our agenda for the next several years. We had to complete the "Know Before You Owe" mortgage rule to simplify and clarify disclosures to consumers when they apply for a mortgage and when they close on the loan.[9] We also continued to review and revise our initial mortgage rules to improve them and to prevent them from having unintended consequences. And we committed ourselves to a project of "regulatory implementation," where we devoted considerable time and resources to assist companies in making the operational changes to comply fully with our new rules.

The regulatory implementation project set a lasting precedent for all our rules. We did not want to leave it to chance whether financial companies would be able to comply with our rules fully and in a timely manner. If, as we believed, our rules were improving the consumer marketplace, then it would be wrong for us to issue them and take the attitude that "it's your problem now" for companies and consumers to implement them. We could facilitate greater success if we helped companies implement them, so we went out of our way to make that happen. We provided companies with plain-language guides to the provisions of the rules and how-to instructions on how to comply with them. We had a hotline for questions, and with frequent questions we sometimes put out more formal guidance to the entire industry. We canvassed the industry to learn about unforeseen consequences and implementation challenges, which we then sought to address. Even with this conscious focus, our rules were detailed and complex and we didn't always meet people's needs. But we addressed many concerns and won points from our critics for our extensive efforts to help companies cope with the burdens of our new rules.[10]

Although we chafed as further amendments to the mortgage rules ate up our bandwidth when we needed to be turning to other things, modifications are inevitable with such a complex subject. We also knew this largest consumer market is the most important one, and the bureau needed things to go well here above all else. Each of the major mortgage rules underwent further changes, some more than once. In defining "rural" areas, for example, where smaller lenders get some special dispensations to encourage lending, we revised our definition twice, each time expanding it further. The last expansion came when Congress intervened to broaden our definition even more, a change we implemented with yet another rule.

For several years, our rulemaking agenda continued to be dominated by mandatory tasks. This eased some of the normal tensions between a regulatory agency and those it regulates, as everyone knew we had no choice but to do as Congress said. Even so, we still had other rules we were required to adopt. Two of them had to do with collecting and publishing data: on mortgage loans, where we would revise and update existing rules, and on small business loans, where no prior rules existed. In each case, the data would be used to discern local lending patterns, help direct public investments, and determine whether lenders are engaged in illegal discrimination. This made the financial industry nervous, because any new data we collected could expose them to closer scrutiny of their lending patterns and generate discrimination claims. We took them in order and completed the first one—another mortgage rule—though the industry was unhappy when we added some extra data fields to help us monitor and evaluate the effects of our other mortgage rules.[11] The other rule may have been the hardest task we faced, since it is not a consumer rule at all, and we made slow progress on it, given our crowded agenda.

Our discretionary rules—the things we didn't *have* to do yet believed we *should* do—were a source of greater controversy. As the constraints on our rulemaking agenda finally began to diminish, we called on the entire bureau to help us prioritize options for discretionary rules in a data-driven manner. These discretionary rules embroiled us in some of the toughest fights we faced, and they will be discussed more fully later.[12]

REGULATIONS AND THE REGULATED

One thing that surprised me about regulations in the field of consumer finance was how long and complex they are. Almost any rule we wrote could easily run to dozens of pages of small type. The detail was routinely microscopic, and the scope was comprehensive. At the beginning of my tenure, Comptroller Curry gave me a reproduction of the original statement of supervisory principles that the Office of the Comptroller of the Currency (OCC) laid out for banks to follow back at the time of the Civil War. It was full of general principles and admonitions, and it all fit onto one very large certificate. Later I took part in a press conference with Chicago Mayor Rahm Emmanuel; he and his city council were just completing municipal legislation on debt collectors. Both the ordinance licensing them and the ordinance providing for enforcement of their code of conduct totaled only five pages, which I envied. Yet the federal regulatory agencies sometimes produced tomes of extended directives. During my confirmation battle, Senator Angus King of Maine expressed his impatience with this approach by having an aide stack up consumer finance regulations on the table in front of us. Before long, I could hardly see him over the pile!

But perhaps surprisingly, we found that regulated companies often prefer prolix rules. Big companies with automated compliance functions want specifics on every conceivable point. They abhor the uncertainty that affords discretion to those who apply the rules. If there are eight possible scenarios, they want clear and fixed answers on how to handle every one, rather than a general principle that might be construed one way by an examiner, another way by an attorney, another way by an investor, and yet another way by a court. It sounds good on the surface to shorten the text, but this often really means the detail will be provided elsewhere, usually in reams of case law. In the field of debt collection, for example, Congress enacted the Fair Debt Collection Practices Act in 1977 and did not empower any agency to adopt implementing rules. For forty years, debt collection firms and attorneys have been drowning in uncertain and conflicting case law all over the country. The body of judge-made law surely covers more total pages than a normal set of implementing rules would cover, and conflicting decisions cannot possibly provide definitive guidance for anyone to depend on. That doesn't even account for the mounting expense of having to litigate all those cases, without any assurance of ever getting a clear and reliable result. Compared with that alternative, even the deep piles of paper on Senator King's table didn't seem so bad.[13]

The primary exceptions to this worldview are smaller institutions, where compliance is often more manual and the burdens of dealing with long rules can be overwhelming. One concern about consumer finance regulation is that it acts as a barrier to entry, raising costs disproportionately for smaller competitors and driving more consolidation in the financial industry. We tried to fight this problem by tailoring our rules to provide greater leeway for smaller entities, which was something we did where we could with our mortgage rules.

The complexity and detail in modern financial regulations may be a natural outgrowth of broader trends in American law over the past century. Since the progressive era, the general precepts of the common law, which often were not known until judges pronounced them in deciding their cases, have given way to a growing crush of statutory law. These enactments codify and expand on the general principles of the common law, and the statute books have mushroomed accordingly. Elegant simplicity was sacrificed for notice, clarity, certainty, and consistency. Our regulations are part of that larger trend, and we got there for the same reasons.

Economists and Market Teams

The kind of data-driven analysis we needed to support our work required the serious intellectual firepower of research economists and market analysts. But their work created some tension within the agency. These experts sought to be dispassionate and free of political influences or personal prejudices, as we all did, but their rigorous academic mindset made the more zealous consumer advocates feel uneasy about the neutral tenor of their outlook.

The importance of the economists and analysts was twofold for the bureau. First, there was the essential work that they, and only they, were able to do. For every rulemaking, the economists must make critical determinations about the small-entity review process and produce a required economic analysis assessing the costs, benefits, and burdens of the proposed rule. They then must account for the comments and criticisms we receive and provide updated analysis for the final rule. All of these are substantial undertakings, which need to be based on defensible facts and data that they gather, organize, and analyze. The work demands great care: their reasoning would be subject to legal challenge, so the entire rule could stand or fall depending on the strength of their analysis.[14]

Our economists and market teams were also an important public face to the outside world. Their integrity and ability bolstered our credibility. We established an Academic Research Council comprising top economists and social scientists, and our Office of Research was initially headed by Sendhil Mullainathan, a recipient of a MacArthur Foundation "genius" grant. Their credentials were exemplary, though we developed a reputation for adhering to "behavioral economics," which some viewed as a thumb on the scale for our pro-consumer preferences. It surely helped when one of our council members, Dick Thaler, won the Nobel Prize for Economics as a leading behavioralist, but those who favored classical free-market economics, like many of the House Republicans, remained suspicious of this approach.[15]

To showcase our growing body of research, our economists organized a series of conferences. One of our research groups created the consumer credit panel by developing and integrating data about American consumers from many sources in a sample that was nationally representative of millions of credit records. Our methodology relied on anonymized individual financial information to analyze trends without invading people's privacy, and the national sample was thoughtfully put together.[16] Among our goals for the research team were to raise the profile of consumer finance in the field of economics and to convince more economists that the best way to do first-class work on issues of consumer finance is by coming to the bureau. Not only could we construct and access the best data sets for research purposes—a key need for many economists—but also we could provide opportunities to influence policy and bring about beneficial change for millions of Americans. As we made headway with these goals, it felt like we were turning an important corner for the future of the agency.[17]

The research unfolding at the bureau, along with similar work being done at the Federal Reserve in St. Louis, helped raise the profile of household spending behavior—which relies heavily on the use of credit—and how it affects the broader economy. The effect of the mortgage market meltdown on household spending and the general economy was just one dramatic example of the importance of that causal chain. And it reinforced lessons from behavioral economics, as seemingly irrational behavior had led to massive disequilibrium in the economy, with lingering consequences that hurt many innocent people, including those who lost their jobs or saw their home values tank because of foreclosures in their neighborhoods.[18]

Our market teams were an amazing resource. Many analysts came from the financial industry, bringing invaluable knowledge of what companies were doing right and what they were doing wrong. The insights and perspective they brought to our work—especially their practical understanding of how financial products and companies operate—were unmatched from any other source. They proved their worth right away. They first created a set of primers to explain the workings of different financial products and markets. An early primer on deposit accounts, which explained how the banks make money from different categories of customers, was a revelation about how "free checking" really works and who pays for it. Their insights into business-to-business models like debt collection and credit reporting, where consumers have no direct customer relationships and are merely incidental to the objectives of the primary market participants, brilliantly explained why problems could fester in those markets with consumers having little influence, either by raising their voices or by taking their business elsewhere.[19] And when it came to our mortgage rules, the mortgage market team played a huge role in analyzing different scenarios about access to credit, default behavior, and litigation risks, which ultimately bore fruit by producing workable rules that supported the housing market recovery.

These experts also created market monitoring reports for the rest of the bureau to digest. The mortgage chartbook was my favorite. Month in and month out, it mapped the progress of how the mortgage and housing markets were gradually healing in the wake of the financial crisis, including the mostly steady decline in delinquencies, foreclosures, and homes that were "underwater" (meaning the owners owed more on their mortgages than the homes were worth). Keeping close tabs on this data helped us assess the effects of our new mortgage rules around the country. The market teams also tracked business strategies and product developments, which helped them anticipate profit-taking practices that could exploit consumers. Back-end pricing in the credit card market, such as with deferred interest products, was one problem they identified and watched closely for its effects on unsuspecting consumers. They melded public data sources (and evaluated their credibility) and began to mine our own data, such as consumer complaints and supervisory information, for new vantage points. And they were incredibly helpful in many other areas as well: they provided deep analytical capacity for our partnerships with state attorneys general and state banking regulators; they helped our supervisory teams know what to look for at the companies they examined; and they collaborated with our supervisory and enforcement teams to better understand and act on the information they collected. More than any other part of the bureau, they epitomized our aspiration to be a twenty-first-century agency.

WAYS AND MEANS

In addition to our powers to compel action by banks and financial companies, the Consumer Bureau has distinct tools to inform, persuade, and nudge consumers in better directions. In consumer finance, these tools are primarily education and the disclosure of information. Repeatedly and persistently, industry sought to push us back into these more limited channels, away from more aggressive enforcement and regulation. Their efforts to deter us fell flat, but we also pursued initiatives in both education and disclosures, with the potential to bring long-term positive changes for consumers and the economy overall. This chapter and the next will discuss our approach to each set of issues.

Strengthening the Economy

Making the case for personal finance education is an easy sell. People quickly realize just how casual our society has been in neglecting this key subject. Children could learn these lessons at home, but there are two large obstacles. First, many parents are unwilling to talk openly about their finances. Some regard money (or the love of it) as "the root of all evil," and for others, it is a source of great anxiety or bone of contention, not to be aired in front of the children. Among parents who are willing to talk about money, many don't have any training themselves and are unequipped to teach their children even the basics.

The other alternative is to teach personal finance in the schools. Yet surprisingly few children learn much about budgeting or money management in school. In a bygone era, most schools presented courses in home economics to all their students. Those courses included much practical advice about life, including household management. But most of those courses were either left behind or consigned to "elective" tracks that students are not required to take—and don't. One expert in the field of financial education showed me old math textbooks from a century ago that used budgeting problems from the household or farm or business to illustrate the mathematical concepts. Some textbooks are moving back in this direction, which will help.

This lack of financial education is a glaring omission in our society. The one subject that everyone needs to grasp is how to handle their own finances. In a nation like ours that is founded on personal responsibility and organized around a free-market economy, this subject is crucial. I saw the effects of financial ignorance on families up close as a local official, and we all saw it as entire communities foundered during the financial crisis. Many people made bad choices about home loans, often because they just didn't know any better. Predatory businesses took advantage of consumers, with full awareness that they did not know better. And the entire economy sank under the weight of these excesses. Had consumers made better choices, had they known more about how to assess and resist those tempting but irresponsible loans, the crisis might have been averted or at least mitigated.

Strengthening financial literacy will produce a more robust economic foundation, but it requires developing a knowledge base that can be passed down from adults to children, one generation to the next, in a more systematic way. This is unlikely to happen at home, and we need our schools to fill the yawning gap. We teach children about the fine points of geography or how to classify animals, but not about money—the one subject they are always keen to know more about.[1] Having omitted this subject from their education, we nonetheless expect them to become adults and suddenly, as if by magic, know how to operate "on their own," including making all the big and small decisions involved in managing their finances. The situation is made more urgent by the greater accessibility and complexity of the financial marketplace. Today, more access to credit means both more opportunity and more danger. People need to be better armed to cope with their greater vulnerability. If we choose not to teach students personal finance, we are choosing to release them unprepared into a dog-eat-dog financial world, where they will be unequipped to fend for themselves, and where even one or two bad decisions can ruin their entire lives.

Inevitably, then, this essential subject is also a matter of citizenship. As Americans, we have made a choice that has stood for over two centuries, to organize our society around a vibrant private sector and to accord each of us a wide realm of individual responsibility. But to own that responsibility, our children need to know more than just how to vote or that our government is divided into three branches, subjects that are required to be taught everywhere. Each of us also needs to learn how to manage our own affairs and make the most of our economic opportunities. People cannot enjoy their fundamental right to the pursuit of happiness if they are ensnared in delinquency and bankruptcy, hounded by debt and despair.[2] We have an important job to do here, and we are not doing it. Personal finance education must be taught to everyone, everywhere in the country.

Homespun Lessons

At the bureau, I warmly embraced our mission of improving personal finance education for all Americans. During an earlier stint as a tax collector in local government, I saw first-hand how often people's misfortunes and hard times were compounded by their lack of know-how in managing their money and making sound financial decisions. When people fell behind on their property taxes, we were able under state law to offer them a payment plan, which gave them more time to pay what they owed. To get this reprieve, people had to come in personally and explain their circumstances to help us figure out a realistic plan. From the stories they told us, we found that simple overspending was rarely the culprit. Instead, it was job loss, or death or illness or injury in the family, or other misfortunes that reduced their income, drove up their expenses, or both. Another cause of tax delinquency was divorce, which adds costs by splitting one household into two and often adds new legal expenses into the bargain. What I learned in meeting with people in financial trouble mirrored almost exactly what Elizabeth Warren had found in her academic research into the causes of personal bankruptcy.[3] We came from very different starting points but arrived at the same conclusions.

In many situations, however, we saw that people's troubles were magnified by their inability to make sustainable choices and engage in realistic financial planning. As we devised payment plans and discussed household budgets, we found that few people we were working with had done anything like this before. Nobody had ever explained to them the importance of tracking the inflows and outflows of their finances, or how to do it effectively. Instead, most people and especially young people are left to learn things the hard way by making their own mistakes through a costly process of trial and error. And they make the same kinds of mistakes as those who came before them, with the same results and the same regrets.

As a local official who wanted to do something about it, I formed a committee on financial literacy, and we started by gathering information about school programs for children and community programs for adults, including those available through Jump $tart, the Urban League, the YWCA, and scouting groups. The agricultural extension program at Ohio State reached out to rural communities with an emphasis on budgeting, as was true of 4-H programs. But it was pretty much hit and miss, mostly miss, for young people to get useful training on how to manage their affairs. And for adults, things were worse. Government programs had been designed to educate people on how to become homeowners, but they thinned out over the years. Some nonprofits helped people deal with their finances, often as a sidelight to helping them learn how to start a business. But most people had no background to build on and no idea where to go to make improvements.

Eventually, we became more ambitious and set a goal to pass legislation requiring every student in Ohio to receive education on how to handle their finances before they could graduate from high school. It is not easy to change the high school curriculum, but we formed a broad coalition of parents, personal finance teachers, and business leaders. Ultimately, the legislature passed a mandate that was quite loose and could mean many different things to educators in the more than six hundred local school districts located throughout Ohio.[4] By this point, I had been elected state treasurer, and we formed a statewide commission on financial education, which I cochaired with State Representative (later Congresswoman) Joyce Beatty. The same coalition that had helped pass the law on financial education helped us implement it, by developing curricula and organizing trainings for teachers from hundreds of school districts. Those already teaching personal finance were thrilled to find like-minded allies from elsewhere, and our sessions were highly motivational. We also continued a program of financial seminars on "Women and Money" for adult women around Ohio, covering issues like budgeting, household credit, insurance, and retirement savings. These events were popular, routinely drawing hundreds of people, and several businesses allowed us to take these programs right into their workplaces, to teach the same subjects to their employees. We also worked with colleges and universities to highlight the need for financial education on campus. What we heard back from people confirmed our sense that we were doing important and much-needed work.

The Bureau's Role

One of our overarching goals at the Consumer Bureau was to install more and better personal finance education in K-12 classrooms. But we lacked any ready-made way to achieve this goal, as a federal agency with no jurisdiction over the schools. Nor did we control any meaningful funding stream to make it happen. All we had were our ideas and our arguments.

The bureau was perfectly suited to serve as a neutral clearinghouse for existing resources. For teachers who want to focus on financial education but are unaware of what is available, we could be a trusted reference to assess the pros and cons of different programs or point them to the many free resources available.[5] We also published a resource guide to help policymakers develop strategies to advance and implement financial education in the states. For those motivated to make change, this was intended to serve as a "how to" guide. It explained how to make the case for financial education (which research shows can improve credit scores and savings rates while reducing delinquency), what components of financial education are most needed, and how to carry out K-12 initiatives. We pushed this guide out to state officials, such as treasurers and state legislators, as well as to business trade groups that we thought would have clout with them. To help educators and parents talk to one another and build a more integrated community to espouse the cause of more and better financial training, we created webinars, chat rooms, and other mechanisms.

We also were carving out a research role for ourselves. Early on, we compared the amount spent in the United States every year to provide financial education versus the amount spent on marketing to influence consumer decisions about financial products. We dug into the public research data, including tax documents and market studies, and we conducted our own interviews with financial providers, government officials, nonprofits, and other experts. Our methodology was consciously conservative, so there could be no argument that we were skewing the results, but even so it was no contest. For every $1 put toward financial education, $25 is spent on financial marketing, making it hard for consumers even to find objective information that is not biased by marketing pitches. The financial industry spends over $17 billion each year on direct marketing and awareness advertising, by means of television, the internet, mailers, and other media. By contrast, spending on financial education only totals about $670 million per year, the bulk of it from nonprofits, some from government, and only $31 million from financial institutions.[6] Googling pretty much any financial topic, such as mortgages or credit cards, produces the same picture. Even some of the informational websites that appear neutral turn out to be funded in part by financial companies. The market for objective information on consumer finance is badly broken, which further undercuts any idealized notions of informed decision making.

Another part of our research involved the effectiveness of financial education in improving people's financial decisions. Some critics, backed by a small and incomplete body of research, contend that classroom instruction on financial literacy has not worked and will not work. We were convinced this view is wrong, and that the apparent evidence for it mostly reflected the scattershot nature of the efforts made to date.[7] We thus commissioned research comparing states that adopted extensive financial education mandates, with well-documented implementation, to adjacent states without mandates. The initial results showed that—holding other things equal as much as possible, which is always a difficult point in economic research—rigorous financial education programs tend to improve credit scores and reduce delinquencies for young adults in the years following implementation of those programs. The effects were not limited to acquiring knowledge alone but reflected changes in actual financial behavior. The study also revealed weaknesses in the prior research, which often assumed that all state mandates are alike and ignored differences in implementation based on timing and intensity. The point it made was reinforced by more recent studies.[8] Perhaps it would not convince the skeptics, but it was a good start to putting things on the right track.

Other indicators point to the effectiveness of financial education as well. The worldwide Program for International Student Assessment (PISA) measures the progress of fifteen-year-old students in several subjects, including financial literacy. In 2012 and 2015, the United States ranked at or just below average among the eighteen countries tested, trailing China, Australia, New Zealand, and several Eastern European nations. In discussions with our counterparts from some of those countries, we learned that they have been doing more to educate their children in financial literacy, and they have been at it longer. Common sense leads to the same conclusion. Nobody truly doubts that education, worked at over time, increases people's understanding and augments their abilities in virtually every field of life. More than a century of consistent effort through mandatory public education has indisputably lifted literacy and numeracy among the American public. It took time, it took repetition, and it took dedication and commitment, but with those elements in place, I am convinced the same can be true for financial literacy.[9]

Our team also launched groundbreaking research to establish a more scientific basis for how teachers can engage young people to deliver financial education more effectively. Among their work was an innovative approach mapping existing research on childhood development against how young people can benefit from financial instruction at each stage of their educational growth. Called the "Building Blocks of Youth Financial Capability," it began with existing research on executive function to plan ahead and control impulses, starting in early childhood and continuing thereafter; progressed to developing financial habits and norms, beginning in middle childhood; and culminated with learning how to obtain financial knowledge and make decisions to act on that knowledge, from adolescence to adulthood. This research opened new paths to work with educators, including grade-level guides, classroom activities, teaching strategies, and assessment and measurement. The universe of these resources amounted to what we called a "teaching pedagogy," which is a guide to helping students develop lifelong decision-making skills in personal finance. It was an impressive body of work that spoke the language of educators in ways that would encourage and propel them to have the interest and the confidence to take up the subject of financial education.

We also examined the pros and cons of so-called rules of thumb as one approach to financial decision making. This approach is designed to address the growing concern that the current marketplace presents too many choices, producing both informational and decisional overload for consumers. Reminders, shortcuts, and other means of simplifying choices hold out promise for helping people cope with the complex challenges they face in their financial lives. Examples are "pay yourself first" as an impetus for saving and "don't spend what you don't have" for budgeting. The results of prior research were mixed, so we conducted focus groups with hundreds of consumers to consider how they use rules to thumb to make decisions about savings, borrowing, budgeting, and spending. We concluded that such rules often prove unrealistic or too rigid for many consumers, so we recommended that they be customized into "financial rules to live by" that people can adapt in more individualized ways. We also found that consumers do tend to rely on such shortcuts as a kind of default mode, and they may be open to rethinking this mindset in moments of personal crisis and adopting new strategies to guide them in the future. This remains a fertile area for experimental research about how practical tools like these can help people make realistic progress in improving their financial choices.

A Good Time to Get Busy

One conundrum we faced throughout my time at the bureau was how to take constructive action even as we were undertaking new research that was slow to mature. If we did not yet know the results of our research, how could we be sure we were doing the right things? This question confounds all practical work on public policy issues. But to establish leadership in this field, we needed to create a hive of new activity around financial education, and we could not afford to fall prey to the paralysis of uncertainty. So, it seemed that "now" is always the best time to get busy.[10]

From the beginning, we capitalized on opportunities to build partnerships, enhance education in schools, and create more workplace training on personal finance. We also made the CFPB's website, consumerfinance.gov, a destination for information. Along with our modules for helping people think about how to make big financial decisions—like "Buying a House" and "Paying for College"—we used public input, including consumer complaints, to generate "Ask CFPB," a growing set of answers to over a thousand frequently asked questions on consumer topics, such as how to correct errors on your credit report and how to stop harassing calls by debt collectors.

Anyone could access this universe of information, including members of the public, librarians, and teachers. It is real-time information, easily accessible whenever it is needed, which we updated periodically.[11] In this way, we were putting into practice the sensible observation that an informed consumer is always the first line of defense against abusive financial practices.

In developing partnerships, the Financial Literacy and Education Commission (FLEC) was a tremendous boon. Congress had created it in 2003 and tasked it with developing a financial education website and a national strategy on financial education. The Treasury secretary chairs the commission, and the Dodd-Frank Act later inserted the CFPB director as the vice chair. These kinds of extra responsibilities often are passed off to designees, but our team and I made it a point to show up and take part in every meeting, to convey our serious commitment to the subject. The FLEC is important because it convenes twenty-one agencies, nearly every part of the federal government that provides any kind of financial education: the Defense Department for the military, the Agriculture Department for rural communities, the Social Security Administration for retirees, and so on.[12] We seized the opportunity to build partnerships with each agency and to focus the group's agenda on three constituencies—students in the classroom, employees in the workplace, and seniors.

Beyond the federal government, our partners included large and small nonprofits, social service providers, labor unions, housing counselors, legal aid lawyers, and, perhaps most important, libraries. Libraries, which already have earned the public's respect and trust, can be found in every community throughout the country. During the financial crisis, I had seen how much the computers in our local libraries were being used by people to help get back on their feet, either with finding a job or managing their finances. We focused intently on building our library initiative, beginning with nine flagship library systems, big and small, from coast to coast. Eventually, we brought the American Library Association, the Institute of Museum and Library Sciences, and thousands of library branches into our initiative, distributing materials and hosting programming on financial education of all kinds. Our most efficient outing was with Senator Jack Reed, where we signed up Rhode Island's single library system, which swept in every library branch in the entire state.

In the classroom, we encouraged more of everything. We showed how financial education can be effectively built into many other courses—including word problems in math classes, essay topics in English classes, and economic lessons in social studies. Educators are affected by how questions are framed on the SAT and ACT, so we pushed for more emphasis on financial education there too. In the schools, we supported any approach that teachers like, from stock market contests to video games to "reality fairs," where students role-play by adopting an adult's financial identity and spend time coping with the challenge of making ends meet, given all the demands of housing, food, transportation, childcare, and so on.[13] We also forged a partnership with the Financial Services Roundtable, made up of many large financial companies, to highlight all the financial literacy programs they were already supporting in schools. For parents, we started a "Money as You Grow" book club, featuring children's books that focus on financial issues and providing guides to help parents use the books to discuss money choices with their children.

We also pressed hard for more financial education in the workplace. Most employers already deal with key financial topics as part of their benefits programs, which may cover retirement, health insurance, life insurance, student debt, and tax administration. We urged businesses to add household finance as a complement to those other offerings. We also published a research report on financial wellness in the workplace, showing how financial distress reduces productivity, increases absenteeism, and undercuts employee health. At a roundtable, employers recognized this phenomenon, calling it "presenteeism," where workers are physically on the job but not able to function well because they are mentally and emotionally distracted by their own financial problems.

As we traveled the country and saw various workplace programs, we highlighted promising practices that businesses were pioneering, including better use of the employee onboarding process, peer-to-peer support, and leveraging technology. We created a "how to" resource guide to help employers figure out how to launch financial wellness programs. We were especially keen to interest the financial industry in doing more for their employees, which seemed like a natural idea that could have real reach, covering about six million people over a broad spectrum from entry-level employees to top executives. Ruefully recalling the old adage that "the cobbler's children have no shoes," Bill Rogers, the head of SunTrust Bank, made a tremendous commitment to a financial fitness program for his workforce, including incentives. We also realized that we could not reasonably ask others to do this work without making the same commitment ourselves, so we created a financial fitness program for our own employees with access to information and services, including in-person and online financial coaching. We encouraged the rest of the federal government to do the same by making a strong push through the Office of Personnel Management.

Measuring Progress

Our team also designed and conducted research on the concept of "financial well-being." The International Network on Financial Education, of which we were now part, describes financial well-being as the "ultimate goal" of financial literacy. Yet the concept itself was lacking a firm definition or a standard way of measurement. Research efforts to refine the definition were underway in multiple countries, especially Britain and Australia, and we joined the effort in a bid to better understand whether people are making progress at improving their financial lives and what works or doesn't work in financial education. In addition to identifying objective criteria such as credit scores and likelihood of delinquency, our team conducted survey interviews around the country with adult consumers and financial practitioners to dig deeper into how financial knowledge and personal traits relate to financial behavior. They also closely examined the relevant academic literature from economics, psychology, sociology, education, and other fields. Finally, they consulted with an expert panel of practitioners and academics in consumer finance to develop testable hypotheses that could guide further research studies.

The definition they proposed is elegantly simple. Financial well-being is "a state of being wherein a person can fully meet current and ongoing financial obligations, can feel secure in their financial future, and is able to make choices that allow enjoyment of life." They noted that, though specific individual goals and visions of a satisfying financial life can differ greatly from one person to another, two common themes are remarkably consistent: security and freedom of choice, both in the present and in the future. They also distilled from the consumer surveys four central elements of the concept of financial well-being:

(1) Having control over day-to-day, month-to-month finances
(2) Having the capacity to absorb a financial shock
(3) Being on track to meet your financial goals
(4) Having the financial freedom to make the choices that allow you to enjoy life

About a year later, we issued a follow-up report and we devised a testing tool to produce a quantitative measure of people's financial well-being, which could be tracked over time. By answering ten questions about their current and future economic security and freedom of choice, people could see how they compare with others and with their past and future selves. Our new financial well-being scale could also be used to assess the effectiveness of financial education programs over time.

This research was years in the making, and its definition and measurement components capture a much more complete picture of individual well-being than a simple measure of income or wealth. Our team's work soon gained backing and support from all over the world, becoming a key piece of the published empirical work in this area. It also was being adapted and used by practitioners, first in Norway and then elsewhere. Here at home, the Pentagon agreed to use the scale as part of its military readiness efforts and as a means of assessing how the financial circumstances of servicemembers and their families may be changing over time.

We used the new scale in a nationwide survey of more than six thousand adults that was published in September 2017. The average financial well-being score for US adults came in at fifty-four on a hundred-point scale, compared to fifty-nine for both Australia and New Zealand, which published results the next year. But we were interested in more than just raw results. By coupling our measurements with other data on individuals and households, we were able to investigate how a range of characteristics, opportunities, experiences, behaviors, skills, and attitudes may be associated with financial well-being. Our results offered a new perspective on the financial conditions of US adults, aside from traditional measures such as employment and income. Although we found, as expected, that underlying financial circumstances make a tangible difference to financial well-being, so do financial know-how, confidence, and day-to-day money management skills. These findings open the door to developing compensating factors and strategies that can boost financial well-being for people at all levels of the economic spectrum, further supporting the value of financial education in helping people take more productive control of their financial lives.

KNOW BEFORE YOU OWE

The Consumer Bureau's "Know Before You Owe" project was an innovative strategy for improving consumer financial markets. As the financial industry tried to herd regulators toward more education and disclosure rather than tougher measures, we opted to use all the tools that Congress had made available to us. To adapt a poker phrase, we would "see" the industry's bet on education and disclosures and "raise" them on regulation and enforcement.

Starting in the first year, while we were building the agency and before we opened our doors, we began focusing on improving disclosures. Elizabeth Warren especially warmed to this theme, focusing on three questions. First, can consumers understand the financial product? Second, can they figure out the costs and risks and make decisions based on that knowledge? Third, can they compare products in the marketplace and have confidence in deciding to choose one over another? If consumers could do these things, they would be in a much better position.

Disclosures in Consumer Finance

The trouble was that the financial marketplace often did not work this way. With physical products, people can pretty much see what they are getting, and apart from the financing, the pricing is clear. But a financial "product" is typically just an intangible contract comprising various monetary terms. Congress passed laws requiring some initial disclosures, but financial products became more elaborate and providers complicated the terms, making them so opaque that it was practically impossible for consumers to compare prices, costs, and risks. And even if people could make comparisons, they might find themselves dealing with a moving target, as these contracts—written by the providers—often gave companies the right to change the terms and pricing unilaterally and without warning. Elizabeth spoke frequently about "tricks and traps" that leave consumers unable to make good choices based on reliable information. The credit card market was the prime example, and consumer abuse and frustration were rampant in the years leading up to the CARD Act.

Rather than rewrite the contract terms that were so profitable for them, companies urged that these problems should all be addressed by adding more disclosures. If consumers did not understand the key points, then it was plausible that they should be told more. Explanations of the costs and risks of financial products became long and involved, and companies added dense provisions to cover every conceivable circumstance that could create liability if left unspecified. New disclosures on top of old disclosures long ago passed the point of usefulness, leaving consumers suffering from information overload. The disclosures were having the opposite effect from what policymakers intended—unable to digest the mass of information, consumers were bypassing it altogether and having to take it all on trust.[1]

We believed more clarity would empower consumers and help them root out bad products, but the key was to find the "sweet spot" between too little information, which allows providers to exploit people's ignorance, and too much information, which drowns the important points. Our solution was to conduct extensive testing so we could unpack the overall effect of disclosures into their component pieces. Then we could simplify product descriptions around a more uniform presentation of the core points. With a neutral and unbiased body like Congress or a regulatory agency specifying the essential information to be included, consumers would gain more confidence that they were focusing on the right information and know they could rely on it.

This approach had a lot going for it. It was pro-market, based on improving information flows and trusting consumers, rather than imposing harsh substantive restrictions on which products could be sold. Indeed, it was a kind of deregulation, weeding out ineffective disclosures that imposed costs on the industry but produced little value for consumers. To pursue this angle, we put out a request for ideas about what laws or rules we might modify or eliminate to reduce burdens for the industry. To our surprise, we got very little back in response.[2] Nonetheless, we had a slogan, and it stuck: every consumer should be able to "know before you owe." And this was not a critique of consumers for failing to protect their own interests. Instead, it was designed to shape up the dysfunctional market for information, which might seem to benefit everyone.

But inevitably, clarifying the bargain would not benefit everyone: if this approach helped protect consumers, it would do so at the expense of banker profits. Some historical background here is helpful to explain why. At the common law, it is accepted that an individual's consent to a contract is vitiated by either force or fraud. If a consumer relies on material statements of fact that turn out to be untrue, the court can void the contract and compensate the consumer for any harm done. But the common law also put heavy burdens on the buyer to fully understand the contract, exhorting "let the buyer beware" and imposing a "duty to read." Over time, judges had shown growing unease about holding people responsible for terms buried deep in the fine print, recognizing that prolixity alone can mask or conceal vital information. Some economists even cited the novel concept of "confusopoly" (a term coined in the Dilbert comic strip): amidst the complexity of the financial marketplace, providers could overwhelm consumers with information and thus confuse them into making product selections they didn't understand and that disserved their own interests. Even though this approach is not illegal, because it does not constitute actual fraud, it could directly undermine consumer choice. Bringing more clarity to the marketplace would help reduce or eliminate any advantage that financial providers can gain by this tactic.

Nonetheless, "Know Before You Owe" was the rare regulatory concept that elicited no overt disagreement from anyone. Advocates of consumer responsibility saw it as each person's obligation to gather the right information before making a sound financial choice. Consumer advocates saw it as the responsibility of financial companies to provide accurate information that consumers could process effectively before agreeing to a transaction. At several of our events, President Obama seemed especially taken with the phrase, which he regarded as the essence of common sense in consumer finance: of course, consumers should "know" before they "owe," and they had a right to expect that they could in fact know "before" they owe.

Against this backdrop, we began examining consumer financial markets and figuring out how to generate effective summary disclosures. These summaries would identify the key prices, costs, and risks associated with financial products and present them in a uniform format. This would produce apples-to-apples matchups, enabling consumers to compare products and shop more effectively for those best suited to their needs. We realized that the project would likely take distinct forms in different markets, varying by the nature of the products and the extent of our authorities. But we had an overarching vision to guide us, and with this vision in mind, we set to work.

Know Before You Owe—Credit Cards

Right away, Elizabeth Warren set an ambitious goal of boiling down the key disclosures for financial products onto a single page. We first sought to do this with credit card agreements. Before coming to the bureau, she had called out the credit card industry for the hidden fees that lurked in the form agreements they imposed on customers. These contracts are typically not negotiable—either you take the product with all the conditions preset by the provider or you do not get the product at all. The *Wall Street Journal* reported that the average credit card agreement had ballooned from about one and a half pages in 1980 to over thirty pages in 2008.

In 2006, the General Accounting Office (GAO) examined customer agreements from the largest credit card issuers. "Usability" experts reviewed the disclosures, and what they found was damning. The disclosures were written well above the level at which about half of adults read. The disclosures buried important information in the text, did not group or label related material, and used small typefaces. Testing and interviews showed that many cardholders simply did not understand key terms, such as when late payments would be charged and what actions would lead to interest rate hikes. The GAO concluded that these problems stemmed from federal regulations that were ill suited to reflect the complex pricing and terms of current credit cards, and from lawyers who kept adding more content to avoid lawsuits.

We sought to streamline and simplify these agreements, but we had two problems. First, it is extraordinarily difficult to take a contract for a complex financial product and reduce it to a single page. In fact, existing law mandated disclosure of many items: definitions, interest rates, fees, payments, transactions, billing rights, defaults, account closure, account information, communications, dispute resolution, and more. Although a thirty-page document seemed excessive, there was a lot of important information that people need to process, and it was unclear how simply omitting it would better inform them. Second, changing the mandatory items would require embarking on a formal rulemaking process, which inevitably would take a long time. We didn't even *have* any rulemaking authority until July 2011, and after that our early bandwidth for writing rules would be fully occupied by the mandatory slate of new mortgage regulations.

To add to these conundrums, the laws and rules for the credit card industry had recently been revised. The CARD Act had just taken effect in February 2010, and the Federal Reserve had modified disclosures and made substantive changes in how credit cards work. In addition, the credit card laws already required a summary disclosure known as the "Schumer box," which requires any promotional material or application to clearly outline the costs and terms of credit cards. This includes the annual fee, interest rate, payment grace period, method to calculate finance charges, and other transaction fees. All credit card issuers had to use the same format in presenting this information, and font sizes were specified to make it all readable.[3]

In some sense, then, a "Know Before You Owe" summary disclosure was already required in the credit card market and had been for twenty years. Obviously, though, it had not succeeded in informing consumers well enough to prevent the kinds of abuses that prompted the CARD Act and that we were seeing in our early rounds of credit card complaints. So, how should we proceed? We adopted a strategy of visibility and transparency. We worked to develop a prototype credit card agreement that would be shorter and clearer, presented in plain language and an attractive format, at a reading level accessible to most of the American public. We made sure we were disclosing all terms and conditions that were legally required. And we would engage in extensive research directly with consumers to determine which disclosures, practically speaking, help clarify how credit cards work in ways that matter to cardholders.

Our team spent many months reducing the typically verbose credit card agreement down to a two-page document, leaving aside the definitions, which could be presented elsewhere, such as on a website. It was not a single page, but it was enormous progress. Yet companies still had the option of whether and how to adapt it. Perhaps the shorter agreement itself would be attractive to consumers as they shopped around among different credit cards, preferring one with a more understandable presentation that could help gain their trust. But neither we nor the companies knew if this was very likely.

At a field hearing in Cleveland, we rolled out the prototype agreement. Pentagon Federal Credit Union, with its million members, agreed to use it and give us direct feedback. We also made the prototype available on our website, along with a database of agreements used by every company, which would allow consumer advocates and the public to compare them with one another more easily.[4]

Even without a formal rulemaking to mandate its use, our streamlining work had some good effects. Our public database spotlighted the length and contents of these agreements, allowing more direct comparisons. Our sample prototype showed that it is possible to shorten the customer agreement and make it more readable. And our attention to this issue put pressure on the credit card companies to do so.

But overall, the results have been mixed. The average agreement has shrunk: virtually none now exceeds twenty pages. Some of the most aggressive card issuers, such as Discover and Capital One, have agreements that are only five or six pages long. Pentagon Federal from our pilot project and other credit unions use a simple three-page customer agreement along the lines of our prototype. Some larger banks, however, continue to use agreements with page totals that run into the teens, and their continued large customer base suggests that consumers do not find it worthwhile to shop around just to secure shorter and simpler customer agreements. Even if that approach could be changed, it would probably take Congress enacting a law to do it.

The more important question is whether the push for simpler and clearer agreements has enabled people to shop more effectively for better pricing and terms. The limited effectiveness of the "Schumer box," which requires issuers to present information about complex pricing models but does not restrict the use of such models, casts doubt on whether that is so.[5] This question is at the heart of the "Know Before You Owe" philosophical debate, and the verdict is not yet definitive.

KNOW BEFORE YOU OWE—MORTGAGES

In the mortgage market, we focused on the mortgage loan disclosures rather than the underlying contracts, but here we had more robust authority. The

Dodd-Frank Act *required* the bureau to adopt a new rule addressing mortgage disclosures, in part to deal with redundancy in the existing system, where two different federal agencies each had its own set of disclosure requirements.[6] That redundancy caused people shopping for a mortgage to get two distinct forms at the outset and two distinct forms at the end. They naturally found this confusing, with the inevitable question being: Why are there two forms and how are they different?

Congress had created the problem decades ago, and made some half-hearted efforts to resolve it, but now they were finally keen to get it done. The details were technical and complex, however, so they simply ordered our new agency to fix it. By not including this task in the initial basket of mandatory mortgage rules, they gave us more time between the proposed rule and the final rule to be data driven and get extensive public input. First, we held a symposium on mortgage disclosures with industry and consumer groups. We then designed a prototype of the combined forms, which highlighted the key features and risks associated with a mortgage loan, and we posted them online for public input. We received over twenty-five thousand comments, and we also did qualitative testing with consumers to see if the forms helped them compare and choose among loans. We later conducted quantitative testing to evaluate the effectiveness of our new forms compared to the old forms. The results showed that people's comprehension was markedly higher with the new forms (it also showed, interestingly, their marked preference for the thirty-year fixed-rate mortgage product, which is a distinctively American form of home loan). When we issued our final rule, we provided a generous implementation period, over twenty months, for everyone in the mortgage and real estate markets to get ready to use the new forms.

We also embarked on a project to "whack the stack." Everyone who has been through a real estate closing remembers the huge pile of intimidating paperwork at the closing table.[7] Our new streamlined forms well summarized what borrowers need to know to make informed decisions, and we sought to get the rest of that paper out of the way so as not to distract or confuse people. We did not want our form, which carefully highlighted the key terms and prices, to be ignored, just one more piece of paper sitting on top of (or buried within) the customary stack. But we learned that we could not achieve this goal because much of the paperwork is required by state law or dictated by legal concerns; lawyers find it much easier to *add* something to the stack than to *remove* something that might expose their client to any legal risk.

To address this problem, we encouraged the industry to move to electronic closings, which some in the industry had been pushing for years. Electronic closings provide greater convenience (including allowing parties to attend remotely by phone or video) and reduce paperwork costs. We convened industry leaders and ran pilot projects with multiple banks, credit unions, and mortgage companies to promote electronic closings, and things are moving in that direction. But the cumbersome process is so massive that many sectors must evolve together—lenders, realtors, title agents, lawyers, local recording officials, and so on. A key move to drive this process forward is for every state to adopt model legislation, already in place in a growing number of states, to modernize the law so that licensed notary publics can perform their key role in validating the transaction online. That is happening, but not immediately. In the end, we did not advocate for entirely paperless closings. Instead, we envisioned our new Closing Disclosure form as the *only* piece of paper at the closing table, which would make it stand out, with everything else presented online so people could read the rest if they wanted, without otherwise having those documents obscure the central issues.

After completing the "Know Before You Owe" mortgage rule, we moved into our now-standard project of regulatory implementation, and there our team did an extremely thorough job. We created a webpage with resources for mortgage professionals and a small entity compliance guide. For the industry, we published an explanatory guide to the forms, a readiness guide, and our exam procedures to help companies prepare to establish their compliance with the rule. For consumers, we debuted an online set of decision-making tools and resources called "Owning a Home," to help people in an interactive format learn about loan options, explore interest rates, familiarize themselves with a closing checklist, and walk through a step-by-step guide to the mortgage process. And we redesigned a booklet that lenders must give to people no more than three days after they apply for a home loan. We redesigned "Your Home Loan Toolkit" to slim it down, put it in plain language, and provided worksheet space for people to compare options. As we continued to build the brand of the Consumer Bureau, we knew that it soon would be in the hands of millions of Americans.

Our new rule required companies to provide the Closing Disclosure to people at least three days before closing on the loan and to require an additional three-day review period if certain major changes occurred after the document was provided. We imposed the notice period because one of the classic "tricks and traps" had been to ambush buyers with surprise fees at the closing table, creating a "take it or leave it" scenario and forcing them to swallow costs they had not agreed to beforehand. Many consumers had been hurt by this unsavory practice. As we worked with companies to implement the rule, however, they pushed back on this requirement. They argued that it might cause closings to be rescheduled or snarl homeowners in unexpected transitions between one housing situation and the next, but the concerns were greatly overstated.[8] As the effective date approached, some companies sought to blame us for what they portrayed as a coming train wreck that could disrupt real estate markets. We were quite resistant to giving any relief from the deadline set almost two years before. On the eve of the effective date, however, we found that we had made an embarrassing paperwork error in filing the rule with Congress—ironic for a rule that was all about paperwork—which meant we had to delay the deadline briefly after all. All sides were relieved when we pushed it past the beginning of the school year, a busy period in the real estate industry, producing an unexpectedly beneficial result.[9]

We monitored the effects on the market carefully. At first, the average time frame for closing a home loan expanded by a couple of months, but before long, it decreased to less than before. The number of loans closed had dropped off significantly just after the effective date, but it recovered within six months. Consumers reported positive experiences with the forms and the process, which were helping them avoid situations giving rise to regrets. That would benefit the good performers in the real estate industry too, which is heavily based on repeat customers.

This result was fully consistent with our original premise: that people deserve to know before they owe. More than three years earlier, I had introduced our proposed rule at a speech before the National Council of La Raza (now renamed UnidosUS), the largest Latino advocacy group in the United States. The theme was "no más" to costs and risks buried in the fine print and "no más" to last-minute closing shocks. I had concluded by saying: "In a reformed and improved system, people will no longer be afraid to put their hard-earned savings toward a down payment. They will be able to reach an informed decision on a loan to buy a home, make a sound investment in their future, and build toward a prosperous tomorrow. Investment in communities will grow. That is good for each of us. That is good for all of us. And that is good for America." It still rang true.

A short time after the rule went into effect, I had lunch with Senator Warren in the Senate dining room, and she asked me how this project had turned out. I said consumers saw themselves as better off, disruptions to the market had been minimal, and most of the industry was adjusting well. Electronic closings can enable software functionality to ensure that consumers have direct and substantive interaction with the new forms, especially the Closing Disclosure. She then asked if either of the final forms had been reduced to a single page. Ruefully, I had to admit that, though the new forms are considerably shorter than before, we had not managed that—the Loan Estimate is three pages, and the Closing Disclosure is five pages. She suggested that we might consider going back to Congress with a list of legal provisions that would need to be changed to make it possible to get the forms down to a single page. I had to admire her tenacity, but I don't believe it will ever be accomplished!

Know Before You Owe—Student Loans

For many families, aside perhaps from buying a home, paying for college is the biggest single investment they will ever make, and the same goes for many other kinds of training. An investment in our skills and capabilities is likely to pay off in the long run, with a better career and better pay. With any large investment, however, paying for it can be virtually impossible without borrowing money. Understanding how to make sound use of credit is thus essential to most educational opportunity.

This is emphatically true in America today. Over the past generation, the cost of a college education has risen dramatically, far outpacing the cost of living. State governments have reduced their investment in higher education, even as this credential is more in demand. Higher education is accessible in this country, but it comes at a high cost, and the availability of student loans and other means of financing poses all the usual perils of accessing credit. When we met with our counterparts from other countries, they often drew a blank on the problem of student loans—unlike mortgages, credit cards, and auto loans. Many other countries ration access to higher education, restricting how many young people can get it, but they do not burden students with substantial debts after they graduate. In the United States, we approach these issues differently, and our approach has pros and cons.

Early on, Raj committed the bureau to undertake a "Know Before You Owe" project on student loans. He noted that about 40% of young Americans are college graduates, but those who had to borrow to get there now were carrying, on average, over $20,000 in debt. We reached out to the Department of Education, where Secretary Arne Duncan was happy to work with us on financial issues around higher education. Together we created the "Financial Aid Shopping Sheet." Refined with the help of over twenty thousand comments, our shopping sheet was just a page long—we finally found a market where we could do it!—and it served as a model disclosure form that colleges and universities could use to clarify up front the costs and risks, before students and their families decided whether and where to enroll. It also presented a standard format that would help people compare financial aid offers side by side, see the full costs of attendance, distinguish between grants and loans, and estimate both total debt and monthly payments after graduation.

Some of the bureau's earliest research showed that student loan debt had exceeded $1 trillion, and it was now the highest source of household debt next to mortgages, exceeding both credit cards and auto loans. These numbers helped people appreciate the magnitude of the problem, as did President Obama's willingness to speak publicly about the personal experiences he and Michelle Obama had with carrying student loan debt for years. In April 2012, President Obama signed an executive order requiring all schools that received tuition assistance and GI Bill money to provide the shopping sheet to military students.

Vice President Biden also aggressively promoted these efforts as a major focus of his White House Task Force on the Middle Class. In June, Secretary Duncan and I joined the vice president and ten university presidents—representing over a million students—who agreed to adopt it as well. Our discussion prior to the event nicely captured the challenge of simplification, as illustrated by the adage, "If I'd had more time, I'd have written a shorter letter." As we sat around for a few minutes looking over the shopping sheet together, people began noting what else might be usefully included. We were amused to realize this was exactly the problem we had to surmount—everyone could find ways to make the form longer, but keeping it short was much harder to do.

By July, the Department of Education was ready to unveil the final version of the shopping sheet and to encourage college and university presidents to adopt it for the upcoming college application process. With their backing and continued strong support from the White House, even without mandating its use, within two years more than two thousand schools signed up to adopt the shopping sheet and help families with this important decision.

At the same time, we were working to develop a set of resources to make this entire process easier for educators, students, and families. We called this "Paying for College," which along with "Owning a Home" was part of our initiative to take significant, one-time—and sometimes first-time—financial decisions, which people may never have faced before, and help walk people through the process. Our goal was to build an interactive tool that would allow people to navigate financial aid offers and student loans by inputting all the relevant financial information and assessing their options before finalizing a college decision. Our resources included information about projected debt burdens, monthly payments, graduation rates, estimated average starting salaries, and more. We also shared our data publicly so that others could create their own apps and web tools to help students make more informed decisions, which some began to do.

At the event with the university presidents, the vice president poignantly spoke of his own experience applying to college, which was a new path for his family at that time. He described his father's discomfort and awkwardness stemming from his unfamiliarity with it all. Our tools are designed to ease the way for fathers, mothers, and their children, helping them be more prepared and get more comfortable as they make this huge commitment.

KNOW BEFORE YOU OWE—AUTO LOANS

The four largest consumer credit markets are the mortgage market—dwarfing all others at about $10 trillion—and the markets for student loans, credit cards, and auto loans, each in a range that is closer to $1 trillion of total credit outstanding.[10] We expanded our "Know Before You Owe" project to include new tools for the auto loan market in June 2016, including a shopping sheet that consumers could fill out to compare auto loans. We also unveiled new online resources, such as a step-by-step guide to help consumers know what to look out for, what questions to ask, and how to navigate the process. Before we designed these resources, we conducted focus group research into how consumers experience the process of shopping for auto loans and, of course, reviewed our own database of consumer complaints.

Consumers shopping for a car or a truck, like those shopping for other big-ticket items that engage our sense of identity—like a home or a school—are focused most intensely on making a choice among competing versions of that item. Since that decision absorbs most of their attention, it leaves less room to focus on decisions about how to finance the purchase. We all know the experience of "falling in love" with a product that seems to fit us just right, and how this tends to cloud or crowd out careful decision making about the money side of things. It often leads people to decide on "too much house"—or car or school—and it can lead to sloppy and dangerous choices among alternative modes of financing. Auto financing is further complicated because auto dealers who handle the marketing and sale of the vehicle often intercede in arranging the vehicle financing too.

Rule-writing authority over the auto market had been divided between the CFPB and the Federal Trade Commission under the Dodd-Frank Act. That had limited us in certain ways, but it did not affect our ability to provide education materials directly to consumers to help them prepare for and navigate the financing process in general.[11] Given the size of the market and the importance of reliable financing to help people access work, school, and health care, we thought it was important for us to do so. We applied what we learned in the other "Know Before You Owe" initiatives to develop materials that would help consumers see the entire financing picture, including whether to buy or lease the vehicle. We tried to make people more aware of the total cost and duration of any loan, rather than focusing on just the monthly payment. Our resources also explained the rights that consumers have, the differences between direct and indirect financing, and the advantages of shopping around to secure a loan ahead of time from a bank or financial company. Getting a loan in advance, rather than getting it in the heat of the moment through a dealer, is often less expensive, especially as many dealers are authorized to mark up the interest rates on loans they provide.

Consumers are changing their behavior in shopping for cars and trucks, with many now doing considerable advance research online and making greater use of sources like the *Kelley Blue Book* for pricing and *Consumer Reports* to compare safety and quality. Our goal was to convince them to extend their research to include the vehicle financing, using our materials as a trusted and reliable source. In time, we will see whether many consumers do that, and what effect their more vigorous shopping will have on the marketplace for auto loans.

Summing Up

Our "Know Before You Owe" project across the four major markets in consumer finance offers several lessons. First, overly long disclosures have reached a point of diminishing value and even negative value for consumers. Too much information becomes counterproductive and undermines both consumer awareness and consumer understanding. We were not the first to realize this, but our comprehensive research based on years of working closely with consumers showed the need to be much more careful in weighing the tradeoffs. Shorter, clearer, and more uniform disclosures not only aid people's understanding but also allow more direct and meaningful comparisons among products that improve consumer choice, which is a key foundation for markets to work effectively and one of the rare areas of consensus on all sides.

Still, the variations among these markets matter. In the mortgage market, we made the biggest difference. We unpacked a complicated loan transaction with disclosure forms that consumers told us were more intelligible than those used before. But Congress explicitly mandated us to impose that change on the market. Even though the industry grumbled about the inevitable costs and disruptions, they knew we had to act and could see that we were reducing paperwork and improving customer experience, both positive developments. We were empowered to devise streamlined and customized forms, along with supportive tools like the Home Loan Toolkit, which the law requires lenders to give to every consumer who applies for a mortgage. This scenario represented the zenith of our authority to take effective action.

We faced more practical obstacles, and in some cases legal limitations, in the other markets we targeted. The credit card market had just been overhauled by the CARD Act in ways that were helpful, but Congress had not explicitly directed us to boil down disclosures as it did with the mortgage market. With student loans, we were fortunate to have the close cooperation of the Department of Education and the Obama administration, which facilitated the widespread adoption of our shopping sheet by a huge number of colleges and universities. We were disabled from imposing any requirements on auto dealers, but we were able to develop materials that could help consumers educate and empower themselves in dealing with auto financing.

We found that Congress could not be as precise as we could in deciding what to disclose and how to frame the information to best meet the needs of consumers. Our approach was informed by our ability to do extensive consumer testing, rather than making subjective judgments, but Congress did not have this same opportunity. Moreover, how well a summary disclosure can work also depends on the nature of the product being described. In markets like credit cards, where the product is elastic, involving key terms that are fluid and variable, succinct disclosures are unlikely to give a satisfactory account of the total picture. In the Schumer box, for example, some key pricing information requires an asterisk because the correct answer to an apparently simple question—what is the interest rate on transactions?—could change at any time. This is true if the interest rate is variable, and many companies reserve the right to adjust their risk-based pricing according to algorithms of their own making.[12] Mortgage loan products are also very complex, though here we were helped by the fact that Congress had outlawed or sharply restricted some of the more exotic and injurious features of mortgages. As a result, our summary disclosures did not have to cope with those troublesome concepts in explaining the product to consumers, though there are still many challenging elements for people to absorb.

Given the realities of these products, we cannot, and probably should not, eliminate entirely the kind of extensive detail needed to describe all the aspects of a mortgage or a credit card—mortgage closing documents remain voluminous, and many credit card agreements still run to more than ten crowded pages. But even so, having a neutral and expert source produce a thoughtful summary document, which stands out from the rest of the information presented, is significant. Just as readers often learn to look first for the executive summary of any lengthy report, people naturally tend to home in on the key pricing and terms presented in the summary, especially one they know comes from a trustworthy and reliable source. For consumers who are dazed and overwhelmed by all the information put in front of them, this sharper focus is a real benefit that can help improve the decisions they make. In short, it's good to know (what is most important) before you owe.

In all these markets, financial providers were understandably wary of the work we were doing. They strongly resisted any push to create plain va-nilla credit products, which would have eased the job of creating standard disclosures.[13] And to the extent that some providers moved toward simpler agreements, it was not the case that customers followed them in droves. Instead, the streamlining of product terms that did occur typically came about as the result of legislative or regulatory intervention. While our "Know Before You Owe" project is helpful to consumers, it is far from a panacea for market practices that have the potential to cause them harm. For those problems, there is still no substitute for better laws and rules with stronger enforcement.

PART III

PITCHED BATTLES FOR THE AMERICAN DREAM

A GREAT BIG COUNTRY

The scope of the task for our new agency was a monumental challenge. Starting from the ground up, we needed to support and protect 320 million Americans nationwide. Even fully staffed, this *still* would represent about 200,000 people for every one of us. We needed to break down the immensity of it all. In doing so, we had two key strategies: visiting communities across the country to meet people and understand the issues in their local areas, and focusing on the needs of specialty populations, such as servicemembers and veterans, students, older Americans, and low-income consumers.

TAKING THE SHOW ON THE ROAD

The Consumer Bureau held monthly field hearings to get out of Washington and talk to consumers in their home communities, helping us better understand the vastly different issues in different parts of the country. In the Bay Area, for example, immigrant groups were creating "lending circles," where people form a group to pool their money and lend it to individual members, whose payments can be used to build up credit history that improves access to other forms of credit.[1] In North Dakota, we heard about the unexpected problem of having "too much money," with the erratic cycles of the fracking oil boom making it difficult for community banks to know how to chart the future. In Alaska, we learned about the challenges of loans for "hangar houses" in remote areas, where the built-in transportation structure was not a garage but a hangar for the family's personal plane.

Whenever we held a field hearing, we also made it a point to meet with local consumer advocates, community bankers, and credit union officials. In these meetings as well, we learned more about the local issues, and we saw how national organizations like the United Way, the Urban League, and legal aid clinics had adapted their own work to the special needs of each community. In the Mississippi Delta, for example, the extreme poverty means access to financial services is sharply limited—few institutions are willing to serve these customers, branch outlets are few and far between, and credit is sparse. Life-saving help comes from community development financial institutions, which are banks, credit unions, or other types of funds that operate on a quasi-benevolent basis to bring opportunity to deprived areas. By contrast, in New York City, consumer life bustles and the biggest problem is warding off sharp practices. The consumer advocates have developed a keen antenna for predators. They have secured far more protections under state and local law than we found in many other places, and they insisted that we needed to be just as aggressive on issues like high-cost lending, online scams, and debt collection abuses.[2] We learned about rampant foreclosures in Phoenix, Las Vegas, and Tampa; student loan issues in Sioux Falls and Miami; and debt collection problems pretty much everywhere.

The first field hearing after my recess appointment was in Birmingham, Alabama, on one of our biggest target areas—payday lending. When we arrived, we found an enormous crowd. We would see this happen again and again. The field of consumer financial protection is so polarized that when we set a topic for discussion, the mere awareness that consumer allies would show up in large numbers often drove the industry to show up in large numbers too, to make sure they were presenting the other side of the debate. That was just what we wanted—not a one-sided discussion, but one that we and others could learn from. We usually convened a panel of experts with experience in the industry as well as consumer advocates, and all sides got a chance to make their points.

We also took comments from the audience, which made things unpredictable but set a receptive tone. Our view was, as Justice Brandeis once said, that the best way to combat falsehood and fallacy was by "more speech, not enforced silence." In our first payday lending hearing, the companies marshaled customers and employees to make the case for the importance of having small-dollar loans easily available, especially in emergency situations. On the consumer side, borrowers spoke compellingly about being ruined by these loans, and faith leaders described the devastation that high-cost loans were creating within their congregations by trapping people in unaffordable debt. When the hearing went long, as it inevitably did, we kept at it until everyone had a chance to comment.[3]

Our monthly field hearings required us to come up with a steady stream of timely topics. That put great pressure on our workflow, and often the artificial deadline of setting a field hearing created special challenges to speed up what we were doing. At times, that sparked dissension, but in general it kept us moving. In addition to our regular field hearings, we tried to have a presence at every major industry conference or consumer group meeting that we could manage. Experts from the bureau were frequently asked to speak or to serve on panels, which often forced us to work through policy issues and positions internally to make sure we were presenting a unified message externally—a familiar challenge for any organization, including government agencies. When we attended industry gatherings, we learned a lot from banking and financial executives about their market dynamics, the practicalities of some of our efforts, and the pros and cons they saw in various decisions they had to make—not only about how we affected them, but also how they conduct their business generally. All these interactions influenced our thinking about our specific projects as well as our larger goals.

We also convened groups to seek their perspective as we worked to complete specific tasks. Our statute required us to have a consumer advisory board, and we decided to populate it mostly with consumer advocates, but also with financial executives, academics, and others of diverse backgrounds. The board met regularly to help guide our efforts. We also created a council of community bankers and another of credit union officials, to get the input of smaller lenders that we otherwise dealt with only rarely. Sometimes we used these forums to sound out issues at an early stage or to indicate our interest and encourage people to consider moving in certain directions. We held public events, for example, to push for streamlining the mortgage closing process and to prod auto lenders to rethink the pricing of their loans to reduce the potential for discrimination. Of course, not all of these efforts achieved their intended goals.

SERVICEMEMBERS AND VETERANS

Consumer protections for service members are vital to military readiness. Those in active service must be able to focus on their dangerous mission of protecting our country against its adversaries. But they are often based far from their original homes and may be deployed or preparing for deployment abroad, compounding the difficulty and distraction of coping with financial problems. They also must maintain security clearances and remain flexible in responding to orders that can change at any time, and this can greatly complicate their personal and financial circumstances.[4]

Recognizing these concerns, Congress enacted the Servicemember Civil Relief Act in 1940 and the Military Lending Act in 2006. Both laws offer some protections to active-duty military and their families against predatory lenders and high-cost loans, primarily by capping interest rates and staving off certain lawsuits to collect debts or foreclose on their homes. In the Dodd-Frank Act, Congress reinforced these efforts by requiring the CFPB to have an Office of Servicemember Affairs.

We were fortunate to have Holly Petraeus lead our efforts to protect servicemembers and their families. Holly had spent the previous six years working as the director of the Better Business Bureau's Military Line, a program providing consumer advocacy and education for servicemembers. She came from a military family of five generations, so she had broad knowledge of the hardships and vulnerabilities these families face. The military leaders greatly respected her judgment, and she secured ready cooperation from every branch of the service. We saw that first-hand, when all the services met with us early on and established close cooperation between the Judge Advocate General's Corps and the bureau to identify and address issues affecting servicemembers. All told, it was a rare instance of how one individual's extraordinary personal qualities could make our government work better than it ever would otherwise.

Holly and her team visited military bases all over the country and around the world, heard the concerns of military personnel and their families, and brought back special problems for us to address. In the throes of the housing crisis, for example, they pointed out that permanent-change-of-station (PCS) orders—which are not optional—require servicemembers to move, even if they cannot afford to sell their home for a loss. These situations sometimes forced families to split up for as much as three years or more, or suffer financial hardship either by selling the home for a loss or bearing the load of carrying two houses and trying to rent one for whatever price they could get. Holly understood the problem first-hand, having moved twenty-four times in a thirty-seven-year span, which can be part of life in any military family. To solve this problem, we had to work with multiple agencies: the Department of Defense; the state and federal parties to the national mortgage servicing settlement; the mortgage lending giants Fannie Mae and Freddie Mac; their regulator, the Federal Housing Finance Administration; and the Treasury Department. We eventually achieved an agreement that PCS orders would be treated as a qualifying hardship to secure loan modifications and other assistance, including eligibility for "short sales"—where the sale price of the home does not cover the shortfall on the mortgage but the lender agrees not to pursue the seller for the remainder.[5]

Another program that the Office of Servicemember Affairs championed was financial coaching. They found that new recruits receive some financial education during basic training, but this seemed like poor timing. Not only are the recruits exhausted and stressed by the many demands of their regimen, but also they arrive at boot camp already carrying an average of $10,000 in debt, perhaps anticipating the income that lies ahead. Instead, we refocused these efforts on the Delayed Entry Program, the period when a recruit has committed to the military but not yet reported to basic training, which may last for up to a year. We planned a short curriculum that could be delivered during this period by smartphone or computer, to help prepare recruits in handling their financial affairs. The military leadership—which, after all, is focused on protecting our nation against foreign enemies, not specializing in consumer finance—eagerly embraced this approach as a better way to promote military readiness.

The Office of Servicemember Affairs also worked jointly with the Pentagon on the special financial challenges that servicemembers face when they leave the military. At that point, their financial situation changes dramatically, including changes in housing, taxation, benefits, and legal protections. For servicemembers who have spent their whole careers serving their country, the transition can be jarring, and many issues are new and unforeseen. With broad input from veterans, the team devised a program for financial coaching to ease this transition back to civilian life. Preparing people to recognize and manage these changes would save them both money and heartache.[6]

Looking Out for Students

We also had an Office of Students, headed by a "student loan ombudsman" appointed jointly by the CFPB director and the Treasury secretary—a position that was held in turn by two creative and aggressive leaders, Rohit Chopra and Seth Frotman. Student loan debt is an issue of huge and growing visibility, and it commanded substantial attention from us. Runaway costs are making it harder and harder for American families to afford higher education. The market for private student loans collapsed in the wake of the financial crisis, and Congress decided to cut the banks out from serving as the middlemen for federal student loans. As a result, almost the entire market now consists of federal student loans extended directly by the US government. The Department of Education is responsible for overseeing the loan programs and the Treasury is on the hook for the unpaid debts. The total amount of student loan debt is skyrocketing, and loan defaults have risen to about one million per year.

There was little we could do about controlling the cost of higher education, but we could seek ways to help people cope with student loan debt. At a field hearing in Miami, we learned about the special challenges that confront new immigrants who do not qualify for federal student loans. Many were using credit cards as an expensive source of financing, when they can qualify for them. And some young people who do qualify for federal loans come under extreme pressure to max out their borrowing limits and use any extra funds to help support their families. Given the government's now-outsized role in the marketplace, our ability to be productive depended on building a constructive relationship with the US Department of Education. Fortunately, Secretary Arne Duncan's strong support for the CFPB led to the fruitful partnership on our "Know Before You Owe" efforts, which started with the financial aid shopping sheet and grew into the broader suite of tools we called "Paying for College."[7]

We also took the initiative to promote the promising federal program that provides for public service loan forgiveness. Back in 2007, Congress enacted this program to incentivize young people to consider modest-paying careers in public service. The law provides that after ten years of full-time work for a qualified employer, those who have made 120 months of qualifying payments can have the remaining balance of their federal loans forgiven entirely, with no tax implications. It is meant to help police officers, teachers, firefighters, and many others working in government or certain nonprofit organizations. The recordkeeping for such a program would seem simple enough, but the Department of Education and student loan servicers created so much complexity and confusion over the eligibility criteria that they almost gutted the program. The problems were so great that after the first ten years had passed in 2017, when many student borrowers should have become eligible for loan forgiveness, fewer than a thousand people received the benefit, rather than the tens of thousands who were expected to qualify. We tried to raise awareness of the benefit with a "how to" toolkit we provided for employers and employees, and we signed up local governments to popularize the program with their employees, but it would not be enough to help people work through the administrative mess that has been made, which has now spawned multiple lawsuits and is not yet fixed.[8]

Students also face financial risks on campus. Many colleges and universities struck secret agreements with banks to share information about students and alumni and to grant exclusive marketing arrangements for financial services, in return for annual payments worth millions of dollars. The CARD Act requires greater transparency about these agreements that cover credit cards issued to students. But schools often go to great lengths to avoid doing the obvious and easy thing, which is to post the agreements on their websites, where the public and consumer groups can review and assess them. As a general principle, resistance to transparency is often a sign of problems. We pressured the colleges to fully comply with the law, and we posted the information publicly ourselves.

Congress also required us to issue a report every year about these credit card marketing agreements, which we found to be on the decline. We decided to expand the scope of this report to discuss the risks to students from similar agreements at some schools that cover other types of banking services. We worked with the Department of Education to craft strong new rules to crack down on abuses with campus debit cards. And our reports called attention to the fact that many colleges have agreements where they are paid to allow banks to offer accounts with higher fees or fewer protections than are widely available elsewhere. By publicizing this issue, we exposed this harmful practice that enriches colleges at the expense of their students.[9]

PROTECTING OLDER AMERICANS

From my days serving at the state and local level in Ohio, I had seen fraudsters and scammers target seniors. Many seniors have access to some money, and growing numbers of older Americans live alone without family nearby. Their abilities may be diminishing, and their loneliness may make them susceptible to approaches that they would have spurned in prior years. When I was a county treasurer, we saw elderly property owners who became delinquent after years of faithfully paying their taxes; often this was a red flag of distress pointing to some change in circumstances, such as creeping dementia or the death of the spouse who had always dealt with financial matters. The easy levers of modern communication create new risks, as scams can reach seniors by mail, phone, or the internet. Even seniors who keep in close touch with their families may be easy prey. A colleague realized his mother had responded to a sweepstakes scam when he noticed her receiving huge volumes of mail that stacked up inches high each month; another friend's elderly father, highly educated and clear-minded, agreed to invest in a fraudulent venture that scooped up much of his savings. We heard all too many of these stories.

Our Office for Older Americans tracked scams, and it created alerts and other notices to inform people about them. We aggressively sought out partners to help us spread the word and find ways to protect people. One of the team's innovations was to create placemats with tips on how to avoid or deal with scams, which the Meals on Wheels program agreed to distribute to seniors nationwide. We worked with banks and law enforcement to speed up notification of potential criminal activity. Community banks, often on the front lines in protecting their customers from fraud, worked with us to better understand how much information they can share with law enforcement and others without violating the financial privacy of their customers. We also helped local governments expand TRIAD programs, which are three-cornered arrangements among law enforcement, community groups, and older adults to share information and boost prevention.[10]

We sought to educate older Americans by publishing a report on the risks posed by reverse mortgages, which are often advertised on late-night television. These loans are made to seniors based on the equity they have built up in their homes over the years. The senior makes no monthly payment on the loan; instead, the balance grows each month and repayment of the loan is deferred until after the homeowner dies, sells, or moves out. The basic product can be beneficial, but there are many complications that consumers may not understand and can lead to financial problems. We found that the risks of seniors losing their homes are heightened when money is taken out in a lump sum or in the name of one spouse only. Some reverse mortgages are misleadingly marketed as "risk free," causing seniors wrongly to ignore their continuing need to pay for taxes and insurance. We made recommendations about how the Department of Housing and Urban Development (HUD) could tighten up reverse-mortgage terms, issued warnings to consumers, monitored deceptive advertising, and brought enforcement actions where these problems led to violations of the law.

We also recognized that the caretaker generation is often in the best position to assist seniors who are vulnerable to financial exploitation. People with aging parents can step in and steer them through various pitfalls. For example, one year my father did not receive his income tax refund; when I checked into it, I learned that his handwriting on his tax return was illegible. After that, I took care of it for him, just as so many people find ways to support their aging parents. To help caregivers navigate the financial complexities, we worked with state and federal officials to prepare guides for "Managing Someone Else's Money," including information on guardianships and conservatorships that most people know little about. We promoted these guides through a column in "Dear Abby" that prompted thousands of requests for the information.

And we partnered with the Social Security Administration to develop advice for seniors about when to claim their Social Security benefits. Many people don't realize that the amount of the benefits they will receive depends in part on how old they are when they claim them—wrongly assuming their eligibility to claim benefits is a one-time affair that kicks in at age sixty-two—let alone what the pros and cons of their choices are.

The most poignant aspect of this work is that it relates to everyone, not just those who are already seniors. We may first encounter these issues with our grandparents, then our parents, and finally for ourselves. Elder financial abuse is a crime that continues to proliferate in our society, and sadly it often occurs within families. Yet many of these situations are recurring and predictable, and we should not leave our seniors exposed, especially as they deal with the infirmities of the aging process. As with much of consumer finance, knowing how to be prepared for the problems that lie ahead is a big part of fighting these battles effectively.

Financial Empowerment

Our Office of Financial Empowerment centered on consumers with low or moderate incomes. The vise of income inequality has many Americans firmly in its grip, and even those with modest means are ripe targets for predatory products.[11] We looked for ways to reduce the shockingly high costs and risks of living in poverty. Unlike telephone companies and certain utilities, the law does not impose any principle of "universal service" on the financial companies that would require them to offer all consumers access to their services, including low-income consumers. They are thus free to cream off the more lucrative customers and ignore those stuck at the bottom of the barrel.[12] As a result, poorer Americans who lack basic banking services often pay more just to access their own money, as well as to secure it and transact with it. When each financial transaction is a "one-off" event, prices hover at their highest levels, and customers do not enjoy the comfort and the many benefits they would gain from an ongoing relationship with a financial services company.

We tried to be opportunistic in finding ways to empower consumers. At a field hearing in Louisville, Kentucky, we launched a partnership with some cities and banks, as well as the Federal Deposit Insurance Corporation (FDIC), to help expand people's access to safe bank accounts. America has about fourteen million adults who are "unbanked," which sets them back enormously. They pay hefty fees every time they cash a check; they often deal in cash, which is risky and insecure; they find it hard to qualify for credit; and they have more trouble documenting their financial records. Banks use a screening process to block certain people out of the banking system, sometimes based on fraud risk but often because of prior bad experiences, including bounced checks and unpaid overdraft charges that may have led to account closures. We urged banks to offer safe accounts without overdraft fees, so they would not have to screen out potential customers based on that risk. These accounts are suited not only to those with low incomes but also to those, like many millennials, who mistrust banks for imposing hefty fees. Several of the largest banks have begun to offer this type of account. In the past few years the number of people who are unbanked has begun to decline, though it remains unacceptably high.[13]

We also issued a report that identified and described "credit invisibles"— people who are unable to qualify for credit because they have no or little credit history. This is a huge hindrance to personal opportunity. This group overlaps with the unbanked but is even larger—about twenty-six million Americans. We convened a field hearing in Charleston, West Virginia, to learn more about the problem. One point we noted is that every one of us starts out in life as a "credit invisible," and then, as we move into adulthood, we may generate enough of a financial record to qualify for access to credit. That can happen in good ways, such as having a family member vouch for you to qualify for your first credit card, or in bad ways, such as having un-collected debts reported on your credit file. Our team did extensive research on thousands of people to explore how people make this journey, helping us develop better practical guidance about how people can qualify for credit and what steps they can take to improve their credit records, which many people find bewildering.

Our team also provided new educational resources for social service providers to use in working with their clients. We called this toolkit "Your Money, Your Goals," and like everything else at the bureau, it was based on careful research. We found that as social workers, labor unions, health providers, and many others help people with various life issues that hold them back, almost always there are financial difficulties as well. Our toolkit was designed to assist those providing such services, as they went about their normal work, by giving them the tools to help people address their financial challenges at the same time. We later compressed the information on managing a budget into an even smaller, colorful booklet called "Behind on Bills?" that proved to be very popular as well. All of this material was presented in plain language and its contents were improved by constant feedback. We trained big groups of people to show them how to work with the toolkit, which enabled us to spread it far and wide. In time, we developed versions in Spanish and Chinese as well.[14]

Our empowerment team also keyed into a significant financial moment for many low-income consumers: the time when they claim their annual in-come tax refunds. The earned income tax credit is a bipartisan federal and state policy that has existed for decades to benefit the working poor, espe-cially those with children. We engaged in vigorous awareness campaigns to make sure people know how to claim the money they are entitled to receive, are aware of the many free or low-cost tax preparation services that are avail-able, and then consider using their refund money to pay off high-cost debt or save for the future. Of course, whenever people are known to be entitled to a lump of money, they are vulnerable to scammers or predators who are eager to separate them from it. We recognized that tax preparers in the past had offered high-cost tax refund anticipation loans, the worst of which can eat up the tax refunds that working families desperately need. We made clear to the industry that we would police bad financial products, and we did. Every year, our own peculiar form of March Madness was to put our people on the road to deliver our tax-time messages and materials and to encourage others to do the same.

Digital Outreach

Each of these special populations has its own unique issues, but they also have much in common with each other and with all consumers. Everyone wants to be treated with dignity and respect, and most of us are anxious about how best to manage our financial affairs. Our efforts to address these concerns led us to produce our online decision-making tools and other resources like "Ask CFPB" to help people learn more about almost any problem in consumer finance—handy tools that the electronic media makes available to anyone, anywhere, at any time.[15] Realizing that we started out largely unknown, we sought innovative ways to raise our profile. Our team used blogs, email lists, videos, chat rooms, and virtual town halls to reach people more conveniently when they were ready and willing to interact with us. We raised awareness of our brand through digital advertising and online search optimization, which was one of the only feasible ways to announce ourselves to consumers everywhere. People needed to know about our resources and to engage with us if we were going to make any difference in their lives. This is a major challenge across the entire government, as much potential help is available but goes unused because people are unaware of it. We worked hard to raise our visibility with the public, but it is always slow going.

TEAMING UP FOR CONSUMERS

The Consumer Bureau was set up as an independent agency within the Federal Reserve system. That structure insulated us from presidential control and congressional funding pressures, and even after Republicans won control of the Senate in 2014, the filibuster and certainty of a presidential veto protected us from any overhaul by Congress. Yet politics still interfered with our work, as our opponents continued to launch attacks on specific issues and created considerable friction for us as we engaged in more pitched battles for the American dream.[1]

Nonetheless, the prevailing political climate surrounding the bureau during this period had its positive side as well, and we worked to make the most of it. Our independence was not the same as forced isolation; we benefited greatly from the Obama administration's strong support. Whenever possible, we teamed up with friendly officials on issues with broad appeal, which helped them see how our combined efforts provided more heft that could better serve their constituencies. This allowed us to do even more to protect servicemembers and students, and it yielded other fruitful partnerships as well.

PROTECTING MILITARY FAMILIES

Many young people who enter military service are leaving home for the first time and are not well prepared to make sound financial decisions. They are juicy targets for predatory lenders who know they are inexperienced consumers with a steady government paycheck. Predators congregate near military bases, it has been observed, like grizzly bears gathering to harvest the salmon swimming upstream to spawn.[2] Our Office of Servicemember Affairs brought this dangerous situation to our attention, but it often took the resources of the entire bureau, working with our external partners, to do something about it.

Ari, the young soldier described earlier who bought a used truck, was one of their customers.[3] He saw advertisements near his base for the "U.S. MILES" program, which was a joint venture between a bank and an auto lender that helped finance vehicle purchases for military customers. The term "MILES" in the title of the loan program was an acronym for "Military Installment Loans and Educational Services," which sounded official and relatively safe. But the loan for the truck, which included undisclosed fees and misleading add-on services, ended up costing Ari 70% of his take-home pay. And the loan stipulated that it had to be repaid through the Pentagon's allotment system, meaning the monthly loan payment automatically would be withdrawn before Ari received his paycheck.

After Ari was deployed, his father stepped in to see if anything could be done about the situation. But his protests were ignored because Ari unquestionably had agreed to the loan. Desperate, Ari's father eventually filed a complaint with the CFPB. We dug into the facts and uncovered the hidden fees and misleading add-on services. We then launched a broader investigation and found that the parties jointly offering the "U.S. MILES" program failed to accurately disclose finance charges, loan rates, payment schedules, and total payments on the loans. They also deceived servicemembers by understating the cost and scope of certain add-on products that were sold in connection with the loans. The breadth of the program caused these violations to touch tens of thousands of soldiers, sailors, airmen, and marines stationed across the country and around the world. We issued a formal public order that forced the companies to stop deceiving consumers, revise the loan terms for Ari and fifty thousand other military personnel, and return about $6.5 million to customers who were harmed. We collaborated on the investigation with the Department of Defense and the Judge Advocate General's Corps for each of the service branches.

Our investigation also revealed that lenders were abusing the military allotment system. It was created years ago as a convenience for troops deployed overseas, before online banking made automatic bill payment a standard service that commonly is offered for free. To put their finances in order while their attention was focused on their service mission, servicemembers could sign up for "allotment" of their pay. This enabled them to have the government pay a portion of their paycheck directly to financial institutions or others of their choosing. But lenders were now using allotment as a one-sided collection tool that totaled well over $1 billion in the 2012 fiscal year. By requiring customers to sign up for allotments, they put themselves at the front of the line to get paid each month, and many servicemembers lost control of their finances without realizing it. Some companies even misused allotments to commit fraud; we brought an action against one company that was collecting bogus fees from military customers without adequate disclosures or notifications. More broadly, we persuaded the Pentagon to study the issue further and they ultimately agreed to discontinue allotments for servicemembers on purchases of personal property like electronics or cars and trucks. The bureau's teamwork with military officials helped Ari and fifty thousand other servicemembers get their money back, and it also brought about an important systemic improvement.

The abuses were not limited to auto lenders. We issued an order against Culver Capital, which offered high-priced credit to servicemembers to buy electronics like computers, videogame consoles, televisions, and other products at mall kiosks near military bases. It hid the true cost of the financing in its inflated prices, indicating that the annual percentage rate was 16% when in fact it was as much as 100% or more. We partnered with thirteen states to secure debt relief for Culver Capital's military consumers, totaling $92 million, and we banned the company and its principals from conducting any further consumer lending business. We also teamed up with two state attorneys general to sue Freedom Stores, which located near military bases nationwide and catered to servicemembers by selling furniture and electronics. It violated the law by filing thousands of debt-collection lawsuits in Virginia to pursue consumers who did not live in Virginia or ever buy anything there, making it virtually impossible to defend themselves in these distant lawsuits. Freedom Stores double-charged many of them, improperly contacted their commanding officers to pressure them to pay, and took money from checking accounts of family members without authorization. Our order secured restitution, imposed a fine, and barred them from any further violations.[4]

Determined efforts made by Senator Jack Reed of Rhode Island also led to some rare legislative modifications affecting the bureau. The Military Lending Act (MLA) was passed in 2006 to protect active-duty military and their families against high-cost loans by capping the interest rate on such loans at 36%. When it became law, new regulations were needed to define the scope of these protections. Initially, the Pentagon worked with the existing banking agencies to produce the regulations, which were so anemic they basically gutted the law. Our team convincingly showed that online lenders were still making terrible loans at triple-digit interest rates marketed specifically to the military, complete with flags and "US" designations on their websites—yet every one of these loans was permitted under the narrow scope of the existing regulations. Senator Reed responded by securing a legislative change that authorized the CFPB to join the other regulators in working with the Pentagon to write new rules to implement the MLA. Because of the close relationships we had already forged with the military leaders, they allowed our team to take the lead in fashioning strong new rules that protect the military and their families against a much broader universe of high-cost loans. Senator Reed also had previously gotten the law changed to give the CFPB oversight over the MLA, which now encompassed the new rules as well. These measures were broadly popular and met only muted resistance.[5]

BACKPACKS WITH DOLLAR SIGNS

With higher education now a prerequisite for many career paths, people are stretching to find ways to finance it. As the demand grows, prices are rising as well, outstripping virtually every other financial item including health insurance. But the stakes are especially high: heavy student debt burdens, often compounded by loan servicing companies that mismanage the collection of payments on the loans, are limiting the ability of young people to buy a home, choose where they work, save for retirement, or start a business. All of this is affecting not only the students and their families but also the larger economy, given the scale and rapid growth of student loan debt. Every field that attracts people to spend money becomes a magnet for cunning financial schemes, and this is no exception. When fraud and deception are added to the mix, the problems intensify. Our Office of Students called out sharp or sloppy practices with respect to student loans, but they needed our enforcement team, working together with other federal and state officials, to take effective steps to protect consumers in ways that would also bolster the economy.[6]

Rodney, the veteran who sought a college degree after leaving the military, was a victim of these sharp practices. He used his GI benefits to enroll in a for-profit college and took out gap loans to cover any shortfalls. He didn't know that he was being misled about the value of his degree and his chances of landing a job. When the school was investigated and ordered to stop its fraudulent practices, he was left with no remaining GI benefits, with stranded credits toward a worthless degree, and with gap loans still to repay.[7]

For years, complaints about fraud at for-profit colleges had been piling up. As we began to see the widespread nature of the problems, we put together a group of officials including several state attorneys general who were already conducting investigations, the US Department of Education, the Justice and Treasury Departments, and even the Securities and Exchange Commission, which was concerned about irregular investment activity. We convened as a group and split up the work, then coordinated with our federal and state partners to bring tough enforcement actions against two chains of for-profit colleges—Corinthian and ITT—that had misled students about costs, graduation rates, and job placements.

We found that these for-profit chains preyed remorselessly on people who are seeking to fulfill the American dream. They focused on young people aspiring to be the first in their family to earn a college degree. They recruited single mothers trying to better their lives. And they especially targeted veterans with educational benefits available under the GI Bill. The research showed that between 2006 and 2010, the military education benefits received by twenty of the largest for-profit college chains grew rapidly from $66 million to an estimated $521 million.[8] Some of the companies told one story about default rates to the potential students as they loaded them up with debt, and another story entirely in selling their business model to investors, many of whom made a killing off the backs of defrauded students.

Our investigation found that these schools often misstated their graduation rates, which typically were only half the rate for students at four-year public institutions. They also overstated their job placement rates and the likely salaries that graduates would earn. The cases we filed put both the Corinthian and ITT chains of schools under orders that required significant reforms in how they treated students. When it turned out they could not manage these reforms and went out of business, we followed up by securing cancellation of hundreds of millions of dollars in debts for those victimized by their fraud. Our federal and state partners did the same with other poorly performing schools—some of which were outright frauds that created fake employers, paid employers to hire students temporarily, and counted jobs lasting even just a few days as a "placement." The results from these cases helped thousands of former students get another chance. Some, like Rodney, were able to get back on track with their education once their GI benefits were restored and their debts to the for-profit colleges that defrauded them were canceled. Our work in wiping out hundreds of millions of dollars in debts also saved many students from continued harassment by debt collectors.

The bureau also forged a three-cornered alliance, with the Treasury and Education Departments, to rein in sloppy and abusive practices by student loan servicers that process the payments made by borrowers. We convened a joint session with lenders and about a dozen of the largest loan servicers, where we pressed them to offer more options for loan modification to help students cope with repaying their accumulated debts. At field hearings and public sessions around the country, we heard stories from students and their families about maddening problems of misapplied payments and poor customer service that magnified the pain of their situations and stunted their opportunities to benefit from the education they worked so hard to earn. Many of the stories were much like Joan's story—the teacher who was paying off $42,000 in student loan debt. She was hurt by servicer errors that misapplied payments to lower-cost loans and failed for years to inform her that she could qualify for income-based repayment, which needlessly cost her money and damaged her credit. The experiences people described with student loan servicing closely mirrored the problems that were rife among mortgage servicers, marked by incompetent processes and indifference to borrower concerns—with many perverse incentives to keep people paying on their loans rather than helping them pay down their loans faster. Our alliance bore fruit when we jointly released our servicing standards for federal student loans in July 2016, which we patterned on the requirements previously imposed on mortgage servicers.

As time passed with unsatisfactory progress, we lost patience and prepared a major lawsuit against Navient, the largest student loan servicer in the country. Navient managed the accounts for more than twelve million borrowers, totaling over $300 billion in federal and private student loans. Following a thorough probe of their operations, we concluded that breakdowns and violations had occurred that failed borrowers at every stage of the repayment process. Specifically, we alleged that Navient had hindered people from repaying their loans by giving them bad information, mishandling their payments, and failing to respond effectively when borrowers complained. Rather than working with borrowers to lower their monthly payments and help them cope with their debt load over the long term, we determined that Navient steered them into short-term forbearance plans, causing their debt to grow as billions of dollars in unpaid interest continued to accumulate. Remarkably, our investigation indicated that when disabled borrowers—including veterans injured during their military service—qualified to discharge their loans, Navient misreported some of them to the credit reporting companies as having defaulted, which damaged their ability to qualify for credit.

When we filed suit in January 2017, we were joined by Illinois and Washington. Their attorneys general, both tough consumer advocates, told their own horror stories about Navient and its predecessor, Sallie Mae. The cases brought by the attorneys general covered a broader time frame that reached back before the creation of the bureau, covering not only the servicing problems cited in our complaint but also Navient's alleged peddling of risky subprime student loans that defaulted at extremely high rates. Navient also serviced federal student loans under contract with the US Department of Education, so when we filed these claims, they pushed back hard through all available channels. But more and more people were coming around to our view, now widely held, that the domino effects of student debt burdens and loan servicing problems are holding back the upcoming generation and hampering the economy.[9]

OTHER WIN-WIN PARTNERSHIPS

We also found some unexpected partners. For the most part, the bureau's authority is limited to issues of household credit, where people borrow money in the form of loans. But people have many other financial obligations, which they pay steadily over time, that are defined as "bills" rather than "credit" because they are paid on an ongoing basis without any fronting of money. These types of obligations include household rent and utility bills, such as gas or electric, and now also encompass bills for cable and phone services, which are notoriously dense and confusing. We asked the Federal Communications Commission (FCC) to work with us on a "Know Before You Owe" initiative to make these monthly bills simpler and clearer. We had been carefully testing our template credit forms with consumers, and the project seemed well suited to phone and cable issues as well.

Separately, a significant problem was developing with the big mobile phone carriers. It came to light that they were profiting from "cramming" their customers' bills with unauthorized charges that most people did not even realize were bogus. The monthly cell phone bills had become an opportunity for merchants to charge people, fraudulently, for things they did not buy. It began when the mobile carriers started charging for premium text messages to deliver things like ringtones or wallpaper, then outsourced the billing function to vendors. The mobile carriers did not keep a watchful eye on these vendors, and clever scammers took advantage of their neglect. Scammers cheated people by charging them for what was supposed to be "free" content like celebrity gossip or sports scores, and by placing fictitious charges on their bills without delivering anything at all. It was unclear whether the mobile carriers even realized this was happening, but they got a hefty cut (about a third) of the gross revenue from all the billings. And when customers complained, the carriers mostly turned a deaf ear.

This scenario prompted a sprawling investigation by the FCC as well as the CFPB, the Federal Trade Commission (FTC), and ultimately the attorneys general of every state. At first, it hardly seemed possible that fraud of this scale could have been committed right under everyone's noses. We apportioned the work among our teams and together we found that the problem was even worse than it seemed. Third-party billing had turned the mobile carriers into large-scale payment processors as well, with very little regulatory oversight to protect people from being ripped off. In the end, our coalition took actions against all four of the big carriers—Verizon, Sprint, T-Mobile, and AT&T. All told, consumers were entitled to more than $260 million in refunds, and the companies paid out tens of millions in additional fines and penalties. Importantly, the companies also agreed to make specific changes to tighten up their billing practices, including new processes to authorize and confirm third-party charges and impose new mechanisms for consumers to block such charges.

Part of the problem was the bewildering complexity of mobile phone bills. Although some consumers complained about unexpected fees, many did not notice the problem because they could not distinguish the bogus fees from the rest of the charges on their bills. The fraudulent merchants took advantage of their confusion by couching their phony fees in vanilla terms that looked legitimate, such as "usage charges," buried deep in monthly statements that could be dozens of pages long. The orders in the cramming cases made a start on reforming how cell phone bills are presented by requiring all third-party charges to be presented in a separate section of the billing statement that is clearly labeled. But beyond that, the FCC under Chairman Tom Wheeler agreed to work with us on a broader "Know Before You Owe" project that led to the adoption of "consumer broadband labels" for customers of mobile and fixed broadband internet service. These disclosures require information about price, data allowances, and performance to be presented to consumers in an accurate, understandable, and easy-to-find manner. The FCC, in consultation with us, specified elegant disclosure formats that are not mandatory but provide companies with a "safe harbor" if they agree to adopt them.[10]

Another solid partner was the Navajo Nation, which teamed up with us to bring an enforcement action against companies and individuals who ran an illegal tax-refund-anticipation loan scheme. We found that the scheme steered low-income consumers, including many tribal citizens, into high-cost loans by misstating the loan rates and deceiving people about the status of their tax refunds. Working together with the Navajo Nation's attorney general, we secured about $1 million in money back to victims and penalties.

Other partnerships helped the Consumer Bureau serve more consumers. The Department of Labor teamed up with us to provide financial coaching at job centers around the country, to improve financial capability for consumers with disabilities, and to incorporate our financial education resources into its summer youth employment programs. They also asked us to consult with them on their fiduciary rule, a sensitive and surprisingly controversial measure requiring investment advisers to act in their clients' interests with respect to their retirement accounts. The Department of Health and Human Services worked with us to protect older Americans and to distribute our guides on "Managing Someone Else's Money." When the IRS determined that they had extra room in certain taxpayer mailings, they included our information urging people to consider saving options for their tax refunds; for our part, we warned people on our website about IRS imposter scams and alerted them about delayed tax refunds.

We also found win-win issues with some of the banks and financial companies where we could use the tool of persuasion. We urged all the major credit card companies to make people's credit scores available for free on their credit card bills and other loan statements. Some companies had begun to do so, and many others agreed to do so as well, covering tens of millions of consumers. This proved popular with customers, who now had ready access to a service they used to have to hunt down and pay for. It also helped raise people's awareness of credit reporting issues, such as how to raise your credit score, which not only benefits consumers but also benefits the banks by helping develop more resilient customers who are less likely to default on their obligations.[11] Later we urged the major CEOs to offer low-cost, safe bank accounts to grow their customer base with the unbanked and with millennials. This also elicited some positive response, and it helped more people attain the benefits of dependable financial services.

Fintech Innovators

Financial technology companies, often referred to as "fintechs," are seeking innovative ways to disrupt traditional banking and better serve consumers. Technology is producing many breakthroughs throughout the economy, and this is as true in financial services as everywhere else. Financial products are unusually flexible, with the only essential "components" being money, information, and contractual terms. And the marketplace has been transformed in the past generation. People crave speed, ease, and convenience, and online commerce, built on the massive power of big data, is solving the logistics and reducing the costs of delivering these characteristics, with obvious benefits for the consumer public.

This development means that more financial choices are broadly available to more people. More types of consumer credit now exist than ever before, and fintech entrepreneurs are intent on finding new ways to extend credit and financial services to those who lack access to them. These developments also have the potential to reduce costs, provide more consumer control, and improve customer service. What is more, many fintech providers are finding ways to make the existing consumer finance markets work more effectively on behalf of consumers. They see shortcomings and inefficiencies in the status quo, and they believe they can figure out how to do things better. They can be nimble in tackling these challenges, and they are getting the best of some of them. Many incumbent companies spend considerable time and money trying to reinvent themselves as well, but they also have to consider whether innovations may cannibalize their existing position in the marketplace. New startups have no such qualms.[12]

Fintech companies are claiming increasingly visible niches where they can compete effectively. Marketplace lenders are taking advantage of the slow, staid processes of bank lending. Better and faster customer service allows some fintech lenders to attract high-value customers looking to refinance credit card balances or certain types of student loan debt. Data aggregators are developing new bases for determining credit risk, such as noncredit financial information like payments of rent and utility bills. Others are probing new ways of helping consumers safely access and share their digital financial records. These new approaches may enable more consumers to qualify for credit. Advances in mobile payments and money transfers are expanding competition for such services. Other financial startups are homing in on specialized issues such as improving credit scores, speeding up wage payments, digitizing mortgage applications, extending short-term credit, creating digital currencies, evaluating people's optimal fit with financial products, and managing personal finances.

But innovation is not always benign. At our first event in Silicon Valley to reach out to the innovator community, Raj gave a sobering talk that described how creative innovations in the mortgage market, including home loans with unusual and exotic terms, led not to paradise but rather to disaster. And financial technology, which often requires consumers to provide their personal and financial information to new and unfamiliar companies— including access to their bank accounts—presents many temptations. It also creates risk of the new tools being used in a discriminatory way, whether intentionally or unintentionally. The bureau's first obligation is to protect consumers, in part by ensuring that fintech companies abide by the same rules as their traditional counterparts. We were thus unwilling to give these new companies the privilege of some sort of regulation-free "sandbox"—which is one of the latest fads in financial regulation around the world—instead, we required them to earn their way forward on a level playing field with the less flashy incumbents.

In the Dodd-Frank Act, Congress directed the bureau to help ensure that consumer finance markets "operate transparently and efficiently to facilitate access and innovation." Yet it is far from clear how a government regulatory agency can foster innovation in a market economy, where potent competition for customers already gives every entrepreneur the incentive to build a better mousetrap. Winning market share requires satisfying the needs of customers better than their competitors, including through innovation. We had no power to compel any financial providers to do that; instead, we sought to remove the overhang of regulatory uncertainty that might prevent them from serving consumers in more beneficial ways.

Through our Project Catalyst, we developed several research pilot projects with firms that requested a temporary safe harbor to test new concepts in return for sharing research data with the bureau. One was with Barclaycard, a credit card company, and Clarifi, a consumer credit counseling service, to see whether intervening with credit counseling would benefit consumers at risk of defaulting on their credit card debt. Another was with American Express to test different strategies for encouraging positive savings habits on prepaid cards. Yet another was with H&R Block to explore ways to encourage consumers to use their tax refunds to build savings. We also spent a huge amount of time on creating a policy for no-action letters, to encourage companies to undertake innovative programs by pledging that we would take no adverse action against them for a defined period. Setting the protocols for the type of detailed submission that would justify such a grant of immunity was tremendously complicated, and during my tenure we only managed to issue one no-action letter. The letter went to Upstart, a company that uses nontraditional data and modeling techniques to decide on loan applicants. We waived any enforcement action under the fair lending laws for three years in hopes that the company's approach would lead to expanded credit opportunities for the underserved and improve our understanding of methods of effective fair lending compliance. Although its use was limited, the policy did signal our interest in promoting experimentation to expand credit access.

By far our most successful initiative, however, was our Office Hours program. The head of Project Catalyst met extensively with innovators in Silicon Valley, New York, and elsewhere to learn more about what they were doing and bring back insights into promising approaches. His ambassadorial work kept our finger on the pulse of the latest entrepreneurial endeavors and helped us monitor what was happening. By making them aware of our interest, we put the CFPB on the companies' radar screens. We encouraged them to remain consumer friendly in terms of cost and service, and we took occasional enforcement actions against fintech companies, which established that nobody would be ceded a competitive advantage by failing to comply with the rules governing consumer financial products and services.[13] Several fintech executives served on our consumer advisory board, and their analysis and insights into this brave new world were also invaluable to us.

Sometimes people would ask where we think the fintech movement is headed. For myself, I believe that these scrappy companies with vast ambitions are unlikely to topple the larger financial companies. The financial services market is so entrenched that it will be difficult for new companies to gain the heft and manage the operational compliance necessary to develop any significant market share. The banking incumbents range from small (with millions or a few billion dollars in assets) to big (with tens or hundreds of billions of dollars in assets) to huge (over a trillion dollars in assets). Despite steady consolidation over many decades, there are still thousands of banks in the United States, along with thousands of credit unions and untold numbers of other financial companies that are not themselves banks. Although they compete vigorously for their customer bases, the banks also have built-in advantages that are unique, such as government-backed depositor insurance, a long-standing accommodation with the intricacies of their regulatory regime, and access to capital through the Federal Reserve's discount window. Only the largest technology companies, with their own considerable market shares, would have any realistic chance to cut into these entrenched positions. Nonetheless, many smaller disruptions are already occurring that are affecting consumers and the tools of consumer finance. So, even if few fintech companies are likely to grow to become a PayPal, many will likely be acquired or enter joint ventures with larger companies, which will change the consumer experience for the better.

THE TOUGHER FIGHTS

During the latter years of the Obama administration, we put down deeper roots by being active on many fronts. Much still needed to be done for consumers, and we felt the responsibility to keep moving forward. Accordingly, we took on some very tough fights in complex areas with the potential to have tremendous impact for consumers.

DISCRIMINATION IN AUTO LENDING

Very early in my tenure, we agreed that the Consumer Bureau would work in tandem with the Justice Department to take on the sensitive task of squelching discrimination in auto loans. As discussed earlier, customers seeking to buy a car or truck often are treated differently when they are stereotyped as "good" or "bad" negotiators.[1] This is a subjective assessment, and it may reflect prejudices based on race or gender or ethnicity. Recall the case of Ramon. When he bought a used car, the loan he was offered had a rate that was 3% higher than the better loan he could have qualified for. He was happy with the price of the vehicle and did not know to question the interest rate, which he assumed was the standard rate for any person with his credit record. For the entire life of the loan, he paid more than he should or could have. In fact, he had no way of realizing that he had been cheated, or that he and other Latinos were being treated differently from otherwise similar customers, because he had no way of assessing the company's patterns of customer treatment. A government agency with the data, the resources, and the authority to enforce the law is in a much better position to do that.

The Equal Credit Opportunity Act (ECOA), enacted in 1974, makes it illegal to deny people credit, or to charge them more for credit, based on race, gender, ethnicity, or other specifically prohibited categories.[2] Yet explicit evidence of discrimination can be hard to uncover. Some people know when they are making judgments and taking actions based on prejudice, but others do so without even being aware of it. Therefore, the methods used to prove fair lending claims include not only testimony and documents that substantiate what happened to each individual borrower but also statistical evidence about patterns in the types of loans made. If the numbers show that loans are being made on terms that differ systematically for customers in a prohibited category, this showing proves a violation of the law.

Although these principles of fair lending law have been well established for more than two decades, they remain tremendously controversial. Discrimination claims are highly sensitive and inflammatory, and allegations alone can greatly damage a company's business reputation. Moreover, companies resent being held accountable based purely on statistics if their conduct is not proved to be intentional. To many, legal liability based on crunching the numbers does not feel the same as overt racism, and companies worry that they cannot know until after the fact whether they are liable for discriminatory lending. The industry pushed hard for more detailed guidance about how they could assess their compliance with the fair lending laws. At first, we were slow to respond as we fleshed out our fair lending program and reached consensus with the Justice Department about how to apply the law in different consumer markets. Over time, however, we developed and shared increasing detail about where and how we drew the line in determining liability, both in our orders resolving enforcement actions and in our supervisory exam materials. This allowed companies to monitor their own lending patterns more effectively, and we also offered guidance about the processes that companies could use to engineer and implement sound compliance management systems.

In auto lending discrimination cases, specifically, and in fair lending cases more generally, some companies continued to question whether cases built entirely on statistics were properly actionable under the ECOA. When a closely similar case under the Fair Housing Act was set for argument in the Supreme Court, it was an ominous sign that our legal theory would be disapproved. All the lower courts had been issuing decisions that faithfully upheld the law, with no disagreements. But the Supreme Court had reached out to reconsider the issue in two prior cases—a likely sign of dissatisfaction with those rulings—and was thwarted both times when the parties settled their disputes before the court could issue a ruling. When the court took up yet a third case, the writing seemed to be on the wall. But in a surprising five-to-four decision authored by Justice Kennedy, the court reaffirmed the doctrine that statistical "disparate impact" cases do violate federal laws that ban discrimination.[3]

Although the Supreme Court had upheld the core legal principle, it was still difficult to apply. How systematic must a pattern be to violate the law? And how should the analysis be conducted? How is it most appropriate to fashion remedies that identify exactly who should be compensated and to what degree? On the Hill, our detractors zeroed in on these pressure points and challenged our assessments. The House Financial Services Committee issued a series of reports criticizing our auto lending work and continuing to make the argument that our entire statistical approach was misconstruing the law—even *after* the Supreme Court had ruled the other way.

For five years, we brought major enforcement actions on discrimination in auto lending, and we addressed the issues in many supervisory exams. Our cases, pursued jointly with the Justice Department, delivered hundreds of millions of dollars in relief for consumers like Ramon and assessed penalties to deter other companies. We took enforcement actions against both the banks that made auto loans and the auto finance companies typically affiliated in some way with a specific manufacturer, such as Honda and Toyota. These actions reined in some of the discretion that lenders have in setting interest rates, making it somewhat harder to engage in discriminatory lending.

Ultimately, however, we were unable to fully achieve our ambitious goal of rooting out discrimination in auto lending. In lobbying over the Dodd-Frank Act, auto *dealers* had flexed their political muscle to get Congress to carve them out of our jurisdiction—while leaving us responsible for policing the conduct of auto *lenders*. But dealers and lenders often collaborate in making loans—the dealers work directly with the customers to make the sale and then select among one or more lenders to arrange a loan. Because dealers typically control the customer relationship and can pick and choose which lenders to work with, they have considerable influence over lenders. Without having the dealers at the table, it was thus impossible to produce a lasting shift in lending practices. In 2014, we held a field hearing in Indianapolis and afterward we convened a roundtable with industry representatives to see if we could reach an industry-wide resolution. The auto lenders were resistant, however, and the dealers were effective in pressuring them not to yield. One banking executive noted the pressure that the lenders feel from the dealers, commenting that it is "a retributive market." Two years later, after completing several notable enforcement actions, we tried again to convene the largest auto lenders to discuss a market-wide resolution, but again we failed to budge them.

CREDIT REPORTING

Credit reporting is an important field that for many years was largely unknown to the public. It grew up rather haphazardly, starting in local areas where merchants began to compile and share information on who was bouncing checks or reneging on credit extended to them.[4] The networks for sharing such information gradually expanded, and then took off with the advent of computers that can store and organize data cheaply and effectively. The business is all about volume, and technological advances made possible enormous volumes. Today, the credit reporting market is dominated by three companies—Equifax, Experian, and TransUnion—each with about two hundred million credit files covering most adult Americans.

Although this industry is built entirely on our own personal financial information, it historically has operated in ways that largely exclude us. It is a classic business-to-business market: financial companies are the data furnishers that provide or sell information about their customers to the credit reporting companies. These companies then aggregate that data and sell the information back to the financial companies to help them gauge credit risk for current and potential customers. In this circular market, the businesses are customers of one another; consumers are not exercising any choice or wielding any market power at all. They cannot exert leverage by taking their business elsewhere if they are dissatisfied with how they are being treated. As a result, they often have been treated poorly.

Individual credit reports contain information about your transactions, including loans you have paid off or left unpaid, payments you have made on time or late, and current sources and amounts of debt. When that information is wrong—as it was for Kim, who was being confused with another woman who had the same name; or for Phyllis, who was being dinged for a disputed debt on a credit card account she had closed; or for Stan, who didn't realize he had three unpaid medical bills—it can damage your credit score, hindering you from qualifying for credit or making it more expensive in ways you may not even understand. The problem of "mixed files," where people are confused for one another, arises quite often for people who have shared the same address or who bear common surnames. But it has not mattered much to the credit reporting companies' business model that the information they maintain and provide about individual consumers be scrupulously accurate. If the mass of data is accurate enough to be valuable in improving the credit decisions that financial companies make, they will find it worthwhile to buy the data. For the credit reporting companies, the cost of investigating potential mistakes on individual credit reports is simply too high to justify when the market already has made the judgment that the somewhat flawed aggregate data is good enough. "Going overboard" on accuracy can only hurt the bottom line for their shareholders.

While individual accuracy might not loom large for companies that deal with credit files by the hundreds of millions, it is hugely consequential for the consumers themselves. An elderly woman who stood up at our field hearing in Detroit and told us she had a problem—"the credit reporting companies think I'm dead!"—was blocked from accessing credit, casting a shadow over her entire financial life. And there was a dignitary element to her lament as well: it seemed nobody at the company cared enough to respond to her walking and talking indictment of their performance. Consumers in this market are like accident victims before the courts began to impose strict liability on vehicle manufacturers. There is no incentive for the companies to build in any attention to *consumers'* concerns when no monetary value is attached to those concerns. A 90% accuracy rate for credit files may seem good in the abstract, with no context, and it may be good enough for the companies that buy and use the data. But that number translates into twenty million people whose credit files are distorted by errors that undermine their financial lives, which is plainly unacceptable.[5]

The Fair Credit Practices Act gives people the right to review their credit reports regularly and to dispute any incomplete or inaccurate information. But no state or federal body had ever supervised this market before, with continuous scrutiny of company operations. With the arrival of the Consumer Bureau, all of that changed. When we got underway, the companies were shocked. Not only were they unable to tell us how they went about ensuring compliance with the law, but also they had to admit that their "processes" were haphazard at best. We learned later that when we started making our inquiries, they learned from their own staff that the same tasks were being handled in unpredictable ways by different sets of people. Some of those approaches were inconsistent with reasonable expectations or even with the demands of the law.

Overall, the company processes for dealing with such disputes were astonishingly feeble. If you complained about a mistake in your file—such as whether you were late in paying your credit card bill—the credit reporting company would assign your complaint a three-digit code representing one of its generic categories of problems. The company would then transmit only that code to the source that originally furnished the data, seeking a response. With no further description of the problem and no real incentive to investigate, the original furnisher naturally assumed that its information was accurate, so errors rarely were corrected. Even if the consumer submitted supporting documents or other materials, *in many instances the credit reporting company would not forward them for consideration.* The whole process could hardly be dignified with the phrase "going through the motions." Some people who persistently pursued their disputes kept shoeboxes full of futile communications and correspondence they had endured with the companies, which could stretch over months or even years.

The law also requires the credit reporting companies to "maintain reasonable procedures" to ensure the "maximum possible accuracy" of the information contained in people's credit reports. As with the companies' approach to responding to disputes, however, we found they had interpreted these phrases very loosely. We set two large goals: first, to refine the accuracy of their huge credit files, since any appreciable error rate affects millions of people; second, to improve the cumbersome, ineffective process of fixing errors. To influence their performance, we exerted steady pressure by regularly supervising their operations.

This pressure was strongly reinforced by a major enforcement action led by the New York attorney general. It produced a tough order that required improvements in the dispute resolution process, including personnel with special training to handle disputed cases and new oversight to ensure the credit information provided by data furnishers is accurate. It also built in delays for reporting medical debt, which tends to be highly inaccurate. Customers are often confused about medical and health insurance billing, which can lead to unexpected debts, including small fees and co-pays that consumers may be unaware of or may disagree with. Some debt collectors simply "park" small medical debts on people's credit reports without informing them, knowing that blocking their access to credit will prod many to pay off the debts. That is what happened to Stan, for instance, who gave in and paid several disputed medical debts to avoid further hassles and qualify for the auto loan he urgently needed. As we continued to oversee the credit reporting companies, our close coordination with the state attorneys general was valuable, especially in designing effective remedies to correct potential violations of the law.[6]

We also applied pressure to the companies by raising the visibility of these issues among consumers. Most people don't know they have rights against these companies, including to review their credit report, for free, from each company once a year; to dispute errors in their reports and get incorrect negative information removed; to place a "security freeze" that seals information in their reports from being released to others; to have negative information removed according to specific schedules; to sue to enforce these rights; and more. By boosting people's awareness, we spurred more engagement between the public and the companies. No longer were the companies isolated by the moats they maintained around their business-to-business model. Our authority to enforce the law meant the companies had to become more responsive to each individual, because the CFPB itself was now focused on their responsiveness.

The credit score initiative is an excellent example of how this worked. By encouraging the credit card companies and other lenders to share people's credit scores on their monthly bills, for free, which many of them did, we made these issues more salient for consumers.[7] Seeing your own credit score, and especially seeing that it changes from time to time, made millions of people realize that they wanted to know more about how their scores were calculated and what they could do to improve them, which led to much more direct interaction between consumers and the companies. This was a much more effective approach than any generic public awareness campaign. The companies gradually began to make changes that improved their performance as they absorbed our key goals, which were to have each company reach 100% accuracy of individual credit reports and to get consumer disputes resolved promptly and fairly.

The essence of our work was to shift the priorities of the credit reporting companies to elevate their attention to addressing the needs of consumers. The companies are so massive that reforming their complex computer processes inevitably is slow going. With credit files on 200 million Americans each, they receive data from about ten thousand information providers who transmit over thirty-six billion updates annually. The industry was feeling the strain and cost of making these reforms, then suffered a terrible blow when one of the companies, Equifax, sustained a huge data breach, in which hackers stole the sensitive personal and financial information of 150 million Americans. The breach included credit history, social security numbers, passwords, account numbers—all of it valuable information that might now be in the hands of scammers and other types of criminals. This catastrophe spurred debates among the public and in Congress over a further issue: whether the CFPB should have *more* authority to protect consumer privacy and data security, where our mandate previously was limited, and how we might work with the Federal Trade Commission to better protect consumer financial information against these kinds of threats. Getting Congress to expand regulatory authority in this era of gridlock is a steep uphill battle, however, and so far, the issue remains unresolved. People continue to worry about the privacy and security of their credit data, and they still have many painful problems with their credit reports.

Debt Collection

Debt collection infects every consumer market. In a world where consumer finance is a larger and more intrusive element in people's lives, so is debt collection. All financial providers sustain defaults and must decide how to deal with customers who miss payments. They have every right to make reasonable efforts to collect what they are owed.

But consumers, even those who owe valid debts, have rights too, along with the reasonable expectation that they will be treated with dignity and respect. The Fair Debt Collection Practices Act lays out many specific rights and obligations of debtors and collectors alike. Coupled with federal restrictions on unfair, deceptive, and abusive acts or practices, there is considerable law governing the relations between debtors and creditors and collectors. Among the specific protections for consumers, for example, are time limits on contacting people (8:00 a.m. to 9:00 p.m.), a ban on communicating with the debtor at the workplace without consent, limits on various forms of harassment and threats, and a prohibition against making false claims.[8]

There are three ways debts are collected. First-party debt collection is when a provider is collecting a debt within the confines of an ongoing customer relationship—that is, the customer is behind on a payment and the provider is simply trying to get paid. Third-party debt collection occurs when the debt is passed on to someone else to collect under a contract with the original provider, and it also includes another model, where the provider sells off the debt for someone else to own and collect, generating whatever revenue it can but retaining no further stake in the collection of that debt. Because almost anyone can get licensed to become a debt collector, the market ranges widely from law firms and large computerized shops to small mom-and-pop outfits that hang out a shingle, get hold of some sort of client list, and go to work. The existence of an ongoing customer relationship tends to temper the conduct used to collect debts; the original provider wants to get paid, of course, but would also prefer not to lose a customer (even one who does not always pay on time) or have its business reputation tarnished through bad behavior.

Many of our investigations of financial companies began with a focus on other violations but ultimately turned up debt collection abuses as well. People who borrow money and fail to repay are enticing targets, and both businesses and collectors become deeply frustrated with people they regard as "deadbeats." Some providers refuse to grant credit unless customers first agree to have payments automatically debited from their accounts, which is against the law. Some collectors violate the law by calling at all hours of the day or night, making threats or false claims. Those were the kinds of problems Donna had experienced before our consumer response team stepped in to stop her from being harassed. Others use legal processes, seeking to turn a debt into a court judgment, which enables more muscular collection mechanisms, such as garnishing people's wages or placing liens against property they own. To improve their odds, some collectors engage in "sewer service," committing fraud in the processes they are supposed to use to notify people that they have been sued. Many debt collection lawsuits end up in default judgments against people who do not understand that they have a court case against them or, if they do understand, cannot afford legal representation. Small claims courts were devised to help people assert their rights on small monetary claims without having to pay for a lawyer. But they can be subverted into debt collection mills, and state and local courts can be as well. In these courts, hundreds of cases at a time *against* consumers are moved through on a fast track with little judicial oversight or any inquiry into the facts of individual cases. Indeed, at times we found debt collectors using the same "robo-signing" techniques to fabricate evidence to bolster their cases, just as mortgage servicers were doing to salvage their foreclosure cases—and they often were getting away with it.

These are horrifying situations for people who are pursued by debt collectors they never agreed to deal with but cannot easily shake off. As with credit reporting, consumers have no choice of debt collectors (other than the original provider) and therefore have no leverage in this market. But the problem is massive—seventy million Americans have one or more debts outstanding—so we employed all our tools to help. We fielded hundreds of thousands of complaints on this issue, outpaced only by the complaints we received about credit reporting. On closer review, some didn't pan out, but others led back to situations like Noelle's mother, who was being dunned for a debt she had already paid, or Jeffrey, who was being pursued for an unknown debt when it turned out he had been a victim of identity theft. We handled many of the simpler problems directly with the companies, but the bigger problems or those that reflected a pattern of misconduct led us to open investigations or conduct examinations to determine whether broader action was necessary.

We brought two sets of major enforcement actions that addressed a comprehensive range of issues in the debt collection market. One action was against a first-party collector, JPMorgan Chase Bank. The other was against two third-party collectors, Encore Capital and Portfolio Recovery, who at the time were the two largest debt collectors and debt buyers in the country.

The action against Chase involved "zombie debts," which are very old debts that the company has written off as not worthy of further collection efforts. Rather than discarding them, however, it is tempting for companies to squeeze out small amounts of added revenue by selling them at a discount to debt collectors that are willing to work them further. They do so in disregard of the misery that may descend on their former customers for years to come (as the debt may be resold still more times) and the fact that aging debt information deteriorates and becomes less accurate over time. Working with the Office of the Comptroller of the Currency (OCC), forty-seven states, and the District of Columbia, we found that Chase sold over a half-million zombie debts to third-party debt buyers, including accounts that were inaccurate, settled, discharged in bankruptcy, not owed, or otherwise not collectible, and also that Chase had "robo-signed" fraudulent court documents. We ordered Chase to stop collecting, enforcing, or selling more than 528,000 consumer accounts, and to adopt new restrictions on when and how it could sell debts or file collections lawsuits, including notifying consumers with information about debts that were sold and not allowing those debts to be resold. Refunds to consumers, along with fines and penalties, cost the bank $216 million. This action helped many people in situations like Noelle's mother and Jeffrey, who were being pursued on debts that were erroneous or already discharged. It also put other banks on notice to clean up their own debt collection practices, which no doubt benefited many more customers.

The other major enforcement actions were against the two largest US debt buyers and debt collectors (each did both). Together, these companies owned the right to collect on over $200 billion worth of debt on credit cards, phone bills, and other accounts. When they bought debts that were inaccurate, undocumented, or unenforceable, they too sought to shore up their files and churn out lawsuits by "robo-signing" false documents. They also used false statements to pressure people into paying and filed lawsuits where they had no intention of proving the debts but counted instead on winning default judgments. One company harassed consumers with calls at all hours of the day and the other misled them into agreeing to receive auto-dialed cell phone calls, which the company could not otherwise make. Our orders imposed an array of remedies much like those we imposed on JPMorgan Chase and required the companies to pay refunds and penalties or stop collection on over $200 million of debts.

The facts and the remedies laid out in these public enforcement actions set the model for what other debt sellers and debt buyers needed to do to comply with the law. Although some would regard it as "regulation by enforcement," the transgressions usually involved obvious misconduct and the necessary remedies were all made very clear to the industry. Indeed, some cases were flagrant. We joined the New York attorney general in suing a set of debt collectors in Buffalo for illegally tacking on $200 to every account they acquired, quoting balances that exceeded 600% of the amount owed, and faking calls and emails to make it appear that the communications were coming from law-enforcement officials, court officers, and government agencies. We resolved an enforcement action against another company for illegal practices such as altering caller ID information to pretend that debt collection calls were coming from pizza deliverers, flower shops, or even family and friends. We also sued bad actors who harassed and deceived consumers in a scheme to collect phantom debts, After buying personal information from debt brokers and lead generators, they used it to falsify debts and threaten people with arrest, wage garnishment, and fictitious "financial restraining orders." Other companies claimed to provide debt-relief services that helped consumers consolidate, reduce, and pay off their debts, but some took millions of dollars in unlawful up-front fees and never delivered on their promises. We brought several cases against debt-relief firms that preyed on desperate student loan borrowers in this manner.

We also supervised hundreds of companies for problems in handling debt collection, which was essential work because collecting on accounts due is an integral part of virtually every business. The steps we took to clean up illegal practices were described in our periodic editions of "Supervisory Highlights," which instructed the industry on what to do, what not to do, and what should be done to avoid crossing these red lines. Debt collection is also a market where private lawsuits are authorized, and lawyers around the country sometimes pointed to our orders in bringing their private claims on behalf of people who were subjected to similar mistreatment.[9]

We sought to give people more ability to assert their own rights, by crafting tools for our website that they could adapt for themselves. One key resource is a set of stop-contact letters that any consumer can send to a harassing debt collector. They are sample letters, with tips on how to use them for specific purposes: to dispute a debt that is not owed, to get more information about a debt, to halt any further contact, to refer any contact to a lawyer, or to specify authorized means of making contact. We shared these pertinent resources with people who filed debt collection complaints, and our allies and partners around the country made them widely available to the people they serve.[10]

We also laid the groundwork to initiate a rulemaking that is badly needed to improve debt collection practices. The Fair Debt Collection Practices Act became law in 1977. For more than thirty years, Congress did not allow any federal agency to write rules to implement this statute, even though the world was changing rapidly around this industry. Instead, all the law that evolved on how to collect debts came via lawsuits decided in the courts. But the job of the courts is to interpret the terms of the statute to decide specific legal disputes, not to leverage any expertise in the practical problems of the debt collection industry. A statute that still refers to telegraphic communications and pre-dates fax machines, cell phones, email, and a host of other technological advances is woefully ill-adapted to serve its purposes. Congress finally recognized the problem and gave us the authority to write new debt collection rules in the Dodd-Frank Act.

Surprisingly, the industry itself was crying out for more guidance, not only to update the law, but also because debt collection law has become a patchwork of conflicting court rulings that breed uncertainty and confusion. For example, when debt collectors call someone to discuss a debt, they often get an answering machine or an answering service. Any message they leave must provide specific information they are required to provide to the debtor, yet it runs the risk of being heard by someone else, which raises privacy concerns also addressed in the statute. Courts in different parts of the country have rendered very different rulings about how debt collectors are to handle that common situation—whether and what kinds of messages can be left without violating the law—with no easy way to sort things out and reach a clear solution.[11] This dilemma is akin to hundreds of similar puzzles in interpreting the law governing debt collectors. In this unusual setting, even the industry could see the value in sensible regulation adopted by an expert agency that is experienced in dealing with these problems and able to gather data, analyze the issues, and seek public input from all sides to resolve them.

The Wells Fargo Scandal

In September 2016, we brought an extraordinary enforcement action against Wells Fargo Bank. In a joint investigation with the Los Angeles city attorney's office, aided as well by the OCC, we uncovered a stunning situation. For years, bank employees had been pushed to cross-sell more products to their customers. For instance, if you had your savings and checking accounts with Wells Fargo, they pressed you to have your credit cards and auto loans and mortgages with them as well. The executive leadership touted their cross-selling numbers on their earnings calls as showing the strength of the bank's customer service and its overall financial health, which boosted their stock prices. There is nothing inherently wrong with any of this; every business wants to sell more products to its customers and works hard to see that its customers want to buy more products from it.

But at Wells Fargo, what was originally a sensible program had gotten way out of hand. The obsession with cross-selling had become disproportionate to any realistic goals. The CEO coined the slogan "Eight Is Great" to set the tone for how employees should be pressured to get every Wells Fargo customer to have eight distinct types of products from the bank. Branch and supervisor bonuses were tied to meeting these improbable goals, and employees were sometimes fired for not making them. The pressure was intense and relentless. At some point, employees began looking for some way—any way—to appear to meet their goals even when they could not. Some started opening accounts in people's names without their consent, funneling some of their money into those accounts, and then closing them after the employee numbers had been recorded to make their goals, keep their jobs, and get their bonuses. Early on, the *Los Angeles Times* had done excellent investigative reporting on the issue, which highlighted how this high-pressure program could lead to the abuse of employees, though it did not yet focus on how customers were being abused as well, which may have started a bit later.[12]

Those press reports, and the initial concentration of the burgeoning problem in Southern California, prompted the Los Angeles city attorney, Mike Feuer, to investigate and file a lawsuit against the bank. His office had statewide jurisdiction, under an unusual state statute, but the bank was trying to stonewall his lawyers and tie them up in protracted discovery, which is a classic defense strategy in difficult cases. We had broader authority to seek information and take testimony, and we used it aggressively. We also had better access to the confidential supervisory work being done by the OCC (as well as similar work we already had underway ourselves). Our enforcement team forged a common interest agreement with the Los Angeles city attorney's office, and we worked together for months to flesh out the case they had initiated. With massive artillery now brought to bear on these issues, the bank's resistance began to crumble, and they finally signaled a willingness to resolve the matter with all parties.

Things went relatively quickly from that point, but two issues proved contentious. First, as in any enforcement action, we insisted on exposing the key facts, which would detail for the public the nature and scope of the customer abuse. We had documents and analysis showing how widespread the problems were: *thousands* of employees had misused the money and data of their customers, and *millions* of credit card and deposit accounts had been opened without people's knowledge or consent. The bank fought hard to control the spin and minimize the issue, suggesting that the number of problem accounts was only about 1% of its total accounts. But because we had access to the undisputed facts, the bank could not keep us from revealing how many consumers were defrauded and from describing everything that happened.

Second, we had to decide on an appropriate penalty to fit the situation. This was perplexing, because the entire episode had caused relatively small amounts of actual consumer harm. The mere opening and closing of accounts had not caused financial losses for many of the consumers, and what losses there were in terms of fees or charges often were fairly small amounts, adding up to only a few million dollars across all customers. Nonetheless, the conduct was plainly "abusive," almost perfectly matching the law's definition of acts that take "unreasonable advantage of . . . the inability of the consumer to protect the interests of the consumer in selecting or using a financial product or service." Customers were outraged to learn that their trust had been violated in this way. Any penalty needed to recognize the dignitary interests of individuals who had relied on a relationship of trust with the bank, only to find that their accounts were being manipulated to advance the financial interests of the bank and its employees.

Thus, it seemed a large penalty would be warranted. But how large? Under our statutory framework, we could make a technical case for a penalty in the hundreds of millions of dollars, given the large number of discrete violations. Yet the Supreme Court had placed constitutional restrictions on penalties that vastly exceed the amount of harm as measured by compensatory damages, suggesting that any ratio of more than ten to one between the two amounts would likely be impermissible except in rare cases of especially egregious acts.[13] Our teams were aggressive and they recommended that we demand Wells Fargo pay a $100 million penalty to us, a $35 million penalty to the OCC, and $50 million to Los Angeles, which amounted to a ratio of more than fifty to one over the amount of actual monetary harm as we estimated it at the time. But this was a clear example of such a rare case involving especially egregious acts. Wells Fargo agreed to pay these amounts—the largest penalty we had imposed to date—no doubt realizing that the ugly facts underlying this outcome fully justified it.

The public reaction was immediate and overwhelming. We had taken a few enforcement actions against Wells Fargo before, and they tried to spin this one as just another speed bump that went with the territory of being a large bank with many customers. But their spin was crushed by the facts—including that millions of phony accounts were involved and that the bank had let go more than five thousand employees in response to these problems—and by the ensuing public outrage. Many other banks also made it clear that they were glad to see us root out these abuses, which they regarded as giving all banks a bad name.

The result also drew Congress's attention. A Senate hearing was quickly set, where my partners and I told our story and panel members on both sides of the aisle excoriated Wells Fargo executives, with Senator Warren calling for the company to claw back bonuses and for federal officials to launch a criminal investigation. The House Republicans also set a hearing, but their attempt to cast blame on the federal regulators fizzled when none of us who brought the enforcement action was permitted to testify. Indeed, our effective teamwork in the matter had made a crucial difference. The Los Angeles city attorney's office deserved much credit for bringing the initial action and pursuing Wells Fargo relentlessly. But the tools and resources we and the OCC brought to the table, including nationwide jurisdiction, broader investigative powers, and our penalty authority, led to a faster and more comprehensive resolution.[14]

The Wells Fargo enforcement action was a seminal moment for consumer financial protection. Eight years after the financial meltdown, and six years after the passage of the Dodd-Frank Act, it showed once again that some banks cannot be trusted to treat their customers well without close monitoring. And the large aftershocks for Wells Fargo reinforced this message: the CEO and other top executives were sacked, bonuses were clawed back at least in part, shareholder actions cost the company hundreds of millions of dollars, public finance business was withheld by various states and cities, and public investigations were launched by the Securities and Exchange Commission and others. The damage to the bank's reputation was unprecedented, and it was forced to embark on a long-term campaign to pursue public rehabilitation.

As we had done with credit card add-on matters, we followed up on this enforcement action by teaming up with the OCC to launch a comprehensive review of all the other major banks to determine if any of them had engaged in similar practices. What we found over the next year, notably, was that a few banks had some problems, but not on the scale of Wells Fargo's abuses. We wrapped up most of those situations through supervisory actions, though some investigations took more time to proceed.

The Wells Fargo matter is an object lesson in how small risks can balloon into large ones in any profit-making entity if they are not monitored closely. In the earlier case of credit card add-ons, the risk came from the bank turning over a marketing program to outside vendors, who were guided by financial incentives to produce financial results, without the bank carefully keeping track of how they did so. Here Wells Fargo's employees were in-house, yet they similarly had strong financial incentives to meet goals that the bank desperately wanted to achieve and believed in wholeheartedly. But here again, the bank failed to visibly and effectively supervise how the cross-selling was done. To give broad guidance to all financial companies, not just the banks, the bureau put out a compliance bulletin on "Detecting and Preventing Consumer Harm from Production Incentives." It instructed companies to pay more attention to their internal programs involving sales incentives and explained how automated monitoring of these programs could help make sure, as a routine matter, that the goals they set are appropriately met.

The extensive fallout from the Wells Fargo situation sharply reinforced the need for a strong consumer agency that firmly enforces the law. More generally, it underscores how essential it is to have steady law enforcement across the entire government if we expect corporations and the public to obey and respect the law.

PART IV

TAKING ON THE TRUMP ADMINISTRATION

UNDER FIRE FROM ALL SIDES

In the wake of the Wells Fargo matter, it was dawning on many in the financial industry and on the Hill that no better case could be made for the Consumer Bureau. This debacle was a striking demonstration of what the large banks could do to hurt people and what we and our partners could do to make it right. We had now survived a full congressional session under Republican leadership with no serious setbacks. Our mission had just been amply reaffirmed. We were making progress on many fronts, and consumers could see and feel how we mattered to their lives.

THE BUREAU GROWS UP

By the fall of 2016, we had made great strides to becoming a more established agency. We were just approving our sixth annual budget, with a process that was becoming more standardized and predictable, while being regularly audited without incident. Every year, we submitted our budget to Congress and for four years we had engaged in informal "hearings" with the House and Senate appropriations subcommittees that had gone well.[1] We were now close to fully staffed, though at slightly lower levels than we had originally anticipated. Early controversies involving employee grievances over performance reviews and promotions had died down, largely through the positive contributions of our new union leadership, which helped us understand and address issues more effectively as we consciously built a more cohesive culture.[2] We finally met a key technological goal of achieving the independence of our computer network from the Treasury Department. A long-simmering controversy with Congress over renovations to our building—which our foes baldly mischaracterized to make the bureau seem fiscally irresponsible—faded as the renovations were now almost finished. The 1970s building, located near the White House, had deteriorated badly over the years, and the renovation work restored what a former tenant had once curtly described to me as "a dump" to a serviceable office building.[3] None of these internal issues was of much interest to consumers, but they had a lot to do with our capability to do our best work, so they occupied considerable time and attention. More and more, the bumpiness of our earlier days was being smoothed out.

In some ways, our improved administration did directly benefit consumers. We completed an inclusive bureau-wide process to reshape our priorities—guided, as always, by what we were hearing from the public through the consumer complaint process. We instituted quarterly performance reviews, where bureau leaders could sit in on presentations about the work being done in other areas, which fostered more collaboration and cross-pollination of ideas. And we began a series of regular roundtables with banking executives to share our latest guidance, discuss issues of mutual interest, and hear feedback about our supervision and examination work.[4]

The bureau's civil penalty fund exemplifies how our administrative work could benefit consumers. The penalties we levied and collected from the big banks and financial companies went into a special fund. This money could be used for either of two purposes: for consumer education programs or to compensate victims in other cases who had not been made whole for the damages they suffered, usually because the perpetrators had no resources or went out of business. Early on, we decided that we would almost always direct this money to victims if we could. Yet that is much easier said than done. Most companies that operate scams or fraudulent schemes keep poor records (as better recordkeeping would simply document their wrongdoing), and identifying those they hurt and to what extent is not easy. But our team was relentless in their careful detective work. They dug into the records of payment processing companies and investigated other payment channels that criminals use to separate people from their money. Bit by bit, they pieced the evidence together in each case. Over time, they succeeded in returning hundreds of millions of dollars to people they identified who were wronged, and their valuable work continues. Every time we sent out a batch of payments, the Consumer Bureau was standing up for people and bringing more justice into the world.

A Setback in the Courts

But our smoother path was not destined to last. Just a few weeks after the Wells Fargo action broke, the US court of appeals in Washington issued a surprising ruling that held the bureau's leadership structure to be unconstitutional. The ruling came in an unusually complex case with a tortured history.

The bureau brought an enforcement action against PHH, a New Jersey mortgage lending company. Our Notice of Charges made the following allegations. In the heady years leading up to the financial crisis, PHH sought to expand its reach by leveraging its strong position in the mortgage lending market to gain a foothold in the lucrative market for mortgage insurance. It created a subsidiary to offer mortgage reinsurance, which is a backup product that assumes some of the risk for companies that provide mortgage insurance to borrowers. The subsidiary had no employees of its own and performed no underwriting to price any of the reinsurance risks it was supposed to assume. The bureau alleged that PHH then began to refer its own loan customers to mortgage insurers who signed up to kick back to PHH's subsidiary part of the premiums they received from those customers. There was nothing subtle about the arrangement: we alleged that PHH had created a "dialer" and placed the mortgage insurers who agreed to make the payments on the dialer to get their share of referrals for mortgage insurance business. One of the telling facts in our complaint involved an insurer that decided to stop playing ball in 2008, was removed from the dialer, and saw its business decline by more than 99%; after a few months, it gave in and six minutes later it was reinstated on the dialer (which one executive referred to as the "captive dialer"). We contended that this arrangement produced profits for PHH of over $150 million in about a decade. The question was whether it was illegal.

The Department of Housing and Urban Development's (HUD) inspector general had opened an investigation, which was later referred to the Justice

Department to consider bringing a case. When the CFPB was created, the authority over the investigation transferred to us. Although the facts seemed clear enough, the wording of the relevant statute posed difficult interpretive issues, which may be why the Justice Department had been hesitant to proceed. Among the open questions under the statute were several disputed issues about whether these arrangements violate the law against receiving kickbacks in real estate transactions; how many years we could go back to bring such claims, especially as a new agency; and how to calculate damages for any violations. The law prohibits kickbacks (accepting a "thing of value") in exchange for doling out mortgage business because such payments can distort the market. Through the years, HUD had been back and forth in how it construed the law and had indicated that these arrangements might or might not be illegal, depending on the specific details of how they were set up.

This constellation of uncertainties created a perfect storm of controversy surrounding the case. We filed the enforcement action not in a court but in an administrative proceeding before the bureau itself, which allowed us to bring claims extending further back in time. That is permissible under the statute, but it was rare for us in a case involving contested facts rather than an agreed consent order.[5] An able administrative law judge that we borrowed from elsewhere in the federal government held a trial and found PHH liable for violating the law. After evaluating the effects of the violations, however, he assessed damages at only $6.4 million. In this posture, the case was then appealed to me as the agency head. Under the statute, I concluded that PHH's acceptance of lucrative market share in the mortgage reinsurance market in return for making referrals of mortgage insurance business was a "thing of value" and thus violated the law.[6] I also had to determine the amount of damages. Depending on how one read the statute in terms of which contract payments were encompassed by PHH's violations, the figure came to either $6.4 million or $109 million. In a thirty-eight-page opinion, I explained my legal reasoning for adopting the higher figure, which set off a firestorm. This decision would lead to significant risks for the bureau, though those risks were not germane to determining the proper legal analysis.

With so much at stake, PHH lost no time seeking further review of the case with the US court of appeals, challenging not only my decision on its merits but also the constitutionality of the entire agency. The latter issue had not been a fit subject for decision in the case up to this point, as federal agencies cannot opine on their own constitutionality, but the courts could certainly do so. Both PHH and the business groups that supported the company with friend-of-the-court briefs let us have it with both barrels. They argued that, in a proceeding where I alone was the final decision maker, I had misread the statutes, retroactively held PHH liable without fair notice, and overreached by upping the amount of the judgment more than tenfold. They asserted the dangers of unfettered agency independence and argued that the bureau should be invalidated on constitutional grounds, which would require the ruling against PHH to be vacated. At oral argument, PHH went even further, contending that because of its constitutional infirmities, the bureau should be struck down completely and prevented from operating any longer.

The case was argued in April 2016, and then, as these things often do, it sat with the court for months. In October the decision was handed down, and it was a setback. The court held that the bureau's leadership structure, with a single director outside of direct presidential control, violates the separation of powers. Then-judge (now Justice) Kavanaugh wrote a 101-page opinion declaring that the "concentration of massive, unchecked power in a single Director marks a departure from historical practice" that makes him or her, in essence, "the President of Consumer Finance." To find the structure unconstitutional, he distinguished away contrary Supreme Court precedents, adopting instead academic theories of the "unitary executive," which judicial conservatives favor to tame independent agencies and hobble the post–New Deal administrative state. The heart of the ruling blunted our independence by holding that the president could replace the director at any time, for any reason. The court, however, explicitly refused to invalidate the entire agency. Instead, it sent the case back to the bureau for further consideration, but it interpreted the relevant statutes in ways that would sharply limit our ability to hold PHH liable for its course of conduct.[7]

Less than a month later, Donald Trump was elected president and the Republicans maintained control of both the House and the Senate. Inauguration Day was only two and a half months away, and we would now be under fire from all three branches of government.

A New Crisis

The reshuffled political landscape created new opportunities for the financial industry to try to weaken the bureau, especially since the court ruling had undermined the independence of my position as the director. We had several major regulatory fights pending. Our rule to provide new consumer protections on prepaid accounts and prepaid cards was being challenged by a company that had millions of dollars at stake. Our proposed rule to address payday lending by requiring companies to make a reasonable assessment of the customer's ability to repay the loan faced frenzied opposition from the whole industry, which feared it would cost them billions. And our proposed rule to bar companies from using mandatory arbitration clauses to block consumers from suing them in class actions cut across the entire universe of consumer finance companies, many of which use these clauses to sharply limit their financial exposure.[8] All of these financial interests saw that if they could get me fired—or use the threat of firing me to cow us into inaction—then they might finally succeed in defanging the CFPB.

Throughout this period, the *Wall Street Journal* joined the financial industry and Republicans on the Hill in continually calling for me to be removed from office. In short order, the newspaper printed editorials entitled "The Unconstitutional Mr. Cordray," which called for my firing, and "The Fastest Way to Fire Richard Cordray," which was presented as a kind of "how to" guide. The new court ruling seemed to open the door to doing so without having to offer any justification at all. But even apart from whether that ruling would hold up on further review, the new energy swelling around this topic encouraged our foes to develop arguments to have me fired "for cause," even under the statutory provisions that had been thought to protect my tenure and with it the agency's independence.[9]

We responded by filing a petition to have the full court of appeals review the *PHH* case, which temporarily put the prior panel ruling on hold, leaving it uncertain whether the president would be able to rely on it to fire me without cause. And, of course, until January 20, the president was still Barack Obama, who strongly approved of the work we were doing and championed the independence of the bureau. As we looked beyond Inauguration Day, however, the view was quite foggy. And our unease was heightened by the bizarre encounters we were having with the president-elect's transition team. At first, as other agencies and departments were contacted to gather information and prepare transition reports, we ominously heard nothing at all. When we reached out to learn more, we found that they had assigned an individual to the CFPB who had no background whatsoever in consumer finance. The sessions we had with her were strangely filled with irrelevant asides and odd comments. We submitted volumes of documents that she requested, though she never discussed any of the information with us. Eventually, the transition team recalled our contact person, and we had some further meetings that were more substantive and reasonable, but we never learned whether any transition report was ever prepared for the CFPB.

Still, the threat that I would be fired as soon as President Trump took office loomed over everything. It made sense to prepare a lawsuit to contest a firing, but the situation was fraught. Our lawyers researched the matter and concluded that any such lawsuit would be personal to me, meaning the bureau could not represent me or pay for my legal representation. Instead, I would have to manage on my own. Moreover, because I was a public official, conflict-of-interest rules prevented any lawyers doing business with the CFPB from representing me. Our lawyers also concluded that there were severe constraints on whether I could accept any donation of legal services, which would be tantamount to a personal financial benefit.[10] With my options narrowed, I spoke with the ethics lawyers at the Office of Special Counsel, who determined that under federal law, if a friend of long standing was willing to represent me for free, that would be permissible. Incredibly, Harry Litman, a former US attorney and my close friend since we clerked together at the Supreme Court almost thirty years ago, was willing to take the matter on, no matter the consequences. When I asked him what his law firm would think, he told me that if they didn't approve, he would resign. You can imagine how moving that flat statement was to me: a friend indeed.

With that settled, Harry and I went about working up a lawsuit. Getting a court to issue an order blocking the president would not be easy, and the precedents were sparse. Our best case in support involved an obscure tiff that occurred a quarter century ago over an effort to remove members of the US Postal Service Board of Governors in the waning days of the George H. W. Bush administration. The court offices still had the papers that had been filed in that case, which were helpful. We didn't know on what grounds a firing would occur, so we had to plan for all contingencies. If I were fired without cause, then we would make the constitutional arguments against Judge Kavanaugh's *PHH* ruling. If I were fired for cause, then we would have to address each of the grounds alleged as justification. With so much media chatter about these issues, the grounds being contemplated were evident enough. They included claims about supposed maladministration, including the bureau's spending on the building renovations, as well as cases in which courts had ruled that the bureau exceeded our legal mandate to protect consumers. We prepared legal and factual responses for all these contingencies, including affidavit evidence to defend decisions I had made and work the bureau had done. Recognizing that a court might defer to President Trump's judgment of my fitness for office, we also requested and secured a letter from President Obama, while he was still in office, attesting to my fitness and praising our good work for consumers. If the sitting president's viewpoint were deemed to be authoritative, then at least there would be dueling perspectives to present to the court.

Another difficulty was that even if a court determined that the president had fired me illegally, if it nonetheless found that he had ousted me, then the court might not be willing to restore me to the position. Many of the cases on the legality of purported removals from office—including the leading precedent from the Supreme Court in the 1935 *Humphrey's Executor* case—involved only claims for backpay, not claims to remain in office. The closest historical parallel we found was President Andrew Johnson's attempt to remove Secretary of War Edwin Stanton shortly after the Civil War. When Stanton barricaded himself in his office for several months, the Senate and the courts supported his position. The controversy ultimately led to impeachment proceedings against the president, who was barely acquitted. But neither the Senate nor the House would be on my side this time, and even Stanton had agreed to resign eventually. The threat confronting us remained very real.[11]

The New Administration

On Inauguration Day, I awaited news of my fate. For the next week, at the beginning and the end of each day, I would make inquiries in the office to learn whether I had been fired yet. As the days passed, nothing seemed to be happening on this front, but once in office, the Trump administration began to take other aggressive steps. They froze government hiring and seemed determined to halt all new regulations. Although the campaign's populist tone had augured potential support for consumers, the early Trump appointments tilted sharply toward the financial industry. The first executive orders called for any new federal rule to be offset by rescinding two other rules, with no overall increase in costs. Whether these orders applied to an independent agency like ours was a murky point, and the lawyers debated it inconclusively.

The atmosphere was tense for three weeks after the inauguration, with no clear word from the Trump administration. Our pending request that the entire court of appeals reconsider Judge Kavanaugh's opinion in the *PHH* case made it harder to fire me, as doing so would interfere with the court's ongoing review.[12] I remained ready to file a lawsuit and made clear that firing me would prompt a legal battle. But the Trump administration uncharacteristically shied away from forcing a confrontation. On February 16, the court of appeals gave us a boost by granting further review in the *PHH* case, setting aside the panel decision, and scheduling the case for reargument before the full court in May.

Gary Cohn, the new head of the National Economic Council at the White House, then reached out and arranged a dinner for the two of us at the new Trump Hotel downtown. He told me that he had been given the task of deciding what to do about my situation.[13] He also said he did not think that starting a big fight would be very productive—though he made clear that plenty of others at the White House would probably think otherwise. He was interested in knowing whether I expected to serve my full term. I told him that I was not sure, but for as long as I did stay, we would continue to do what we thought was best to protect consumers and would keep him informed about significant actions. He acknowledged that, and by the end of the dinner, we negotiated a temporary truce to await further legal and political events. For the first time in a month, I did not have to fear being fired at any given moment. When community bankers met with the president in early March, he raised the issue of what to do about my situation. He questioned whether firing me would be worth the "political backlash" and suggested that it would not be worth it, in view of the risk involved in taking out a regulator who was protecting consumers against abusive lending.

I began to feel a reprieve from the sword of Damocles that was hanging over my head. Yet the day after President Trump met with the community bankers, Preet Bharara, the US attorney in Manhattan, was unexpectedly fired, despite having received public assurances from the president himself that he would remain on the job. Two months later, FBI Director James Comey learned from news reports that he too had been fired, after President Trump had earlier decided to keep him on the job. These dramatic events underscored how little we could count on any assurances from the volatile Trump White House.

Amid growing internal disagreement about whether to push forward with our rulemaking agenda, we decided to do so, prompting expected resistance from the financial industry. But as spring stretched into summer and then into fall, the White House left me alone, and we continued to function much as we had before the change of administrations. The *PHH* case was reargued in May, and it seemed to go well for our side on the key issue of whether the bureau's structure with an independent director was constitutional.[14]

Although both houses of Congress and the president now were arrayed against us, the filibuster continued to protect us from any broad legislation to weaken or overhaul the bureau. Far-reaching reform measures to curb our powers passed the House on a party-line vote, as they had before, but they were dead on arrival in the Senate. Frustrated, the House Republicans continued to make incessant demands to produce reams of documents, backed first by subpoenas and then by threats to hold me in contempt of Congress. They even threatened CFPB employees with criminal prosecution if we did not comply to their satisfaction—which, from their adamant posture, we could see that we never would. Our people were under tremendous pressure, as they tried to satisfy a shifting set of demands that were utterly unreasonable.[15] It was evident that the threats were intended to prevent us from continuing to forge ahead. We understood the point they were making, but we had other plans.

THE LAST BIG FIGHTS

Shortly before leaving office, President Obama encouraged me to stay in place for as long as I could be reasonably effective. In January 2017, we had three big fights underway and each represented years of work to protect consumers. The fights were to preserve our rule protecting consumers who use prepaid cards, to uphold consumer rights to take legal disputes to court rather than being required to submit to arbitration, and to finalize a rule that would rein in the damaging consequences of high-cost payday loans. Moving forward with these objectives would put us out of step with the anti-regulatory thrust of the new Trump administration, but as an independent agency we set our course based on the data and evidence we had compiled. On each issue, consumers needed our help, and once again we judged that the Consumer Bureau would gain strength by pushing forward to provide that help.

Defending the Prepaid Rule

Strong new consumer protections for prepaid accounts were urgently needed to fill a gap in the regulatory framework resulting from the evolution of consumer use in the marketplace. Prepaid accounts accessed by use of a card had been developed for limited purposes, and in the 1990s they evolved into a form that could provide a reasonably functional substitute for a bank account. Consumers could receive direct deposits of funds from multiple sources on their prepaid cards and use them to conduct transactions at point-of-sale terminals or to withdraw cash at ATM machines. Some types of digital wallets can now play a similar role by holding funds for a wide range of electronic transactions. The amount of money loaded onto prepaid cards for general use in the United States rose dramatically from about $1 billion in 2003 to about $65 billion in 2012, as the number of transactions involving prepaid cards approached ten billion annually. The market is global, with hundreds of billions of dollars in value being deployed in this manner around the world.

This new product grew out of people's love affair with payment cards. General-use credit cards first became popular in the 1960s because of their versatility. A variety of "closed loop" prepaid cards, usable for a single purpose or at specified locations, also began to proliferate, including telephone calling cards, transit farecards, and merchant gift cards. Other types of banking cards, including ATM cards and more recently debit cards, became a convenient and inexpensive means of accessing funds held in deposit accounts. In the 1990s, governments at all levels began to experiment with easier and cheaper ways to help people receive and use funds that were distributed to them. This effort was stimulated by the growing approval of "open loop" cards that can be used anywhere they are accepted. Over the same period, some employers began to adopt payroll cards as a means of transmitting wages to employees without bank accounts. The computerized foundations of these various products made them increasingly adaptable, and improved technology reduced the risks they pose as compared to cash. From these origins, the general-purpose, reloadable prepaid card emerged as a product that consumers like and find increasingly useful. The resulting spectacle of "fat wallets" filled with wads of different cards, along with vigorous market competition, created incentives for companies to offer cards for multiple uses.

A prepaid card can make a huge difference for someone without a bank account. Take Fred as an illustration. He lived very close to the margin, and after periodically overdrawing his bank account—and often being assessed multiple fees per day from penalties on cascading transactions—he was finally forced to close it altogether.[1] He then confronted the high cost of being unbanked. To access his paycheck, Fred had to use a check cashing service, which cost him $50 of the $900 he cleared every two weeks. He also had to carry all his money around in cash, which led to some of it being lost or stolen. But when he reapplied for a bank account, he couldn't pass the screening with his history. Then Fred discovered prepaid cards. Not only could he load his paycheck onto the card at minimal cost, but also he could use the card for the same kinds of purchases and transactions he used to make on his bank debit card. Even better, now he was limited to spending only the amount on the card, so he could not run the risk of incurring high fees from an inadvertent overdraft. He also felt more comfortable and more secure dealing with a card rather than cash—though here his confidence was misplaced.

Fred, like many consumers, did not fully understand the differences among distinct types of cards, such as debit cards, credit cards, and prepaid cards. Some of those differences are in the fees and charges that can result, and consumers are generally aware of those, especially with credit cards where they may struggle to pay off their monthly balance. But most assume that the same *legal* protections apply to any of these types of cards. At the time we set to work, that assumption was quite wrong. Debit cards carry the standard protections under federal law that go along with bank accounts, from which funds are accessed, including the right to have errors corrected and disputes resolved. Credit cards are governed by a different set of rules because money is advanced in the form of a loan that is later repaid, which brings into play additional federal consumer protections around extensions of credit. But with general-purpose prepaid cards, the accidents of their historical evolution and their distinct functionality meant that they were not covered by either set of federal protections. This was risky in such a fast-growing market, and we undertook to plug this troublesome gap.

One of the reasons prepaid cards have become so popular is that they are accessible, low-risk products that involve no credit; people simply load money on them and use them to transact. Millennials especially like them as an alternative to credit cards, which they see as risky, and to debit cards, which can lead to expensive overdraft fees if (like Fred) you misjudge your bank balance.[2] The rule we proposed generally mimicked the consumer protections that have long applied to debit card transactions, but with some adjustments to account for the distinct nature of the product. It also essentially barred overdraft on prepaid cards by applying credit card rules to them, which made any overdraft fees impractical. Adding credit features to "prepaid" cards was, by definition, a contradiction in terms that would create additional risks for consumers—many of whom had turned to prepaid cards precisely to avoid these kinds of risks. We crafted the rule to ensure clear disclosures about how the prepaid card works, its costs, and other fees; rights to get disputes resolved and errors corrected; limits on losses from unauthorized uses, such as from lost or stolen cards; and free access to one year of account information to keep track of account balances, transaction history, and fees.[3] Our rule also applied to payroll cards, certain types of government benefit cards and mobile wallets, and new types of electronic prepaid accounts.

Most providers of prepaid cards were already voluntarily providing many of these protections as a matter of good business practice and perhaps in anticipation of our next steps. But without a rule, consumers remained at risk. We also made clear that a regulation was coming, and we would be monitoring the market closely while it was put in place. A timely enforcement action just before we finalized the rule showed the risks. When Rushcard, a prepaid card company, ran into a transitional processing glitch with its payment processor, a unit of MasterCard, tens of thousands of users were locked out of their accounts, unable to access the money they had loaded onto their cards. Some users' cards were declined, and others racked up late fees and penalties because their direct deposits were mishandled. The disruption dragged on for weeks, compounded by a shortage of personnel to respond effectively to customer concerns, before it was finally resolved. The bureau recovered $10 million for customers hurt by having their funds wrongly frozen, required processing changes to avert future problems, and imposed a penalty of $3 million.

We finalized the rule in October, a month before the election, but some in the financial industry began pushing Congress to overturn it. Only a few companies were directly hurt by the decision to restrict credit features—overdrafts—on prepaid cards, though no doubt others were watching these developments carefully. Yet one company, Netspend, stood to lose millions in revenue, and it mounted an all-out effort with its home-state delegation from Georgia to nullify the rule under the special process set up by the Congressional Review Act (CRA). Congress was invoking this law to overturn about a dozen regulations across federal agencies in the first few months of 2017, all with President Trump's backing.[4]

The main objection to the rule remained the restriction of credit features on prepaid cards, but as companies began to implement the rule, they raised other concerns as well. We announced that we would consider revisions to address these issues and delayed the rule's implementation. The delay was helpful because it meant that companies would not have to pull large amounts of preprinted packaging for cards sold in stores. We also made some changes to the rule to reduce fraud and provide more flexibility around digital wallets. But we did not yield on the main issue of restricting credit features, and the opponents were unable to muster the votes to kill it by the May deadline. One senior Republican Senate staffer commented that this regulation seemed to be exactly the kind of work that the Consumer Bureau was intended to do. That victory was a shot in the arm for our continued rulemaking efforts.

HAVING YOUR DAY IN COURT

Our arbitration rule, five years in the making, was more contentious. In the last few decades, more and more companies have inserted clauses in the fine print of their consumer contracts requiring that any legal disputes be resolved through individual arbitration. The arbitration process is private, operating outside the oversight or control of the courts, according to its own special set of rules. If a problem later arises, these clauses allow companies to force their customers out of court and into arbitration, and to stop them from banding together with other customers to bring group claims. In most transactions, people are unaware that the arbitration clause even exists and do not understand its consequences. And even if they were to object, mandatory arbitration clauses are often offered on a take-it-or-leave-it basis that customers must accept if they want the product or service.

Eleanor, for example, went to a nearby auto mall to buy a new car. After settling on the car that she wanted and negotiating what she thought was a fair price, she sat down with the loan staff to work out the financing. The documents for the loan were long and tricky, and she did her best to read them carefully. One provision that caught her eye was the prominent assurance that she would be offered "the LOWEST interest rate you qualify for based on your credit history." After an hour of going back and forth, she agreed to a sixty-month loan at a 9% interest rate. She later learned from her credit union that the quoted language was false; many of the dealers at that auto mall had arrangements with lenders that if they could talk customers into higher interest rates, the lender would split the difference with them. In fact, Eleanor's credit history would have qualified her for a 6% interest rate. Hundreds or maybe thousands of other customers had likely been similarly victimized by the same company. But her loan agreement contained an arbitration clause that barred her from filing a group lawsuit in court. Because she stood to recover less than $2,000 in her own individual case, she could not find a lawyer who was willing to take her claim to arbitration. She was stuck, and the lenders and dealers she sought to hold responsible were able to continue gouging other customers.

Arbitration began as a way for businesses to resolve disputes with each other faster and less expensively. The Federal Arbitration Act of 1925 was designed for business-to-business disputes between parties of relatively equal bargaining strength. After decades passed, however, the US Supreme Court began to apply this law, with its presumption in favor of arbitration, to disputes between a business and its individual customers, cases where the parties rarely have equal bargaining strength. For these individuals, the practice of mandating arbitration operates as a kind of legal lockout. With the stroke of a pen, companies have the power to extinguish your right to bring your case before a judge in a court of law, no matter what the consumer financial laws say. Even more, companies that marry arbitration clauses with class action bans can use these provisions to sweep aside laws that specifically give people the right to bring a group lawsuit. In contracts for loans and financial products of all kinds, arbitration clauses have become a key feature that protects the corporate bottom line by limiting the company's exposure to legal liability.[5]

Companies accomplish this result by cutting off class actions, which allow many people to sue together as a single group and thus make bringing such claims much more efficient and cost-effective. Class actions are especially important in consumer finance, because often a company's illegal behavior causes small amounts of harm to large numbers of victims. When the amount at stake is low, as it was in Eleanor's case, nobody is likely to find it sensible to bring a claim on their own. As one judge observed, "Only a lunatic or a fanatic sues for $30." But if a $30 fraud is perpetrated on a million customers, the company profits by $30 million. And if nothing can be done about it, then the company pockets the $30 million and continues along the very same path. In response, the companies argue that average individual awards are larger in arbitration cases, but that is no answer—with consumers effectively disabled from bringing small-dollar disputes, the only cases they bring in arbitration are large-dollar disputes, which inevitably means the average arbitration case will be worth more than the average court case. That is a sign of failure, not success, in pressing their rights.

Moreover, class action lawsuits are not simply about money. They also provide a mechanism that permits courts to modify corporate behavior and clean up problems for future consumers. By using arbitration clauses to stifle this option, companies can prevent the courts from identifying and remedying corporate actions that violate the law. In earlier class action cases involving consumer finance issues, for example, courts had issued orders preventing banks from maximizing overdraft fees by reordering transactions and stopping auto lenders from setting interest rates in a racially discriminatory manner. Moreover, unlike court judgments, which are public, arbitration orders are private, which mutes broader awareness of corporate misdeeds and any corresponding deterrent effect on the violator or others in the industry. It also undermines the traditional system of evolving public precedents that illuminate how the law is being interpreted and applied.[6]

Of course, private lawsuits are not the only way to stop companies from abusing consumers—the CFPB, for example, has enforcement powers—but the resources of the bureau, and those of all the state and federal regulators combined, are limited and insufficient to deal with the vast array of issues that arise in the broad and deep financial markets. The courts have historically been an important check on corporate misbehavior; indeed, they have been fulfilling this role since long before state and federal regulators came onto the scene. In addition, choosing to assert your own rights and demand justice for wrongdoing is a form of self-reliance very much in the American legal and constitutional traditions. It is not merely having a "day in court," but rather having the right to stand before the law as an equal and bring your wrongdoer to the bar of justice. And in situations where it is advantageous to band together to do so, as the law allows, such concerted action has deep roots in our community traditions as well.

In recent years, Congress had begun to recognize the harm that flows from arbitration clauses and to restrict their use. In the Military Lending Act, Congress barred companies from using mandatory arbitration clauses to limit the rights of servicemembers and their families in consumer credit contracts covered by the Act. In the Dodd-Frank Act, Congress banned mandatory arbitration clauses in mortgage loan contracts. It also went a step further by directing the CFPB to study how arbitration clauses affect consumers in other markets and authorizing us to take whatever action we deemed consistent with the results of our study. Much was at stake, as our market analysis showed that more than half of credit card customers and almost half of those with deposit accounts are covered by arbitration clauses—amounting to well over a hundred million consumers.[7]

We spent three years amassing new data about arbitrations and court judgments in consumer finance cases and comparing their effects. We reviewed hundreds of arbitration clauses and thousands of lawsuits and arbitrations involving consumer finance issues. Based on this work, we produced an exhaustive seven-hundred-page report that reached several key conclusions. We found that arbitration agreements limit consumers' ability to get relief from financial companies by cutting off class actions. Although this presumably lowers the companies' costs, we found no evidence that it results in lower prices to consumers. From our review of multiple consumer finance markets, we determined that very few people pursue relief individually, either through arbitration or the courts, whereas millions of people are eligible for relief each year through class action resolutions. From a nationwide survey of credit card holders, we also confirmed that fewer than one in five consumers with arbitration clauses in their agreements were aware of that fact, and very few understood that such clauses restrict their ability to go to court.[8]

Consistent with the results of our study, we proposed a rule to prevent mandatory arbitration clauses in consumer finance contracts from blocking class action lawsuits. It would not preclude people from agreeing with companies to arbitrate disputes once they arose, but it would allow consumers the freedom to choose their preferred course. The proposed rule also would require the financial companies covered by the rule to submit records on individual arbitrations to the bureau so we could assess the fairness of the process and monitor other concerns. This would shed more light on how arbitration works and its outcomes, enabling people to evaluate whether they should opt for arbitration and whether the process could be improved.

Our proposed rule sparked a broad backlash. It covered virtually every consumer finance market and thus united almost the entire financial industry against us. The US Chamber of Commerce openly opposed the rule from the outset and vowed to challenge it in the courts. Some observers noted the irony of businesses banding together under the chamber's banner to go to court to squelch a rule that would allow consumers to do the very same thing, but they were playing for keeps. Once the rule was finalized, we became aware of lobbying efforts to prod our fellow regulators to convene the Financial Stability Oversight Council (FSOC) to overturn the rule. That was a new procedure under the Dodd-Frank Act that had never been invoked, however, and the legal grounds for doing so were shaky. I met with Steve Mnuchin, the new Treasury secretary who chaired the FSOC, to discuss the issue, and he decided not to proceed in that manner.[9]

But Congress itself moved to overturn the rule, and the House quickly voted to do so. As with the prepaid rule, the arbitration rule's foes invoked the CRA, which has internal deadlines that are fuzzy, depending on obscure calculations and estimates based on fluctuations in the congressional schedule. Having challenged our aggressive enforcement actions for five years, the industry now turned around and argued that consumer class actions are unnecessary because the CFPB has robust enforcement powers to deal with any concerns. While the clock was ticking in the Senate, we battled with the Office of the Comptroller of the Currency, now under new leadership, which went out of its way to work up statistical analysis to undermine the case for our rule. We thought their analysis was shoddy and slanted, but it provided talking points to the other side. As we exchanged esoteric memos about the finer points of statistical probability, it was doubtful that anyone else was paying attention to the substance of these discussions.

As the October deadline for action neared, Senate Leader Mitch McConnell set the matter for a vote. Everyone knew it would be close. The Senate was closely divided already, and Senators Lindsey Graham and John Kennedy—two southern senators who appreciate the role that lawyers can play in protecting people's rights against corporate abuses—were leaning our way. On the day of the vote, we heard reports that Senator Murkowski might cast the decisive vote in our favor to save the rule. But our optimism throughout the afternoon faded with the daylight, as the Republican leadership applied heavy pressure to vote with the party on this issue. Late that night, Vice President Pence swept across town in his motorcade to cast the tie-breaking vote to defeat it. We had pushed the entire financial industry to the very limit on an issue they cared deeply about, but they got the better of us. My statement for the bureau summed up our bitter disappointment: "Tonight's vote is a giant setback for every consumer in the country. Wall Street won and ordinary people lost."

As a last-ditch effort, I wrote a personal letter to President Trump asking him to consider how this issue would affect the many people who would be unable to get justice when they were wronged. I realized it was almost certainly futile, but I felt the need to do it anyway. At a private signing ceremony, flanked only by Republican lawmakers and industry lobbyists, President Trump signed the resolution as expected. That result not only invalidated the rule but also would prevent the bureau from adopting any new rule on the same subject without new congressional authorization. The president also took the occasion to survey the room about whether he should reconsider his reluctance to fire me. As they debated the issue, our consumer advisory board was meeting in Tampa. I received an unscheduled call from the White House, and a secretary asked me to hold to speak with the president, but then the call was abruptly terminated. Chief of Staff John Kelly apparently intervened at that point, and I never heard anything further. I knew why the White House had called, but once again I had dodged the bullet.[10]

A few days later, I received a very different call, this time from former congressman Barney Frank. He said he understood how disappointed we must be, but that we had raised the visibility of the arbitration issue in important ways that would pay dividends down the road. He also expressed his confidence that, with a change in the political winds, legislation will be passed to roll back this get-out-of-jail-free card as a general principle—not only in consumer finance but also for employment discrimination, oversight of nursing home abuses, sexual harassment, and many other areas as well. It was an encouraging call, and the continuing work that many are doing on this issue suggests that perhaps someday he will turn out to be right.

Reforming Payday Loan Abuses

Our last big fight was over the payday lending rule. This project dated back to the first public hearing we held in Alabama. We had devoted years to analyzing and addressing problems with millions of payday loans, which create repeated debt traps that hurt many customers and ruin others. Borrowers secure these loans in a variety of ways: by giving a postdated check, by authorizing the lender to take payments directly from their bank accounts, and by putting up their vehicle title as collateral. When people use their title as collateral, this can lead to the added blow of losing the vehicle if they default—leaving them much worse off, perhaps unable to get to work, to the store, or to the doctor. Our research showed that more than four out of five payday loans are rolled over or followed by another loan within two weeks, and half of all loans made are part of a sequence at least ten loans long. And paying down the balance on these loans over time is often difficult; for longer loan sequences, the current balance is more likely to go up than down, and growing loan balances are naturally associated with higher default rates.

The typical loan carries an annual percentage rate of around 400%. That sounds staggering to most people, but it is the norm in this industry. And, in fact, that is not the worst of it—in Missouri, we learned about loans offered at rates as high as 1,950% annually, with predictably dire results. People get stuck paying to roll these expensive loans over for many months while their financial problems snowball. Rachel, for example, was a receptionist making $11 per hour. Behind on her rent and utilities, she tried to fix her money troubles by taking out a $2,000 loan, giving the title to her truck as collateral. She made the payments faithfully over the next ten months, which added up to $4,685. By that point, she had paid down exactly $1.16 of principal on the loan, and the compounding interest charges meant she still owed $2,421— more than she had borrowed in the first place, putting her on the unavoidable road to bankruptcy. These loans are like hailing a taxi for a cross-town trip and getting trapped for a far longer and more expensive journey. Online loans create other dangers as well; some lenders misuse customer data, and others market loans deceptively or in states where they are illegal.

In our enforcement actions against payday lenders, we saw these problems on vivid display. Our first order required Cash America, one of the country's largest payday lenders, to pay $14 million in restitution to consumers for "robo-signing" documents in connection with debt collection lawsuits and for making loans to servicemembers at rates that violated the Military Lending Act.[11] We also resolved a matter with ACE Cash Express, another large payday lender, after finding they used harassment and false threats of lawsuits or criminal prosecution to collect on unpaid loans. Our investigation uncovered a training manual that we read as showing how they bullied people into a cycle of debt—by creating a false sense of urgency to pressure overdue borrowers into taking out additional loans they could not afford and piling on new fees. The key graphic explaining their loan process portrayed an endless circle, with arrows leading from the initial loan to collection efforts leading to further loans. Our order required them to stop using these abusive techniques and pay $5 million in refunds as well as a $5 million penalty. Texas officials helped us pursue the matter.

The Mississippi attorney general joined us in a case against All American Check Cashing. That case also alleged abusive practices, such as directing employees to hide check-cashing fees from customers by counting out the money over the fee disclosure on the receipt and explicitly forbidding employees from telling customers what the fees were (the training manual instructed: "NEVER TELL THE CUSTOMER THE FEE"). Our investigation also led us to conclude that the company deceived payday loan customers about the fees they charged, describing the program internally as a "huge income booster" because of the extra fees. One email that was sent to all stores had a cartoon of an employee pointing a gun at a borrower and saying, "Take the $ or die!!" The case got snarled in the courts for years, after the company challenged the constitutionality of the bureau.

We also saw rampant fraud with many online lenders. Our case against the Hydra group was a pointed example, involving a massive cash-grab scam that forced unauthorized loans on potential customers and debited their accounts for payments without their consent.[12] "Lead generators" are companies that serve as online middlemen for the lenders. The lead generators first secure your information and then try to match you to a loan. But consumers typically know little about this process and nothing about the lead generators themselves, who often set up and shut down operations with minimal capital, leaving them largely unaccountable for any damage they do to people. These companies have little incentive to vet lenders with care, and some of the lenders they work with, like the Hydra group, misuse customer information for improper purposes, with devastating effects on people's finances and credit records. Other lenders simply offer loans that have sky-high interest rates—sometimes of 700% or more—and may not even be legal in the states where they are offered online. The problems with lead generators are not limited to online lenders; we also pressed cases where they teamed up with debt collectors and misused consumer data to try to collect on phantom debts that were never owed.

Not all payday lenders were violating the law in such egregious fashion, but harm to consumers was widespread, and we believed the industry needed to be reformed. Dating back to colonial times, state usury caps had limited the interest rates that lenders could charge on most loans. In more than a dozen states with over ninety million people, these caps remain in place, and payday lending does not exist. But starting in the 1990s, most states loosened their laws by exempting short-term payday loans from the interest rate caps to jump-start this industry. Before long, over twenty thousand payday loan stores had sprung up in those states—more locations than McDonald's, Wendy's, and Burger King combined. Although the basic payday loan product is costly for consumers, who pay billions of dollars in fees every year, it produces an inefficient business model, with high default rates and expensive marketing, including the cost of so many brick-and-mortar storefronts to maintain high visibility in targeted communities. Online lending might be expected to reduce these costs, but the default rates are even higher, as is the cost of acquiring new customers. Lenders pay lead generators hundreds of dollars for each potential new borrower, a telling indicator of their expectations about what will happen with those borrowers, given that this up-front cost would not be made up until a payday loan has been rolled over at least several times.

Reflecting its unease about high-cost lending, Congress first addressed the issue in the Military Lending Act by imposing a rate cap of 36% on loans made to active-duty military and their families. In the Dodd-Frank Act, Congress expressly authorized the CFPB to rein in payday lenders through its powers of supervision, enforcement, and regulation but, at the same time, declined to allow us to impose interest rate caps. Given this limit on our authority, we looked to the same principle that both Congress and the bureau had applied successfully to mortgage loans and credit cards.

The gist of our payday lending rule rests on a simple proposition: before making a loan, a payday lender must reasonably assess that the borrower is able to repay it. In a healthy credit market, both the borrower and the lender succeed when the transaction succeeds—the borrower meets his or her need and the lender is repaid. But if lenders can succeed by setting up borrowers to fail, that is a telltale sign of a malfunctioning market. The rule we proposed in June 2016 sought to prevent predatory lending by requiring lenders to verify the borrower's income, borrowing history, and certain key financial obligations to make a reasonable determination of whether the borrower can pay the full amount of the loan when it comes due, without needing to reborrow. The proposed rule provided further protections to prevent lenders from pressing distressed borrowers into rolling over the same loan or taking out several loans in quick succession. It also would crack down on objectionable collection practices that the industry uses to extract payments from consumers' bank accounts. When those attempts fail because the account has insufficient funds, our research showed that the lender often makes repeated attempts to collect, which usually fail but rack up additional penalty fees, harming the borrower further and in some cases causing the bank to close the consumer's account. Our proposed rule would require lenders to give borrowers advance notice of these attempts, so people could either dispute the debt or cover the amount due, and it limited lenders to two failed attempts without seeking a new authorization, to keep consumers from being slammed by multiple fees.

Our proposed rule posed a mortal threat to any lender whose business model was based not on the consumer's ability to repay but on the lender's ability to collect. This business model depends on making loans aimed *especially* at those who can only afford to pay more fees but not to repay the whole amount of the loan principal. Those who repay the loans more quickly are not preferred because they are not profitable. Our economists analyzed the market and estimated that by curtailing the instances of repeat lending and requiring basic underwriting, our rule would prevent perhaps 60% of payday loans from being made on the same terms they were made currently. Yet it would only stop 6% of consumers from taking out an initial loan. This estimate showed just how much the industry had come to rely on getting customers to reborrow. And though it suggested that our rule would have a significant effect on the business, that effect would diminish if lenders reformed their practices by adjusting the costs and features of their loans and changing the range of products they offer.[13]

The payday lenders and their supporters fiercely criticized the proposed rule on the ground that it would limit people's borrowing options, especially in a pinch. We recognized the need for emergency credit, but it should be made available through products that help people rather than harm them. Our rule still allowed companies to make responsible small-dollar loans to customers facing an emergency, and many better options are already available, such as secured credit cards, traditional installment loans, consumer loans from credit unions and community banks, pawn loans, and payment plans offered by many utilities and government offices.[14] Ninety million people live in states that ban payday loans and get along without them.

Nonetheless, the argument that the proposed rule was paternalistic and limited people's credit choices carried weight with many of our critics.

The payday lending industry knew their arguments backward and forward. They had already spent two decades battling over these issues at the state level, and the creation of the CFPB simply opened a new battlefront at the federal level. The industry is a tough adversary and was implacable from the beginning. They resisted our first efforts at supervision and fought our enforcement actions tooth and nail. They took issue with our extensive data on how the market worked, and they raised what we viewed as specious arguments to contest the methodology and conclusions in our reports. Certain payday lenders, especially online lenders, hid behind shell companies, some located offshore to make it harder for us to crack down on them. Others claimed bogus Tribal affiliations to assert legal immunity from state authorities and from us as well. It was also another way to tie up our enforcement investigations with legal challenges, and it slowed us to a crawl in some cases.

The industry lobbyists were countered by a vast coalition of faith groups, including ministers, rabbis, priests, nuns, and imams who oppose payday lending as a scourge on people and their families. Many faith leaders told us about members of their congregations who brought them heart-rending stories—not because they had financial expertise, but because they would at least care about what happened. The involvement of faith leaders changed the nature of discussions on Capitol Hill by interjecting a moral element into the debate, rather than just financial considerations. We asked the Obama White House to convene a roundtable of faith leaders to publicize the issue as well, and their larger megaphone was helpful in raising public visibility around what was at stake with our rulemaking.

The change of administrations greatly altered the climate both for rulemaking and for the industry, which hurt our cause. Through it all—including reported strategy sessions of industry lawyers and lobbyists at a Caribbean island—it was apparent that the industry never thought we would be able to complete a rule restricting payday loans. When we proposed the rule, we were swamped with a million public comments, as opposed to the hundreds or thousands we received for most rules. We were required by law to consider them all, which created an immense challenge even to process and categorize them, let alone to analyze and respond to them. The threat of lawsuits hung in the air, and the industry was buoyed by the antiregulatory thrust of the Trump administration. We staggered under the load, but with the help of many who pitched in from around the bureau, we managed to finalize the rule in October 2017.[15] When it was published in November, it became the law of the land. As with most federal regulations, however, it would not take effect for many months, opening new avenues of resistance for its opponents.

Our new federal rule did not displace state regulation of payday loans. Its core principle of "ability to repay" provided a federal floor of protections, while allowing states to continue to maintain and modify their own legal frameworks. In recent years, a few states have put the issue of payday loans to the ballot, and voters uniformly have rejected high-cost lending by restoring their former interest rate caps.[16] Legislators have often been less responsive than the voters in pushing for such reforms, but despite the power and money wielded by payday loan lobbyists, legislatures in Washington and Ohio have adopted partial reforms that curb payday lending to some degree. Our rule offers a fresh blueprint for reforming the industry, but the fight over it, already years in the making, promises to rage on for years to come. As new law now on the books, it presents a serious challenge to unwind it, both legally and politically, though efforts are underway to do just that.

A TREACHEROUS TRANSITION

In November 2017, just after we completed the payday rule, I made the decision to leave the Consumer Bureau. With only a few months remaining in my term, there was not enough time to complete any other big projects, and the approaching transition to a successor chosen by President Trump was inevitable. As I stepped down, I knew the bureau would be buffeted by hard political winds, yet I was confident it was now sturdy enough to withstand the storm.

A NEW LEADERSHIP FIGHT

As I departed, however, a fight erupted over my successor. The Dodd-Frank Act appears to designate the deputy director to step in as the acting director when the director role is vacant, just as the vice president does when the president leaves office during his or her term. But the ambiguous wording of a different statute, the Vacancies Act, perhaps would allow the president to appoint someone else to head the bureau on a temporary basis.[1] The issue had not been tested, and the legal question was unsettled. Of course, the president was entitled to nominate a new director, subject to Senate confirmation, but until that possibly lengthy process was completed, the interim leader would serve for a crucial transition period.

I had elevated my chief of staff, Leandra English, to the deputy director position. The administration objected to my attempt to select my own interim successor, even though it was in accordance with the wording of our statute. Leandra's experience at the top levels of the bureau, combined with her prior career in several other federal departments, gave her excellent management credentials that would help keep things steady while awaiting a new permanent director. And if a fight did occur, I knew that she would be able to shoulder the burden of becoming the focal point of the dispute and that she would put the bureau and its employees first, avoiding disruption to any of the substantive areas of work.

President Trump responded by appointing Mick Mulvaney, who served in the cabinet as the budget director, to supplant her. It was an especially unfortunate choice, which directly undercut the bureau's status as an "independent" agency. It also put in place a former Tea Party congressman who had been openly hostile to the bureau while serving on the House Financial Services Committee. Earlier that spring, for example, after I spoke to a group of bankers, Mulvaney later told the group that whenever he walked by our building on his way to the White House, he just wanted to tear the place down. He nonetheless claimed squatters' rights, moving into the bureau during an uneasy period where both contenders were serving alongside one another. A lawsuit was filed to challenge his appointment, but the judge refused to intercede.[2]

Mulvaney ultimately stayed about a year, mainly focusing on public relations stunts. But during his time, he adopted a philosophy of government *inaction* to slow the pace of enforcement and regulation, declaring that the bureau would no longer "push the envelope" to protect consumers. For months, he imposed a "data freeze" based on alleged security concerns that blocked the bureau from gathering information, which paralyzed supervisory exams and enforcement investigations. After he finally conceded that the bureau's data was secure and the work resumed, several existing investigations were closed, and some cases were dropped. Others were completed but produced what appeared to be more lenient results and less money back for consumers, which some observers dubbed the "Mulvaney discount."

In my view, this posture was wholly inconsistent with the bureau's mission, and many in the financial industry rejoiced. Yet it was in line with the Trump administration's approach in numerous areas, including health care and environmental protection: appoint a critic to head the agency and shift it away from its core mission more in favor of the industry it was meant to police. These kinds of shifts tend to occur as new administrations with differing views replace their predecessors, and the work done by these agencies ebbs and flows accordingly, though in this instance the abruptness and extent of the shift was unusually dramatic. And unlike those agencies with a deep institutional history, the bureau was only a few years old, making it potentially vulnerable to a complete dismantling, which Mulvaney had advocated while in Congress, calling the bureau "a sad, sick joke."

Some of Mulvaney's views were bizarre and almost cartoonish. Taking an extreme approach of "strict constructionism" of the statute, he argued that he should refrain from taking any action unless Congress explicitly ordered him to do so. The statute, for example, requires the CFPB director to testify in front of both the House and the Senate at least twice a year. But Mulvaney contended that because the law merely orders him to "appear," he could discharge his obligation simply by coming to the Capitol and sitting in the hearing room while refusing to answer any questions. In another move, he insisted on rearranging the initials of the CFPB to BCFP because the statute at times refers to it as the "Bureau of Consumer Financial Protection." It seemed that the purpose was to downgrade the bureau in the public's mind by demoting the emphasis on consumers and highlighting its status as a government agency. When it was later pointed out that this move stood to cost financial institutions hundreds of millions of dollars in needless changes to various documents, his successor sensibly rescinded his order.

More Payday Controversies

The payday lending industry was quick to renew its lobbying efforts under the bureau's new leadership. After the new rule became law, they tried to get Congress to repeal it, as Congress had done with the arbitration rule. A small group of House members filed a disapproval resolution, but the effort was short-lived, with very few members willing to stand up and affirmatively support high-cost payday loans. That was understandable, as ballot measures in states such as Arizona, Ohio, Montana, South Dakota, and Colorado had shown that payday lending is widely unpopular, and many faith leaders oppose it. It was also hard to make a case against a rule that simply required an ability-to-pay assessment to be made before offering a loan, which is the same principle Congress already had approved for mortgages and credit cards.

As the move for legislative action petered out, the payday lobbyists turned their attention to Mulvaney. While a congressman from South Carolina, he received substantial support from this industry; it was reported that in the 2015–2016 election cycle, he was one of the top ten beneficiaries of their campaign contributions.[3] Early on at the bureau, he dropped or limited several ongoing investigations into legal violations by various lending companies, some of which charged interest rates as high as 900% annually.

The payday lenders' trade association filed a lawsuit soon after the new rule took effect. It later asked the court to halt the process of implementing the rule, and under Mulvaney the bureau took the unusual step of joining the payday lenders—the parties that were suing it—in asking the court to delay the rule. This move had no legal basis—a court cannot set aside a law or regulation simply because someone asks it to do so; the parties must make a showing, based on evidence, that the law or regulation is invalid in some way—so the court denied the motion. The bureau then announced its intention to begin the longer and more arduous process of reconsidering the rule, and again asked the court to halt implementation. In view of the new announcement, the court agreed to put things on hold temporarily, at least while that process moved forward.

Mulvaney then undertook to roll back the payday lending rule. The legal and economic pillars of the rule are firm, grounded in the kind of data-driven analysis of millions of loans that we had stressed from the beginning. With no new research that would justify it in disavowing the rule's foundational facts, the bureau sought to make the case instead that it should have the leeway simply to change its mind about federal intervention in this market. Asserting some of the same arguments that the bureau had previously rejected, based on the need for access to credit and the ability of the states to oversee these companies, the bureau proposed a new rule to eliminate the ability-to-repay provisions of the existing rule. This new proposal must move through the same notice-and-comment process before it can take effect, and then is subject to legal challenges of its own. In the meantime, however, implementation of the current rule remains on hold, and the whole mess is destined to be tied up in the courts, which suits the payday lending industry just fine. Justice delayed here is justice denied, and for now the payday lenders can continue to make high-cost loans to people who are unlikely to be able to repay them, with devastating consequences.

TURNING BACK THE CLOCK

During his interim year, Mulvaney also took other steps that set back the bureau's efforts to protect consumers.

In keeping with his rigid philosophy favoring inaction, he argued that the bureau should no longer supervise companies for compliance with the Military Lending Act. This struck many as an odd move. Congress had always strongly supported consumer protections for the military, and Congress had explicitly granted *additional* authority for the bureau to enforce the protections conferred under the Military Lending Act. If the bureau could bring public enforcement actions in court to force companies to comply with that law, then surely it could use the confidential process of supervising companies as a preventive measure to make sure they are complying with that law. Moreover, the bureau has express authority to supervise institutions for compliance with the consumer financial laws, and Congress has now made clear that the Military Lending Act is one of those laws. Nonetheless, the bureau stopped doing this work, with no good explanation why.

In addition, the bureau was reorganized to downgrade the proactive role of its fair lending work. The new leadership separated the Office of Fair Lending from Enforcement and Supervision, isolating Fair Lending into a role limited to advocating, coordinating, and educating companies, but not investigating or supervising whether they are violating the antidiscrimination laws. Since this change was made, the work we had been doing to prevent companies from making discriminatory offers of credit appeared to be shelved: no new fair lending cases were filed by the bureau or referred to the Justice Department during the year after my departure.

The bureau also took a big step away from the work it had been doing to help student loan borrowers. In August 2018, Seth Frotman, the head of the Office of Students, resigned. His blistering resignation letter described how Mulvaney had suppressed information in a report that showed how banks were ripping off students through account fees that were legally dubious, sided with the new leaders at the Department of Education in supporting predatory for-profit schools and helping student loan servicers avoid regulatory oversight, and abandoned the CFPB's enforcement efforts to secure relief for consumers against student loan companies that violated the law. It was a complete 180-degree turn from the aggressive push we had made, which returned more than $750 million to student loan borrowers harmed by predatory practices.

These moves undercut certain aspects of the work that the bureau was doing to protect consumers; other changes were intended to destabilize things more broadly. Although the bureau had never had a single political appointee other than the director, Mulvaney hired several political appointees, who were then paired with existing bureau leadership to scrutinize what the employees were doing and recommend changes where they saw fit.

Wells Fargo Strikes Again

Even with Mulvaney's stated preference for inaction, continuing problems at Wells Fargo showed once again that government oversight of financial institutions is imperative. In addition to the account-opening scandal, the bureau's further reviews of Wells Fargo's operations revealed two other ways it had mistreated customers. The first unfair practice involved auto loans. Wells Fargo required its auto loan customers to have collision insurance to protect Wells Fargo's collateral. The bank hired a vendor to ensure that each customer had the required insurance. But the vendor did a poor job: it disregarded available information and used an incomplete database that omitted many people who got their insurance through smaller firms. When the vendor sent out notices, many customers did not respond for predictable reasons—perhaps because they had moved and never got the notice, or perhaps because they had reason to disregard it, such as knowing that they already had insurance. But when that happened, regardless of the reason, Wells Fargo then "force placed" the insurance on them, charging their accounts as much as $1,000 per year or more, often for duplicate coverage. In some cases, these charges extended for over a decade, and they affected about 850,000 customers. When people complained, their concerns were typically ignored. Unlike the circumstances of opening accounts without consent, which were outrageous but only produced a few million dollars of direct consumer harm, this practice cost consumers billions of dollars.

The second unfair practice involved how the bank handled "rate locks" on mortgages. Wells Fargo was the biggest mortgage lender in the country for much of this period. Many mortgage applicants are willing to lock in a fixed interest rate, for a set fee, that will last through a designated closing date for the sale of the home. This practice is a standard convenience in the industry. If something happens to delay the sale, it costs more to extend the rate lock for a further period. Under Wells Fargo's approach, if the customer was responsible for the delay, then the customer typically would be charged an extra fee to extend the rate lock, but if the bank caused the delay, it was supposed to bear the cost itself. Nonetheless, Wells Fargo almost uniformly billed the extra fee to the consumer, regardless of who was truly at fault. Our investigation revealed that this practice reaped over $100 million in unjustified revenue for Wells Fargo.

Since we had uncovered both practices through our supervisory examinations at around the same time, they got wrapped up together in the same investigation and enforcement action. But as Mulvaney reviewed these matters, which we had initiated against the troubled bank during my tenure, rumors began to circulate that he might let Wells Fargo off the hook. That seemed plausible, because he had just accused the bureau of "trampling on capitalism" and promised to offer the same friendly ear to financial providers as to consumers. But surprisingly, President Trump weighed in with a tweet from out of the blue, admonishing him that "Fines and penalties against Wells Fargo Bank for their bad acts against their customers and others will not be dropped, as has been incorrectly reported." To date, it stands as the only occasion on which the president has registered any public support for the bureau's work to protect consumers. The CFPB and the OCC fell in line, bringing a public action that levied a joint billion-dollar penalty against Wells Fargo, the second-largest resolution that the CFPB had ever reached in an enforcement action.[4] The result also included some partial relief for consumers—$182 million to car loan borrowers and $98 million to mortgage customers. But the total harm that people suffered was far greater. Ultimately, the fifty state attorneys general reached their own resolution on these issues and secured an additional $575 million in relief for consumers. And Wells Fargo also paid out hundreds of millions of dollars more on the auto loan and mortgage issues, to resolve consumer class actions and shareholder lawsuits. Adding all these actions together, the overall result came closer to making people whole for how they were unconscionably mistreated.

In analyzing this episode, it is apparent that the bank's misdeeds were severe enough that they could not be overlooked, especially with such a high-profile company. And it showed, once again, that the banks are fully capable of engaging in conduct that nobody—including the most industry-friendly officials—could tolerate. It thus underscored the essential role that the bureau performs in leveling the playing field for consumers. When individuals try to remedy these kinds of injustices on their own, too often they are ground under the wheels of inflexible corporate processes, without even being able to match a face to the problem. That was the infuriating story at Wells Fargo, where customer complaints were ignored for over a decade. Moreover, people know only about the single fraud or mistake that was perpetrated against them, not the full scale of the company's transgressions. Here it took the government, acting in the public interest, to fully assess and expose these systematic abuses, especially those that involve smaller losses for individual consumers but can easily add up to millions or even billions of dollars in profits for the banks.

The Dynamics of Federalism

Another important dynamic was also at work. As the Consumer Bureau was sounding the retreat in certain areas, state attorneys general and state banking regulators were stepping up to protect consumers in the financial marketplace. The close partnerships that the CFPB had built with these state officials had a momentum of their own, and this steady cooperation was still bringing to light many bad practices around the country. Even if the bureau were to take the lead less often in such matters, it was hard to pull back entirely from this joint work or to ignore the harm being done to consumers when others were in position to expose it. That was part of the backdrop to the most recent Wells Fargo matter. With all fifty state attorneys general pursuing the bank for unfair and deceptive practices on auto and mortgage loans, it was difficult—even embarrassing—for the bureau and the other federal regulators to abdicate their role in addressing these violations. Similarly, as the Federal Trade Commission pressed its investigation of Equifax for the massive data breach, it was aligned with forty-eight states and the CFPB. That lineup eventually concluded an enforcement action imposing new data security requirements and obtaining money and services worth hundreds of millions of dollars for consumers. The bureau joined the others in imposing these measures and levied a $100 million penalty of its own. Of course, it matters whether the bureau plays a leading or a trailing role in these alliances—for example, it is harder for the states to push for more aggressive restitution and penalties where the bureau is willing to settle for less. But it matters less than if the bureau were operating entirely on its own.

The extent of authority that state officials can count on being able to exercise is a critical factor in their ability to fill such a void. For the most part, state officials enforce state law only, and their reach may be limited by federal law, which often preempts any conflicting state law. Prior to the Dodd-Frank Act, that was a problem for the states in the area of financial regulation. The OCC had adopted a regulation asserting broad authority under the National Bank Act to preempt state officials from interfering with its oversight of national banks. That meant even anemic activity at the federal level could prevent the states from taking any stronger actions to regulate financial institutions. When the New York attorney general sought to investigate the fair lending practices of a national bank, the OCC joined with a banking trade group to block them in court by claiming federal preemption. The case ultimately reached the Supreme Court in 2009, as debates were already underway over the financial reform bill. To the surprise of most everyone, the Supreme Court ruled in favor of the states.[5]

This positive development for state power was taken even further in the Dodd-Frank Act, which provided for an unusual system of dual state and federal authority. Traditional theories of federalism hold that federal officials enforce federal law, state officials enforce state law, and never the twain shall meet. If federal officials pull back from enforcing federal law, while also claiming to preempt state laws protecting consumers, they can checkmate state officials from trying to do more. This standoff has occurred in various areas of American law from time to time, but federal suppression of popular reforms can stoke mounting social and political pressures. To give state officials more power to protect people in the realm of consumer finance, Congress did two things in the Dodd-Frank Act. First, it stated that federal consumer financial law sets a floor, not a ceiling, on protecting consumers. That means states are free to adopt or interpret their own laws in ways that differ from federal law, as long as they provide *more* protection for consumers. Second, Congress stated that state officials, in many respects, can enforce federal consumer financial laws directly.

These are significant changes that create a novel form of cooperative federalism. They present a farsighted response to precisely the shifting policy environment we are currently experiencing, where the federal government itself may be disinclined to engage in tough enforcement of federal consumer law, because of free-market ideology, antigovernment bias, desire to support the financial industry, or other reasons. Regardless, the Congress that enacted the Dodd-Frank Act spoke clearly to say it was not willing to put all its law enforcement eggs in the federal basket. We now have an enhanced system of federalism for consumer financial protection, which reflects a clear congressional embrace of the important role that state officials can play to protect consumer rights.[6]

The Bureau's Enduring Strength

With its critics in control of the presidency and both houses of Congress, the Consumer Bureau nevertheless proved too strong to take down. Even Mulvaney, in his waning days as interim leader, conceded that it is here to stay.[7] Although there have been sporadic efforts to suggest specific reforms, nobody any longer is seeking to repeal the bureau. The strategy we pursued from the start—to deliver tangible results for people harmed by financial companies—elevated the cause of consumer financial protection, and the public will not stand to see it undone. Despite changing leadership and the recent tumult, the dedicated men and women at the bureau continue to do its work, racking up both wins and losses, but taking the field every day to advance its vital mission.

A new appointee to head the bureau, Kathy Kraninger, was confirmed in December 2018. Her arrival calmed the waters after Mulvaney's erratic tenure, though it remains to be seen whether she will make good on her public pledge to wield all available tools effectively to protect consumers. Key markers of her willingness to stand up for consumers will be whether she takes enforcement actions against companies for violating the law; how she handles the ongoing fight over the payday lending rule; and how she proceeds with rulemakings on other issues like debt collection, small business lending, and bank account overdraft practices. The inevitable problems that bubble up within the financial companies will also continue to make a strong case for the bureau to prevent and address harm to consumers, who need and deserve this support.

In the meantime, important parts of the bureau's work are still getting done. Its robust system of consumer response continues to help individuals by listening to them and addressing their concerns. In its 2018 annual report to Congress, the bureau reported that it helped individual consumers by handling approximately 330,000 complaints over the course of the year. Aside from the Military Lending Act, the supervision program remains intact, continuing to serve its preventive role of making sure companies are abiding by the law and fixing the problems they create when they violate the law. And most of the work the bureau does to educate and engage with consumers continues to be widely supported.

But leadership matters, and while much of the core work of the bureau is ongoing, both enforcement actions and regulatory work have backtracked in ways that leave people more vulnerable, though they continue to produce results for consumers from time to time. Some of the advances the bureau has made are now being rolled back, and some of the advances it could be making instead are being ignored. For all our sakes, we need the Consumer Bureau and its leaders to be vigilant and forceful for consumers.

PART V
GOVERNING IN THE PUBLIC INTEREST

CONCLUDING THOUGHTS

The Consumer Bureau brought about an important shift in American domestic policy, akin to the creation of Social Security during the New Deal. In that era, leading officials and the public came together to insist on new measures to help prevent seniors from living in poverty. There was no safety net in place to support people who were no longer able to work for a living, and our government created one that was built to last. In the wake of the 2008 financial crisis, our leaders and the public pushed through further measures to help ensure that consumers of all ages should be treated fairly in the financial marketplace. The Consumer Bureau presents a model that shows how our government can look out for people and their families, helping to remedy individual injustices and correct larger distortions in the market, which had become sharply slanted in favor of the corporations that controlled it. In the process, the Consumer Bureau showed that our government can work to improve people's lives.

The CFPB and Our Families

Across every field of consumer finance, people are bruised by their experiences with loan products and other financial services that have become more complex and sophisticated. Credit is now integral to the

American dream and to the American economy. The scale on which financial products are offered no longer allows for careful negotiation between the lender and borrower. Instead, lawyers for the financial companies write the contracts, and the borrowers—the consumers—must take it or leave it. With the power to write the contract comes the power to set the terms, which financial companies have exploited with dense, complicated provisions that few consumers can fully understand. When things go wrong, consumers are told that they signed the contract, and they have little recourse but to absorb the unexpected costs and accept the indignities. Responsible people end up in difficult financial circumstances that leave them stymied, and the fallout affects them, their families, and their communities. In the 2008 recession, it affected all the rest of us as well. We needed to level the playing field for consumers against the big financial companies and financial predators. The Consumer Bureau's mission was to provide that balance.

On their own, individual consumers do not have the clout to affect the big banks or financial companies. If they complain, the company can ignore or refuse them, with little to lose except a single customer. Theoretically, people could band together, but there is no easy mechanism for them to do so. They can sue—which itself involves a form of government intervention—but companies have increasingly cut off that option, writing terms into their contracts that prevent customers from going to court to pursue relief as a group, and relegating them instead to a secretive process for arbitrating their individual claims. This is frustrating, and it reinforces our feelings of impotence when these efforts turn out to be fruitless.

But the bureau gave people leverage in ways that mattered. Our consumer response function enabled people to bring their complaints to the companies not merely as individuals but backed by an organization willing to use its authority on their behalf. Companies had greater incentive to take their complaints seriously, and many problems got resolved. As people spoke up more frequently, the large volume of complaints showed companies more clearly the patterns of problems that needed—and soon received—greater attention. And as our process made it possible to organize and assess their complaints, we gained a clearer sense of the problems that consumers all over the country are dealing with, which focused our work as well.

We also supported consumers by improving disclosures and financial education. In today's market economy, we expect people to shop for the best deal, know their limits, and make responsible decisions. But contracts that are dense with intricate information about complex financial products and services make it nearly impossible to understand the deal, let alone make sensible comparisons between options. People need to develop greater capability—more know-how—but they also need the choices that are available to them to be more accessible and comprehensible. I sometimes illustrated the gap in consumer knowledge by holding my hands out, one above the other. Making financial products more comprehensible through simplifying disclosures is a way to lower the top hand, and strengthening the skills and aptitude of consumers is a way to raise the bottom hand. Our "Know Before You Owe" efforts pushed down the top, and our financial education work pushed up the bottom. By squashing the two together, we aimed to narrow the gap for consumers, though both aspects of this project remain a work in progress.

Much of the bureau's effectiveness, however, came through enforcement and supervision of companies. As more Americans worry about stagnating wages—what's going into the pockets of working people—they should worry about what's being drained out of their pockets as well. Congress gave the Consumer Bureau broad authority to combat the harm people suffer from surprise fees, from scams and frauds, and from abuses by large financial companies. As a visible cop on the beat, the bureau took actions against corporate violators, putting $12 billion back in the pockets of consumers who had been wronged. The preventive work done by our supervisory teams was less conspicuous but just as important. It applied steady pressure to halt unfair and deceptive practices through regular inspections that monitored how companies treat consumers.

To secure more balance in the financial marketplace itself, the bureau helped implement the laws and shape the rules that govern mortgages and credit cards. These changes strengthened people's ability to understand the products they were buying and outlawed various practices that had cost them billions of dollars. The new mortgage lending framework, in particular, reined in the kinds of reckless and predatory loans that had brought about the financial crisis.

Keeping money in consumers' pockets—through enforcing the law and setting sensible limits on corporate malfeasance—produces more opportunity. And if the kind of progress we were beginning to make was possible in just a few short years, then steady efforts over time could make a tremendous difference for the American consumer public. As President Kennedy pointed out more than fifty years ago, increased efforts to help people make the best possible use of their incomes can contribute as much to the well-being of families as efforts to raise their incomes. Our public policy should insist on aggressive efforts to make sure that our market economy is achieving both results.

THE CFPB AND OUR ECONOMY

The CFPB's mission to support and protect consumers also strengthens the economy. When markets are working as they should, consumers are the primary beneficiaries. Their preferences guide the products and services that companies provide, and competition incentivizes businesses to increase customer satisfaction. But prior to the Great Recession, consumer financial markets had moved into perverse channels where corporate interests and consumer interests were not aligned. Companies used methods of marketing, pricing, and financing to obscure costs and risks and impede consumers from understanding whether they were getting a fair deal that they could live with over time. Lax enforcement allowed many providers to violate the law and get away with it. And specialty markets such as debt collection and credit reporting, which greatly affect people's access to credit and what they pay for it, were operating without any real regard for individual consumers. Instead, they were focused only on satisfying the financial companies that paid them.

How well people function in the financial marketplace is important to the stability of our overall economy. Consumers are the largest economic group in the country, spending far more every year than businesses and the government combined: fully two-thirds of our economic output is consumer driven. As consumer credit expanded in recent years, it facilitated this spending and became a central feature in American life. People who are in financial trouble are weak spots for the American economy. Shoring up their vulnerabilities makes the entire country sounder and more resilient.

The mortgage market demonstrated how a large volume of terrible choices made by lenders and borrowers can weaken and even collapse the underpinnings of our economy. In the runup to 2008, the ripple effects of many individual mistakes multiplied into heavy waves—of foreclosures, loan defaults, and job losses—that washed over everyone across the country, many of whom had neither misused nor abused their credit. The mistakes of some lenders and some consumers caused the system to break down for everyone around them as well. Coming out of the deep recession, consumers and lenders were both treading much more carefully, and we worked alongside them to implement safeguards that would help restore confidence in the consumer finance markets.

Improved market dynamics brought about by thoughtful regulations and backed by evenhanded enforcement can also benefit the financial companies themselves. Many established lenders fared poorly during the "race to the bottom" in mortgage lending. Their refusal to reduce their loan underwriting standards cost them customers, who went instead to competitors offering easy no-doc mortgages with few constraints. This type of market dysfunction tends to develop a self-perpetuating momentum of its own that is difficult to resist, especially when a company sees its viability is at stake. Many executives faced excruciating choices in the face of these pressures. Lenders that insisted on maintaining sensible loan standards—as many had done for decades—were being pushed out of the market by others who were willing to exploit short-term profits at the expense of long-term sustainability. Many of the unsound practices that led to the financial crisis were entirely legal. Banning or limiting them has enabled companies to compete without distorting their products in ways that endanger a functioning market. In both the mortgage and the credit card markets, customer satisfaction rose as new substantive regulatory interventions improved the performance of companies.

Dependable law enforcement is another key to making markets work effectively. It protects ethical companies against those who cut corners improperly and violate the law. At the local level and the state level, I had seen this dynamic at work with businesses that resented seeing their rivals profit from breaking the law and getting away with it—for example, by not paying their property taxes or not bearing their mandated share of employment costs. Effective law enforcement safeguards law-abiding businesses that struggle to compete against cheating competitors. This is, in fact, the worst form of unfair competition, where companies can outpace their market peers by acting illegally.

Effective regulatory oversight also strengthens those parts of the financial companies that focus on customer satisfaction and compliance with the law. In many instances, the CFPB's new level of activity caused companies to increase their staffing and resources to deal with consumer issues.

Companies instituted strong programs to address consumer complaints, implement new rules, and root out bad practices. Eliminating practices that generate litigation, regulatory problems, or a bad reputation with customers takes effort and resources, but in the long run it strengthens the company's bottom line. Our oversight and enforcement pushed companies to listen to the employees who advocated for more responsible behavior, instead of the marketing and sales personnel who often downplayed these risks.

The CFPB faced consistent opposition from those who argue for less regulation and in favor of what they view as a free market. But the "invisible hand" that produces optimal outcomes in a free market works best in conditions that are not often found in consumer finance markets. In these markets, consumers are not sufficiently informed because credit has evolved to be so complex that, without hiring a lawyer, people cannot truly understand or compare the terms of the contracts they are signing. And dysfunctional market dynamics—such as the race to the bottom, unfair competition, and back-end pricing—can push companies to engage in perverse practices that they cannot easily resist. These deficiencies in the market mean that we cannot rely on unfettered competition to discipline corporate behavior effectively. The "visible hand" of government regulation is needed as a supplemental safeguard to protect consumers and to fortify the market against the defects of imperfect competition. Although Americans have rejected the European socialist model of government ownership over large chunks of the economy, they support the concept of regulated industries, where the excesses of corporate market power are checked by government oversight on topics such as food and drug safety, air travel, clean air and water, and many others, including consumer finance. Regulation itself has become a basic element of our governing framework, though vigorous debate continues about how light or heavy its burdens should be.

One shortcoming we saw with the regulatory model is that it can disadvantage smaller companies. If the objective is a level playing field, then the standards should be the same for everyone. Yet larger firms can bear the weight of regulatory compliance more easily and can spread the costs over a greater revenue base, whereas small companies may find the cumulative burdens stifling and unmanageable. There is solid ground for debate over whether the same rules are necessary for firms under a certain size. The smaller community banks and credit unions, for example, are rooted in the local communities where they do business, and they remain subject to the kinds of personal norms that have long constrained and informed their actions. Corporate executives who live among their customers, who belong to the same community groups, and whose families participate in the same local activities and events seem less likely to engage in or get away with unfair, deceptive, or abusive practices. In contrast, leaders of large financial companies are increasingly divorced from the many local communities where they do business, and they may not feel the same pressure from personal norms that would have constrained and informed their actions as a local business. There is also growing concern that these huge companies are becoming too big to manage effectively. At Wells Fargo, for example, executives failed to monitor or understand the systemic fraud that thousands of their employees were committing. Taking these differences into account, we tried to tailor our rules differently for small entities, exempting them from some rules and streamlining others. In 2016, community banks made record profits.

Finally, Congress tasked the CFPB with monitoring consumer credit markets—especially the mortgage market—more comprehensively. By removing blind spots to identify risks and irregularities in their early stages, the bureau can better protect consumers, and it also can help head off problems before they grow into systemic threats to the broader economy. Spiraling student loan debt is one example: by documenting the rise in the total debt burden and highlighting potential consequences for the broader economy, the bureau's research has put pressure on policymakers to find ways to address these issues. Solving big problems is still hard, but better research and data certainly help.

The CFPB and Our Democracy

The Consumer Bureau exemplifies a vision of government that is focused on supporting individuals and families while serving as a check on entrenched interests. Across today's deep partisan divide, many people doubt whether it is even possible for our government to work for them. Those who doubt it range from progressives who worry about a system rigged for the powerful against the powerless to Tea Party activists and Trump supporters radicalized by the effects of the financial crisis. Many people want to see the power elites broken and the established alignments disrupted, even if the system cannot be fixed.

But it *can* be fixed. The work done at the Consumer Bureau shows that our government can be realigned to serve ordinary Americans, not just those at the top of the pyramid. In the case of Ari and his father, for example, the bureau's backing made the critical difference in solving Ari's individual problem when he was cheated on the loan to buy his truck. But in addition, the bureau—armed with the tools and authority of the government—was in a position to identify and resolve two larger problems as well: thousands of others had been cheated in the same way, and predatory lenders were legally abusing the Pentagon's allotment system. And the bureau resolved both problems, getting relief for fifty thousand servicemembers from deceptive terms on their auto loans and bringing about systemic reforms in the Pentagon's allotment system to prevent future abuses.

Only government has the ability and the authority to make these larger corrections. Efforts to get government out of the way erode its ability to do this vital work—work that it uniquely can do—to enforce the laws that protect individual Americans and the marketplace. Steady and efficient administration of the laws is essential if they are to achieve their intended objectives—here, to ensure that people will get a fair shake and have a chance at the opportunity that America promises.[1]

An important proxy for governing in the public interest is to focus on policies that benefit the middle class. In America, the possibility of reaching and staying in the middle class remains a potent symbol of economic opportunity. Over two-thirds of the public self-identify as "middle class," even though by some measures this segment has now shrunk to about half of the population. Yet people increasingly see this status as fragile: almost one-third of Americans believe that at some point the middle class will disappear completely, and almost as many more feel uncertain about its future.[2] Both these perceptions and the reality are also affected by the growing inequality of income and wealth, which seems to be hollowing out the prospects of the average family, lessening opportunity, and diminishing aspiration. Even in a strong economy, many Americans are struggling. Almost forty million people continue to live in poverty, fifty-five million are unbanked or underbanked, and forty-four million young people are staggering under the weight of their student loans. People are anxious about the future, and they feel the indignity of corporate indifference when they raise legitimate concerns. As people lose faith in our ability to correct dysfunctions in the marketplace, their alienation threatens to destabilize the broad and empowered middle class that has long been the cornerstone of our successful democracy.

In much of government, there is sharp tension between advancing the interests of the public and serving the narrower desires of powerful constituencies, which are locked in on specific goals and have substantial resources to pursue them. These influential groups often wield their clout to maintain the status quo that serves them so well. They work quietly below the surface, eluding public attention while achieving their objectives. Bringing issues out of the shadows and giving them greater visibility is one way to combat these unseen efforts to subvert the public interest. But shifting government to advance the aims of the general public is much harder: as President Kennedy noted, every one of us is a consumer, but we are not organized in a self-conscious way and hence our voices often go unheard. We must reorient our government—by banding together, by speaking out, by voting—if we are to make it respond directly and effectively to our concerns.[3]

That is true in consumer finance and in many other areas as well, such as health care, fairness in the workplace, law enforcement, and environmental protection. Some of the specific issues we encountered at the bureau span multiple sectors, such as companies' use of arbitration clauses to cut off people's right to sue them in court for violating the law. The imbalance between individuals and corporations is a perpetual struggle, and if uncontained, it overwhelms people, sapping both their individual resolve and their sense of community purpose.

When public officials ignore these concerns or merely grandstand about them, it corrodes our social fabric even further. People may come to believe that our political and economic systems are incapable of addressing their concerns, and if that belief becomes widely shared, it could undercut respect for our laws and our democracy. More people are already losing confidence in our capitalist market system, which historically has brought so much prosperity and freedom to America. Ill-defined calls for a socialist order auger a new willingness to depart from our common civic values and a mistrust of what can be achieved through our traditional governing order.

The steadfast will to govern in the public interest depends crucially on both the direct backing of political leaders *and* popular support. Entrenched interests inevitably will resist efforts to realign our government in this manner. The Consumer Bureau has shown the capability to address the people's everyday concerns, but the will to do so is vulnerable to pressure and to ideology, both in the bureau itself and throughout the government. It matters whether we choose leaders who are willing to intervene to make a positive difference for individuals and families—who want to push the envelope to protect consumers—rather than leaders who believe that government is the problem and want it to do as little as possible. I believe government can and should strenuously defend and enhance the dignity and worth of every individual. Promoting and safeguarding a marketplace that serves consumers is essential to that goal. We must remain vigilant and active in supporting a practical vision of our government that is dedicated to protecting the public—in short, a government that stands on our side. The health of our families, our economy, and our democracy depends on it.

NOTES

CHAPTER 1

1. As long ago as 1960, Professor Karl Llewellyn powerfully described the dynamic of how one-sided form contracts can oppress consumers: "The one party lays his head into the mouth of a lion—either, and mostly, without reading the fine print, or occasionally in the hope and expectation (not infrequently solid) that it will be a sweet and gentle lion." But, as he went on to observe, "not all 'dominant' parties are nice lions, and even nice lions make mistakes." Karl Llewellyn, *The Common Law Tradition: Deciding Appeals* (Boston: Little, Brown and Company 1960): 362.

2. See, for example, Bob Sullivan, *Gotcha Capitalism* (New York: Ballantine Books 2007) and José García, James Lardner, and Cindy Zeldin, *Up to Our Eyeballs* (New York: The New Press 2008). Early consumer advocates like Colston Warne and Esther Peterson constantly stressed that informed choice lies at the heart of our democracy and the economic system upon which it relies.

3. The figures for "average" credit card debt can vary significantly depending on what groups are being used as the numerator and the denominator. Many people pay off their balance every month, which means the average can be much higher for households that use credit cards as a source of revolving credit.

4. As we learned at a field hearing in Miami, the total amount of educational debt in the United States is likely even greater than the formal numbers on student loans seem to suggest. Students (or their families) who do not qualify for student loans for various reasons, or have exceeded their available limits, may find other ways to finance their education, such as by taking on credit card debt or securing home loans of various kinds.

5. Early on, Rohit Chopra, the CFPB's talented student loan ombudsman (later a Federal Trade commissioner) called attention to this "domino effect," which has since been confirmed and reinforced by further studies. See Prepared Remarks by Rohit Chopra Before the Federal Reserve Bank of St. Louis, November 18, 2013, https://www.consumerfinance.gov/about-us/newsroom/student-loan-ombudsman-rohit-chopra-before-the-federal-reserve-bank-of-st-louis/.

6. The principal fair lending law is the Equal Credit Opportunity Act of 1974. The law was adopted against a backdrop of government officials all over the country who

sanctioned and perpetrated discrimination in lending and housing for decades. More discussion of our efforts to enforce this law can be found in chapters 6 and 12.

7. The Fair Debt Collection Practices Act, passed in 1977, is one of many consumer financial laws whose core feature is the specification of unfair and deceptive practices that have been identified in specific contexts. The same principles, minus much of the specificity, have been developed and applied under state law as well. As the Ohio attorney general, I was in the uncomfortable position of both enforcing the law against troublesome debt collectors and formally engaging in debt collection on behalf of the state.

8. For some years, identity theft has been pegged as the fasting-growing crime in America. Credit reporting problems do not require criminal victimization as a predicate, but identity theft is another cause of unexpected problems that can be very difficult and time-consuming for people to resolve.

9. For years, lawmakers had taken halting steps to make credit reporting issues more salient for the public, such as by mandating access to free credit reports (but not free credit scores, a limitation that reflected fierce industry lobbying). We considered launching some sort of public awareness campaign, but later we decided to promote the Open Credit Score Initiative, which now makes credit scores regularly and freely available to many millions of consumers, as discussed further in chapter 11.

10. The erratic nature of medical debt is so pronounced that it is now an accepted principle that it should be treated differently from any other reported source of debt. Small medical debts that often are subject to billing disputes or confusion simply cannot be regarded as reliable indicators that a consumer is truly unwilling or unable to repay the listed debt. Accordingly, in 2015 the New York attorney general resolved a major enforcement action to ensure that medical debt would no longer be reported immediately to the credit reporting companies but would only be reported after 180 days had passed to allow more time and effort to get it sorted out. This was no light matter, as our research suggested that claims of unpaid medical debt beset forty-three million Americans. These issues are discussed further in chapter 12.

11. See Nicholas Confessore, "Make America Pay Again!," *New York Times Magazine,* April 16, 2019.

12. The Council for Economic Education has published its *Survey of the States* for twenty years to assess state progress in providing financial education to students. The results are very mixed, as fewer than half the states require a personal finance course, include personal finance education in their K-12 standards, or require standardized testing of economic concepts. Progress on these issues has slowed to a crawl in recent years, and the CFPB's efforts to address them are covered more fully in chapter 8.

13. The plight of so many Americans who live paycheck to paycheck has been widely remarked. In a notable study, the Federal Reserve found that four in ten Americans do not have enough savings to cover an unexpected $400 shortfall. See Federal Reserve Board, "Report on the Economic Well-Being of U.S. Households," May 22, 2018. Extensive data also shows that large numbers of Americans do not manage to save enough to provide adequately for themselves and their dependents in the event of their retirement.

CHAPTER 2

1. President Kennedy delivered this speech on March 15, 1962, and that day is now celebrated around the globe as World Consumer Rights Day. He recognized four fundamental consumer rights: the right to safety, the right to be informed, the right to choose, and the right to be heard. The right to be informed corresponds to our "Know Before You Owe" project, discussed in chapter 9, and the right to be heard relates to the CFPB's consumer complaint response role, discussed in chapter 5. The current figure for US household debt, according to the Federal Reserve Bank of New York, hit a record high of $13.86 trillion in the second quarter of 2019—the twentieth consecutive quarter in which it has risen.

2. The Federal Reserve Bank of St. Louis, which is the source for these figures, is known for its close study of US household balance sheets, including the use and scope of household credit.

3. The practice of overcharging borrowers through the yield spread premium is an example of how trusting consumers can be easily exploited. Sitting across the table from professionals they know to be experts—and often assume have their best interests in mind, or at least have interests that are equally aligned—they may not see that the other parties have their own agendas and arrangements, ranging from concerns about securing repeat business to taking outright kickbacks. The Real Estate Settlement Procedures Act was enacted in 1974 to root out such practices in the real estate market, but the details of these arrangements can be highly elusive, making its enforcement troubled and spotty.

4. The Great Depression is now defined as having begun in August 1929 when the economy first entered a recession, prior to the stock market crash. The trough was deep, but by 1936 there were signs of steady improvement before the economy plummeted to a new nadir in 1937–1938, not emerging again until after the severe market disruptions that occurred in fighting World War II. Among the many new mechanisms created to fight the Depression, the National Recovery Administration was struck down by the Supreme Court as unconstitutional, but many others—such as the Securities and Exchange Commission, the Federal Deposit Insurance Corporation, and the Social Security Administration—survived and continue to fulfill their intended purposes.

5. Perhaps the most accessible account of how the collapse of the mortgage market brought on the financial crisis is Michael Lewis, *The Big Short: Inside the Doomsday Machine* (New York: W. W. Norton and Company 2010).

6. See Amir E. Khandani, Adlar Jeewook Kim, and B. Andrew W. Lo, "Consumer Credit-Risk Models Via Machine-Learning Algorithms," *Journal of Banking and Finance* 34 (2010): 2767, 2785 ("In the aftermath of one of the worst financial crises in modern history, it has become clear that consumer behavior has played a central role at every stage—in sowing the seeds of crisis, causing cascades of firesale liquidations, and bearing the brunt of the economic consequences. Therefore, any prospective insights regarding consumer credit that can be gleaned from historical data has become a national priority.").

7. Senator Isakson has told this fascinating story in several speeches, and he told it to me directly during a courtesy call I paid on him during the confirmation process over my nomination.

8. This story was told by Scott McComb, the chief executive officer of Heartland Bank, located in central Ohio with just over $1 billion in assets. See Dave Ghose, "Scott McComb Shepherds Heartland Bank to New Heights," *Columbus Dispatch*, December 30, 2018.

9. The financial crisis and ensuing recession would have been even more disabling— rivaling the Great Depression—if the federal and state governments did not have in place these safety nets, which also produce countercyclical fiscal policies. The seven-year frozen tundra of zero interest rates, never seen before in US history, also had extraordinary and often unnoticed consequences that distorted the economy. At the same time, rampant income inequality is distorting it further, as the top 1% of families receive an income, on average, that is more than twenty-six times the average income for those in the bottom 99%, the biggest gap ever for income inequality in the United States. See Estelle Sommeiller and Mark Price, "The New Gilded Age," Economic Policy Institute, July 19, 2018.

10. See, for example, Rakesh Kochhar and Richard Fry, "Wealth Inequality Has Widened Along Racial, Ethnic Lines Since End of Great Recession," Pew Research Center, December 12, 2014. The top 0.1% of the wealthiest Americans now have 22% of the wealth, their largest share since 1929, and the share of the bottom 90% has declined steadily for over three decades. See Emmanuel Saez and Gabriel Zucman, "Wealth Inequality in the U.S. Since 1913: Evidence from Capitalized Income Tax Data," NBER Working Paper No. 20625, October 2014.

11. Oliver Wendell Holmes Jr., "Lecture 1," in *The Common Law* (Boston: Little, Brown and Company 1881). Many stories in this book illustrate the point that consumers can be hurt just as much by sloppy and unsound practices reflecting the indifference and neglect of corporate processes as by nefarious practices consciously intended by financial predators. In terms of pure economic harm, that is surely correct, but the point here is that for most people it also matters if the *manner* in which they are harmed "adds insult to injury."

12. The government's failure to require that the capital injections made into the banks be passed on to those suffering in local communities was not entirely overlooked at the time, but more cumbersome processes that the government developed to treat this problem—such as mortgage assistance programs like HAMP (the Home Affordable Modification Program) and the so-called Hardest Hit Fund—had only limited success in remedying this deficiency.

CHAPTER 3

1. This mistrust first surfaced in knock-down, drag-out battles over the first and second versions of the Bank of the United States, which was chartered in 1791 and again in 1816 before the charters lapsed and the banks were closed both times. In 1893 and 1907, the machinations of powerful financiers triggered damaging panics that were only quelled by the direct intervention of the elder J. P. Morgan and other

private bankers. This situation caused widespread concern about concentrated financial power, which led in 1913 to creation of the Federal Reserve System, with its unique hybrid apparatus composed of a federal board of governors combined with twelve regional banks. See Federal Reserve Bank of Minneapolis, "A History of Central Banking in the United States," 2019; Ron Chernow, *The House of Morgan* (New York: Simon and Schuster 1990).

2. Elizabeth Warren, "Unsafe at Any Rate," *Democracy Journal*, Summer 2007.

3. The law's unusual designation of a transfer date, set one year into the future, created an uncomfortable period of suspended animation in which we did not even yet refer to ourselves as the "CFPB," but instead only as the "CFPB implementation team," clearly an awkward way to introduce ourselves to the public.

4. See Vasco Carvalho and Xavier Gabaix, "The Great Diversification and Its Undoing," *American Economic Review* 103 (2013): 1697.

5. See Christopher Witko, "How Wall Street Became a Big Chunk of the U.S. Economy—and When the Democrats Signed On," *Washington Post*, March 29, 2016, and Bureau of Labor Statistics, "Finance and Insurance NAICS 52, Workforce Statistics," https://www.bls.gov/iag/tgs/iag52.htm.

6. See M. B. Pell and Joe Eaton, "Five Lobbyists for Every Member of Congress on Financial Reforms," Center for Public Integrity, May 21, 2010; Pete Schroeder, "Banks Spent Record Amounts on Lobbying in Recent Election," Reuters, March 8, 2017. For more background on the passage of the Dodd-Frank Act, see Robert G. Kaiser, *Act of Congress* (New York: Vintage 2013).

7. These legislative victories were all achieved with some measure of bipartisan support; they were, respectively, the Riegle-Neal Interstate Banking and Branching Efficiency Act of 1994, the Financial Services Modernization Act of 1999, and the Bankruptcy Abuse Reform and Consumer Protection Act of 2005. The important Supreme Court ruling on exporting interest rates from one state to another came in *Marquette National Bank v. First of Omaha Service Corp.*, 439 U.S. 299 (1978).

8. We offered this somewhat conservative estimate in 2013 in our first report to Congress on the effects of the Credit Card Accountability Responsibility and Disclosure (CARD) Act, based on annual consumer savings of $1.5 billion in late fees and $2.5 million in over-limit fees, for a total of $4 billion per year. A contemporaneous academic study pegged the consumer savings far higher, at $11.9 billion per year, with no reduction in the volume of credit. See Sumit Agarwal, Souphala Chomsisengphet, Neale Mahoney, and Johannes Stroebel, "Regulating Consumer Financial Products: Evidence from Credit Cards," NBER Working Paper No. w19484, September 28, 2013.

9. See Sandhya Somashekhar, "Tea Party Activists March on Capitol Hill," *Washington Post*, September 12, 2010; Al Gore, "The False Spontaneity of the Tea Party," Huffington Post, February 14, 2013; Jeff Nesbit, "The Secret Origins of the Tea Party," *Time*, April 5, 2016.

10. Audrey Chen, one of our most creative talents, joined us from Comedy Central, of all places. Len Kennedy, former general counsel at Sprint Nextel, described going into the library for months just to research and write about the financial crisis, to figure out what happened and why—then became our first general counsel once the Consumer Bureau became a reality. Nick Smyth, a recent Harvard Law

School graduate, was so intent on joining the new bureau that he enrolled in some more courses to qualify as a student intern before going on to do work protecting servicemembers and as part of the enforcement team.

11. Title X of the Dodd-Frank Act, which is only one part of the voluminous bill, is separately referred to as the Consumer Financial Protection Act of 2010.

12. Again, the unique trajectory of the bureau originated in the Treasury Department before moving over to its permanent home in the Federal Reserve. Yet much of our organizational backbone remained with the Treasury for several years, including personnel support and our information technology network. Even after we achieved total independence from the Treasury, it had become customary for our leadership to meet regularly with Treasury leadership to update them on our progress— including Deputy Secretary Neal Wolin, and Treasury Secretaries Tim Geithner, Jack Lew, and Steve Mnuchin.

13. As Elizabeth departed, several top executives decided to leave as well: Dan Geldon, her long-time strategic adviser; Wally Adeyemo, who served as our chief of staff and went on to serve as senior international economic adviser to President Obama; and Elizabeth Vale, who had come over from the White House to set up all of our external affairs establishing relations with industry and consumer groups.

CHAPTER 4

1. In 2010 in Ohio, we stumbled onto these problems after hearing from legal aid attorneys about irregularities they were seeing in foreclosure cases. Iowa Attorney General Tom Miller and Colorado Attorney General John Suthers formed a bipartisan task force to pursue the issue, and we joined it. A short time later, Ohio filed the only lawsuit nationally on this issue against GMAC, a state-chartered bank; federal law blocked the states from suing any bank with a federal charter. In just a few months, all fifty state attorneys general signed up to take part in the joint investigation.

2. The last holdout to sign on to the agreement (aside from Oklahoma Attorney General Scott Pruitt, who never signed on) was California Attorney General Kamala Harris, who was looking to drive a hard bargain on behalf of her state. Since it would be difficult to get the banks to finalize an agreement without California, she was in a strong position to insist on more relief. In the end, she secured her own state monitor (Professor Katie Porter, later elected to Congress), who helped many homeowners get better outcomes and worked with the CFPB to improve servicer performance.

3. This mostly friendly attitude from opposing senators was a relief because it meant that my reputation was not being assailed in ways that would hurt both me and my family. Moreover, I had my own unique experience with such matters. Twenty-five years earlier, just out of law school, I clerked for Judge Robert Bork. At the end of that year, he was nominated to the Supreme Court. I went on to clerk for Justice White, and over the next few months I saw a confirmation battle up close that became overtly personal. Not only did the Senate reject Judge Bork but also the process was a bitter ordeal. Nothing like that was happening in my case.

4. In a bygone era, this break between the sessions lasted for many months, as the legislators adjourned and made the long journey home until the next election, after which they reconvened for a lame-duck session before Congress ended in March and the newly elected legislators arrived. But America's growth as a national power required more of a full-time Congress that was less willing to leave the president unsupervised for long stretches. The Twentieth Amendment then reconfigured the schedule so that both the new president and the new Congress got underway in January rather than March. And swifter travel meant that even the most remote legislators could get to the Capitol in hours rather than weeks, so as a practical matter, long absences were no longer needed. The recess appointments made in 1903 were not contested in court but they were controversial because the House had not consented to allow the Senate to adjourn and create any recess at all. In my situation too, the House had refused to allow the Congress to adjourn, with some members remaining in the Capitol to hold "pro forma" sessions specifically to prevent President Obama from making any recess appointments.

5. Cleveland was a fitting choice for these events, as many of its communities had been hit especially hard by the foreclosure crisis. In traditional neighborhoods like Slavic Village, clusters of vacant, abandoned, and boarded-up houses had decimated property values throughout the community. When I was the Ohio attorney general, we had organized "Save Our Homes" task forces throughout the state to try to stave off foreclosures, but the efforts we and others made were often overwhelmed by the fraudulent and predatory lending that had blanketed certain areas.

6. The abrupt transition from Raj Date's interim leadership to my sudden installment as the first director was eased considerably by Garry Reeder, who remained as chief of staff. This key role would be filled in turn by Meredith Fuchs, Chris D'Angelo, Eli Corbett, and Leandra English, who each also took on other important roles during their time at the bureau.

7. We later learned that these harmful practices were not limited to US credit card markets; similar problems had occurred in Britain also, requiring regulatory action by our counterparts there. The background to our enforcement actions, which we undertook jointly with other federal regulators, is recounted in more detail in chapter 6.

8. The issue of "available household income" was complicated in part because of changes in the law that had been made to limit marketing of credit cards to students between the ages of eighteen and twenty-one. It was a good example of the kinds of unexpected and unforeseen consequences that can arise in modifying the law, which necessitates almost superhuman omniscience when engaging in legislation or regulation.

9. Representative Frank chaired the House Financial Services Committee during the crucial battle over the Dodd-Frank Act, but after the watershed 2010 elections, control of the committee passed to the Republicans for the next eight years, first under Spencer Bachus of Alabama and then under Jeb Hensarling of Texas. When Congressman Frank retired in 2012, the ranking Democratic member became Maxine Waters of California, a fierce champion for consumers and the CFPB. She became the new committee chair after control of the House flipped back to the Democrats in 2018.

10. The main constitutional challenge to the bureau was brought by a small community bank from Big Springs, Texas. Ultimately, the courts found that the bank lacked standing to pursue most of its claims because it was, like other small banks and credit unions, essentially unharmed by the bureau's actions. After the recess appointments were struck down by the court of appeals, and while that case remained pending in the Supreme Court, Senator Johanns of Nebraska wrote to demand my resignation on the ground that my status as the CFPB director violated Articles I, II, and III of the Constitution. We responded with a point-by-point rebuttal of his arguments, also making clear that I had no intention of resigning in the middle of the ongoing legal proceedings.

11. Although Senator Reid did not invoke the nuclear option on this occasion, the Senate later dropped the filibuster for all nominees other than for the Supreme Court. In 2014, Republicans recaptured the Senate and adopted the same strategy by refusing to take up Judge Merrick Garland's nomination to the Supreme Court for an entire year, despite no real objections to his stellar qualifications. That left a crucial vacancy, and when the White House turned over in 2016, the Senate scrapped the filibuster for the Supreme Court as well. That led to Neil Gorsuch filling the vacant seat on a vote of fifty-four to forty-five, and Brett Kavanaugh filling the next open seat on a vote of fifty to forty-eight. The politics of the confirmation process had been irreversibly altered.

12. Kathleen Sebelius grew up in Ohio, where her father, Jack Gilligan, had served as governor. When she was elected to serve as the governor of Kansas before coming to Washington, they thus formed the first father-daughter gubernatorial team in US history. I asked her to be part of my swearing-in because of my friendship with her family.

13. The Supreme Court decision on the recess appointments was *NLRB v. Noel Canning, Inc.*, 134 S. Ct. 2550 (2014). Out of many different arguments made by numerous lawyers, the court ultimately decided that "pro forma" sessions count as actual sessions of the Senate, and the time between sessions when the appointments were made was only three days, which was too brief to qualify as a true "recess." The CFPB order ratifying all prior actions was challenged and upheld under traditional principles of agency law in *CFPB v. Gordon*, 819 F.3d 1179 (9th Cir. 2016), *cert. denied*, 138 S. Ct. 555 (2017).

CHAPTER 5

1. Most government agencies do not have statutory mandates about responding to complaints, yet they develop some such functions anyway. But Congress showed its special solicitude for this area of the CFPB, not only by legislating about it, but also by imposing mandates and treating the issues in so much detail, as well as specifying all the material required to be included in our annual reports.

2. Although the Federal Trade Commission approaches consumer complaints much differently from the constituent service model, its database, called Consumer Sentinel, is invaluable. Every law enforcement agency is encouraged to pour information into it—and the CFPB does as well—and they all can access the data for

purposes of identifying problems and enforcing the law. The public does not have direct access to the data in Consumer Sentinel, but anyone can go to court under the Freedom of Information Act and try to get the data they seek, with the agency having to foot the cost of losing those lawsuits.

3. This was a common path for the type of public office that had gradually grown up from a smaller office into a larger one, mirroring the growth of the state government over more than a century.

4. This approach to complaints made against auto dealers stemmed from a lawsuit the Ohio attorney general's office had filed against the auto dealer association many years earlier. The case was based on the sales of cars that turned out to be lemons, and it turned into a prolonged and bitter battle. Ever since, the auto dealers had asked to address any complaints filed against them as a first step, which the office started doing on a trial basis until the program proved itself to be effective.

5. Sartaj had run Capital One's credit card operations in Canada and thus was highly familiar with such processes. We benefited at the outset because, as a new and largely unknown agency, we did not immediately generate a huge volume of complaints, which gave us more time to work out the kinks.

6. Sartaj Alag, the initial leader of the team, left and later returned to serve with distinction as the chief operating officer. His successor, Scott Pluta, was a thought leader on all aspects of operational design and customized a complaint-handling process and public complaint database that became the envied role model for other government agencies. Before Scott left, he recommended his deputy Chris Johnson to take over the leadership with Darian Dorsey stepping up to be his capable deputy. Chris is as fine a manager of people as I have ever seen, as shown by the flawless execution of the difficult system pivot that was accomplished by Project Mosaic. Members of the consumer response team also helped organize a regular weekly co-ed basketball game, which, for me at least, was a welcome tonic that helped lessen the strain of the long-distance commute.

7. The problem of agency capture is a recognized concern for government agencies that are intended to pursue the public interest in dealing with the power of special interests in a specific field. See George J. Stigler, "The Theory of Economic Regulation," *Bell Journal of Economics and Management Science* 2 (Spring 1971): 3. It is often exacerbated by the revolving door that swings freely between corporate America and many government offices.

8. The thousands of "afterwords" our consumer response team received from people over the years are nicely summed up in one from November 2017: "Thank you for your service to our country and for what you do to make things fairer for those who can't speak loudly enough on their own to be heard by our leaders."

9. In a cruder way, "naming and shaming" is a controversial but long-standing method to obtain compliance with the law, and I had seen it work to some degree at the local level with "Dirty Dozen" lists of tax delinquents. Our database of public complaints was less pointed than those more ham-handed techniques, but it did bring the issue of compliance out into the open as scholars and researchers began to recognize. See, for example, Ian Ayres, Jeff Lingwall, and Sonia Steinway, "Skeletons in the Database: An Early Analysis of the CFPB's Consumer Complaints," *Fordham Journal of Corporate and Financial Law* 19 (2014): 343, 345 ("The results indicate

that in the aggregate, these complaints provide a veritable treasure trove of data for assessing the work of the Bureau and the companies under its watch.").

10. An interesting example of this phenomenon has to do with the economic data that clouded the picture around the 1992 campaign where Bill Clinton defeated George H. W. Bush. At the time, the country was believed to be in a recession, which spawned the famous campaign slogan "It's the economy, stupid!" But when the data were run and rerun and then further revised years after the fact, it turned out that the recession had ended in March 1991 and gross domestic product growth for all of 1992 exceeded 4%, a very high number that differed greatly from the initial data (and thus the perceptions) at the time. See Federal Reserve Bank of St. Louis, Economic Data, Gross Domestic Product.

11. The Wells Fargo mess over opening fake accounts, discussed in chapter 12, is a vivid example of how such things can happen. Over time, we learned that some banks were adjusting executive compensation to factor in internal complaint handling and how the bank stacked up against its peers in our database. We also learned that in some banks, these areas were getting more favorable treatment of their budget requests to upgrade their systems and hire more people.

12. Notably, the consumer complaint system does not affect the many thousands of small community banks and credit unions, who fall below the statutory threshold of $10 billion in bank assets to be subject to direct oversight by the bureau.

13. This was partly because the natural reaction at lower levels of the corporate hierarchy is to want to try to fix a problem before reporting it "up the chain," which means having to deal with the fallout that would inevitably follow.

14. This is the Deborah whose story was told in chapter 2, up to the point of her frustrating impasse and prior to the point where the bureau intervened on her behalf. See Massimo Calabresi, "The Agency That's Got Your Back," *Time*, August 24, 2015.

CHAPTER 6

1. The pipeline was not entirely empty. A group of attorneys from the Department of Housing and Urban Development (HUD) who joined the bureau brought with them about a dozen relatively minor matters—but including, as it turned out, the noteworthy *PHH* case, discussed in chapter 13, which ultimately generated a dangerous constitutional challenge to the CFPB. We also landed some excellent attorneys from the Federal Trade Commission who brought many ideas for potential consumer finance cases that they could not pursue previously because of the statutory limitations on that agency.

2. See Bagehot's Notebook, "The Governor's Eyebrows: Nudging the Financial Crisis," *Economist*, May 25, 2009, and Jonathan R. Macey, Geoffrey P. Miller, and Richard Scott Carnell, "Examination and Enforcement," in *Banking Law and Regulation* 3rd ed. (Aspen: Aspen Law and Business 2001).

3. This somewhat unwieldy division ultimately encompassed half the people at the bureau and was known as "SEFL," short for Supervision, Enforcement, and Fair Lending. Initially, two counterparts set up the supervision team: Steve Antonakes, who had served as the Massachusetts banking commissioner, was in charge of

supervising the banks, and Peggy Twohig, who had served as the FTC's top enforcement attorney in consumer finance, was in charge of supervising all the non-bank financial companies. During the first year, I led the enforcement team and Patrice Ficklin led the fair lending team.

4. One big change we made over time was to jettison our initial decision to divide our supervision work into "bank" versus "nonbank" oversight, with separate personnel and separate processes. Since our statute intended for us to eliminate this distinction as much as possible, we shifted our approach, determined to treat the two types of companies in the same ways, as they competed against one another in the same markets—including mortgages, auto lending, student loans, and others.

5. Congress had stressed the importance of this work to carry out the ECOA by creating an Office of Fair Lending within the bureau, which we reinforced by providing it with supervision and enforcement staff. We emphasized the significance of this work, and the team helped me prepare a major address to commemorate the 40th anniversary of the passage of the ECOA, which stressed the importance of economic rights in securing civil rights for all Americans. I delivered the speech at my alma mater, Michigan State University, in October 2014. This functional organization for enforcing the fair lending laws was later dismantled, as described in chapter 15.

6. Part of the initial awkwardness we faced in working together was that our fair lending team can resolve matters either by supervision or by enforcement, but the Department of Justice can only bring enforcement actions. Nonetheless, Patrice Ficklin and the rest of our fair lending team invariably managed to surmount the process issues and get results because of the trust they built with the Justice Department's Civil Rights Division—led first by Tom Perez, then by Vanita Gupta.

7. The action against GE Capital resulted in consumer remediation of $169 million for about 108,000 cardholders. In the action against American Express, we found that the bank had also charged higher fees and interest rates and offered less advantageous terms to Puerto Rican customers, all of which produced $95 million in consumer restitution for over 220,000 cardholders who were harmed. Both banks agreed to adopt compliance plans to ensure no future discrimination against consumers with a Spanish-language preference. The bureau imposed no penalties, however, because each bank self-reported the violations—a practice we were trying to encourage among the companies we oversaw.

8. The special difficulties we faced in pursuing our broader objective of rooting out discrimination in auto lending are described and analyzed more fully in chapter 12.

9. Unfortunately, as sometimes happened, the court's review of the interesting factual issues underlying our claims was delayed when they were caught up in preliminary skirmishes over constitutional challenges to the CFPB's structure.

10. During my six years leading the bureau, our cooperation with the state attorneys general was extremely close. Sometimes we took the lead, sometimes they did, and much of our work was truly collaborative. We recognized that by aggregating our resources, we could cover far more of the almost limitless terrain of consumer law enforcement. The systemic underenforcement of consumer laws is a recurrent problem and is a subset of a larger problem in law enforcement generally. See Public Rights Project, "Voices from the Corporate Enforcement Gap" (July 2019).

Distinct strategies for deploying limited resources to enforce consumer laws at the federal and state level have also received insightful attention. See Prentiss Cox, Amy Widman, and Mark Totten, "Strategies of Public UDAP Enforcement," *Harvard Journal on Legislation* 55 (2018): 37.

11. One unusual feature of the bureau's supervisory authority is that it is not directly linked to any authority to revoke a company's license or charter. Yet because of the strong web of related authorities granted to the bureau, and the close coordination that soon emerged between us and other federal and state regulators, this missing link did not seem to undermine our effectiveness.

12. The role of state officials to police the front lines and protect consumers, even or perhaps especially in an era when the federal government is in retreat, is taken up in chapter 15, where it is discussed as one aspect of the consequences flowing from the recent transition in the CFPB's leadership.

13. These matters were discussed in chapter 4. They grew out of supervisory examinations, but the violations were so plain and the liability so great that it seemed totally inappropriate to keep them confidential, so all our orders were issued publicly. In determining when a potentially confidential supervisory matter would be resolved as a public enforcement action, one key criterion was the size of the monetary amounts at stake. Under the securities laws, the banks and most other financial companies would be forced to disclose any "material" resolution to the public in any event.

14. With the credit card add-on matters, we were fortunate in one respect. To their credit, Capital One told us they were embarrassed by what the audiotapes showed about how the vendors marketed the products. Their CEO, Rich Fairbank, made the tough decision to discontinue any further sale of these products, even though we had not mandated that result, because he judged it to be the safest course going forward. Some of the other banks seemed less convinced that they needed to discontinue this practice, but I don't believe any of the other banks recommenced selling these products during my tenure.

15. As we continued to mature, I suggested to the team in one of my weekly messages that we were having to develop a Griffin—a creature from Greek mythology that was part eagle and part lion, combining the best parts of the king of the birds and the king of the beasts. It was a fanciful allusion, but it captured the difficulty of the project.

16. I first learned that companies often know best what bad practices their competitors are engaged in when I was working to enforce even-handed property tax collection in local government. Virtually no business owner enjoys paying taxes, but what they hate most of all is the thought that someone else—especially a competitor—could be getting away with *not* paying them. The same lesson applied here as well.

17. When I became the CFPB director, the position of enforcement chief went to my deputy, Kent Markus, who is an accomplished leader—he implemented big parts of the Crime Bill for the Justice Department in the Clinton administration, including putting 100,000 additional cops on the street—and he grew the enforcement team to around 150 people. He later gave way to Tony Alexis, who also was a respected alum of the Justice Department and a former federal prosecutor, and then eventually to his deputy, Kristen Donoghue. Kent's deputy for several years was

Hunter Wiggins, who devised many creative strategies, including the complex multiparty legal moves that resulted in hundreds of millions of dollars in loan forgiveness for students victimized by the misconduct of several for-profit colleges. Each of these leaders was consistently forceful about the work we were doing to protect consumers.

18. In the same publication, we would also summarize our latest enforcement actions, which had already been made public when they occurred, so all the latest information about consumer finance violations would be readily available in a single source. It was a valuable working guide for compliance officers and lawyers to use in assessing practices at their own financial institutions.

19. When Steve Antonakes became the deputy director, he continued to serve in the role of associate director for SEFL, which was a heavy load. When Steve later left the bureau, his position as the head of SEFL was filled by Chris D'Angelo, who as the bureau's chief of staff had played a central role in working through the bureau's priority-setting process. At that point, the deputy director post went to David Silberman, who bore a similar load as he continued to oversee the bureau's market monitoring and rulemaking work, as discussed in chapter 7.

20. Ocwen was a rare case of a company that failed to comply with the terms of a prior CFPB order. Its failure reflected the enormous difficulties it faced in making the deep systemic changes that were needed to overhaul its operations. In one other case, involving the auto lender SNACC, we found that the company committed fraud in complying with our order by issuing worthless "credits" to hundreds of consumers and failing to provide the required compensation to others. We penalized this transgression heavily, and it served as a deterrent to others.

21. A famous judicial observation, quoted in the Justice Manual devised by the US Department of Justice, makes this very point, as so many courts have done in both civil and criminal cases: "The law does not define fraud; it needs no definition; it is as old as falsehood and as versatile as human ingenuity." *Weiss v. United States*, 122 F.2d 675, 681 (5th Cir.), *cert. denied*, 314 U.S. 687 (1941).

22. The survey, undertaken by one of our enforcement attorneys who is also a law professor, was based on a comprehensive review of every public enforcement action taken by the CFPB during its first four years. See Christopher Lewis Peterson, "Consumer Financial Protection Bureau Law Enforcement: An Empirical Review," *Tulane Law Review* 90 (2016): 1057. Among its noteworthy findings are that virtually all consumer relief obtained by the bureau was awarded in cases where we uncovered evidence that the defendants had illegally deceived consumers, and virtually all consumer relief was obtained in cases where we did not act unilaterally but instead collaborated with other state or federal law enforcement partners.

23. This understanding of how cases set precedents reflects the way the law has always worked. For example, the narrow holding of the *Brown* desegregation case on its face only applied to the Topeka school district, yet it was universally recognized that the constitutional requirements imposed in that case would have to be met by *all* school districts across the country, even though a considerable number of them initially resisted this outcome.

24. The successive editions of "Supervisory Highlights" do not always specify the total amounts of monetary relief that went to consumers through nonpublic supervisory

actions. But from the reports issued during my tenure, these actions appear to have produced hundreds of millions of dollars more in compensation, along with substantial amounts of nonmonetary relief, to over 3.6 million additional consumers.

CHAPTER 7

1. Raj liked nothing better than to review corporate filings before meeting with executives, who often found that he knew nearly as much about their business as they did. Not only did he speak their language, but also he had produced a set of influential papers on topics in consumer finance during his time leading the Cambridge Winter Center for Financial Institutions Policy, a nonprofit organization dedicated to fostering a rational, informed discourse of policy toward financial institutions.

2. Only two other federal agencies—the Environmental Protection Agency and the Occupational Safety and Health Administration—are currently subject to this same elongation of the rulemaking process.

3. The CFPB began assessing the credit card market in mandatory biennial reports to Congress, and we found that the CARD Act and new rules were greatly beneficial to consumers, fixing many problems and saving people billions of dollars each year. The JD Power consumer satisfaction surveys showed a steady positive trend in how consumers viewed the performance of these companies, and other factors were in play as well. Many companies became more responsive to their customers by adopting "net promoter score" indexes ("based on your experience, would you recommend this company to others?") to evaluate their call center personnel. This worked much better than numerical goals, which put pressure on staff to rush customers off the line as soon as possible, as we noted when we visited a facility in South Dakota. In addition, coming out of the Great Recession, consumers reduced their default rates as they modified their own behavior and became more cautious in using credit cards. This unusual "trifecta" of improvements on the part of government, companies, and consumers showed that progress can be made in consumer finance markets in the right combination of circumstances, which was heartening. If it could happen in this market, then it could happen in other markets as well.

4. The World Bank estimates remittances by country each year. Five years later, in 2017, it projected that Americans were sending about $67 billion "overseas" (though that includes huge outflows to Latin America), with about $6 billion in inflows. See World Bank Group, "Migration and Remittances: Recent Developments and Outlook," Tables on Outward Migrant Remittance Flows and Migrant Remittance Inflows, 2019. Yet the CFPB's data for that same year, which may be substantially more complete, pegged the US market for remittances at $175 billion, based on 325 million transactions. See CFPB, "Remittance Rule Assessment Report, Executive Summary," October 2018.

5. The largest US remittance provider, Western Union, took to heart our challenge that they show themselves to be industry leaders in conforming to the new rule. They came back several times to walk us through all the work they were doing to meet the revised deadlines, which underscored for us how much effort is needed to adjust to new regulations. The five years of data about the tentative effects of the

remittance rule are set out in the Executive Summary of the CFPB's "Remittance Rule Assessment Report."

6. A broad group of people pitched in to work up these rules, but the leadership was the key to figuring it all out and delivering workable rules on time. David Silberman, the original head of our credit card team, stepped up to become the new head of the RMR group after Raj became the deputy director. David brought incredible intellect and a relentless work ethic to the mortgage project, while Raj remained heavily involved. First Pat McCoy (a law professor who had written about the housing crisis) and then Pete Carroll (who was a mortgage industry entrepreneur prior to the crisis) led the mortgage markets team that performed much of the underlying market analysis. Ron Borzekowski, who had helped Congress analyze the causes of the financial crisis, headed up the team of research economists. Kelly Cochran led the rule-writing team, and her rare combination of professional conscientiousness and personal kindness helped the team deal with the extreme demands of the situation.

7. This temporary provision, commonly known as the "GSE patch," was crucial to provide more latitude for lenders. It was set to expire either in 2021 or when Fannie Mae and Freddie Mac (the "government-sponsored enterprises," or GSEs) emerged from conservatorship, where they had landed after they cratered in the wake of the financial crisis. As years passed with no action from Congress on reforming these entities, it became clear that the bureau would need to consider further whether to extend the patch beyond 2021, and to reassess the pros and cons for the housing and mortgage markets.

8. Perhaps the most resounding compliment came from our fellow regulators. Congress required several other agencies jointly to adopt an important mortgage rule confusingly known as "QRM" (qualified residential mortgages) as opposed to our "QM" (qualified mortgage) rule. Their rule would require mortgage lenders to maintain "skin in the game" by retaining some risk on the loans they made. But after carefully considering the contents of our rule, the other agencies decided not to adopt the QRM rule, saying they thought our rule adequately addressed the underlying problems. They garnered some criticism for that, but not much.

9. The "Know Before You Owe" rule for mortgage loans is discussed more fully in chapter 9.

10. Another way we sought to provide more clarity in consumer financial law was by filing "friend-of-the-court" briefs in cases that raised difficult or contested points of legal interpretation. We did so in many cases—most often on debt collection issues, but also on issues of mortgage servicing, credit reporting, fair lending, foreclosures, payday lending, and the Truth in Lending Act.

11. This rule, which amended regulations issued under the Home Mortgage Disclosure Act, accompanied a major operational change to move the process of collecting and publishing mortgage data from the Federal Reserve to the bureau—a transition that some lenders worried would layer on even more unwelcome burdens. The systems upgrade turned out to be a bright spot, as improved technology eased compliance burdens for reporting lenders and made the data much more accessible for end-users and the public. Indeed, the team's work on this project won awards for innovative government technologies.

12. These rules on new consumer protections for prepaid cards, arbitration of consumer disputes, and underwriting restrictions on payday loans generated fierce opposition from the banks and financial firms that would be affected, and the stories of those political and legal fights are told in chapter 14. One discretionary rule that we resisted, though it was constantly urged on us, was to write a regulation to define the term "abusive," even though it is already defined explicitly in the Dodd-Frank Act.

13. Although large banks and financial firms prefer more detail, they often chided us in public for being out-of-touch bureaucrats, given the length of our rules, and they usually skewed the math by counting not just the text of our rules but all the pages of our comment summaries and supportive analysis as well. But behind the scenes, they constantly peppered us with questions seeking more detailed guidance, and they were dissatisfied if we failed to provide actionable answers in writing—answers, you might say, that they could "take to the bank." The total volume did not much concern them, because their computer processes for automating compliance are so powerful that the added weight is largely incidental.

14. Even as the heavy burdens of our rulemaking calendar put a strain on the research team, they were also involved with many other aspects of our work. In fair lending enforcement actions, they provided the close statistical analysis needed to justify taking enforcement actions, devising appropriate remedies, and making them stick. They also took part in most key meetings, to assess and call out any flaws or biases in our approach.

15. This school of economics builds in more realistic assumptions about how people behave and make economic decisions in the real world, recognizing that people operate on imperfect information and have human shortcomings that are sometimes predictable and systematic. As Professor Thaler has put it, we should base our models on actual "Humans," not hypothetical "Econs" who know everything and always behave rationally. We found this approach persuasive, and it has moved well into the mainstream of modern economic theory.

16. Working with the consumer credit panel, our economists did innovative research on "credit invisibles" to highlight the millions of Americans who have either no credit profile at all or a profile that is too skimpy to allow them to qualify for credit of any kind. The practical point of this research, which is discussed further in chapter 10, was to help us better understand what holds people back from enjoying the benefits of credit and how it might be possible to empower consumers on a broader scale.

17. Macroeconomics seeks to explain the overall economy, whereas microeconomics focuses on individual economic behavior. Yet the microeconomics I learned as a student was focused primarily on the "theory of the firm," explaining how businesses operate and make decisions about hiring, contracting, producing, and the like. What was missing in that theoretical universe was a corresponding focus on the "theory of the household," of how consumers make decisions and why. Our work at the CFPB demonstrated that individual consumer behavior not only helps drive people's personal welfare but also, taken in the aggregate, can have a big impact on the direction of the economy. After all, consumer spending makes up about two-thirds of total domestic spending in our economy, and it cannot safely be ignored by presuming it will always be a stable and predictable element of that economy.

18. These are classic externalities that economists recognize as one category of market failures that can justify some form of market interventions to try to correct for the resulting distortions.

19. These dynamics of the marketplace, or of other social and political organizations for that matter, are insightfully analyzed in a famous treatise. See Albert O. Hirschman, *Exit, Voice, and Loyalty* (Cambridge: Harvard University Press 1970).

CHAPTER 8

1. Several groups make it a point to call out how well or poorly each state is faring on financial education. See Champlain College, "National Report Card on State Efforts to Improve Financial Literacy in High Schools." Its latest report card in 2017 shows some movement both forward and backward among the states, but little overall progress. The Council for Economic Education began publishing its *Survey of the States* every two years beginning in 1998. Although the 2018 report found slow to no growth in financial education, there were bright spots—in 1998, only one state required students to enroll in a personal finance course, but now Michigan, Georgia, Utah, and Texas are leading the way by requiring personal finance and economics courses to be taken and by implementing state standards and standardized testing.

2. One obvious way to ensure that all students receive personal finance education thus would be to build these topics into civics education, which is already required in every state but could be broadened to include the study of our rights and duties and capabilities in the economic as well as the political sphere.

3. See Teresa A. Sullivan, Elizabeth Warren, and Jay Lawrence Westbrook, *As We Forgive Our Debtors: Bankruptcy and Consumer Credit in America* (New York: Oxford University Press 1989); Teresa A. Sullivan, Elizabeth Warren, and Jay Lawrence Westbrook, *The Fragile Middle Class: Americans in Debt* (New Haven: Yale University Press 2000).

4. Offerings for personal finance education in different states, and within states, can vary dramatically. The spectrum ranges from merely making it available to students as an elective, to folding it in the curriculum designed for other subjects (usually math or social studies), to requiring a stand-alone course as a condition for high school graduation, to insisting on testing to ensure that students can meet fixed proficiency standards. Obviously, some approaches do not ensure that a given student will receive financial training at all. Any alternative that does not require all students to learn about finances, in some manner, is likely to be inadequate to prepare young people for the rigors of managing their own affairs.

5. When I was in local government, for example, we arranged for FDIC personnel to train teachers on how to use the Money Smart program, which was a big hit. Little did I know that later, as the CFPB director, I would serve on the FDIC board as we expanded the program to Money Smart for Adults. Where we could, we also synthesized work done by others. During President Obama's first term, he convened an Advisory Council on Financial Literacy, chaired by John Rogers, a well-known investment adviser. John recruited Beth Kobliner, a financial writer, who

built an excellent website called MoneyAsYouGrow.org, with content and activities for parents and caregivers. After the council issued its final report, they generously allowed us to incorporate this website as one of our financial education resources at the bureau. They also asked us to join the council ourselves, which we did, and we did so again during the president's second term.

6. The report, called "Navigating the Market," was published in November 2013. About two-thirds of the total annual spending was for direct marketing of products to get consumers to make an immediate purchase, and about one-third was for awareness advertisements that generally promote financial services. In the report, we observed that this great disparity in resources reinforced the need for the CFPB and others to provide more high-quality sources of unbiased financial information to consumers.

7. A profound and related question is always the issue of how knowledge affects behavior. It is one thing to know more about how to conduct our affairs, but it is another thing entirely to have the discipline to execute on that knowledge in our day-to-day lives. Yet surely there is an important link between the two, and this objection seems more relevant to the "how" of financial education rather than the "whether" and "why." It's an argument for role-playing and practical exercises, rather than just academic training and testing, but it's not an argument for forgoing financial education altogether.

8. See Carly Urban, Maximilian Schmeiser, Michael Collins, and Alexandra Brown, "The Effects of High School Personal Financial Education Policies on Financial Behavior," *Economics of Education Review*, March 2018; Alexandra Brown, Michael Collins, Maximilian Schmeiser, and Carly Urban, "State Mandated Financial Education and the Credit Behavior of Young Adults," Federal Reserve Finance and Economics Discussion Series 2014-68, August 2014. The literature remains mixed, but there is now more data to consider, with more state programs in place and more time to gauge the effects. Nonetheless, further research must take care to distinguish among states based on the strength of implementation of their programs and other meaningful variables, such as teacher training.

9. See Organization for Economic Co-operation and Development, *PISA 2015: Results in Focus, vol. 4, Students' Financial Literacy*. Almost fifty thousand teenagers worldwide took part in the test, which covered subjects from simple decisions on everyday spending to more complex issues such as income tax. Unsurprisingly, US financial literacy was found to be strongly correlated with mathematics and reading performance. As an encouraging note, two states—Massachusetts and North Carolina—piggybacked on the PISA test by collecting their own data for further review.

10. The brunt of this impetus for action was borne by the head of the Consumer Education and Engagement Division, Gail Hillebrand, who had been a leading consumer advocate in California for thirty years. Her division encompassed not only our financial education team but also our offices whose work focused on specialty populations, as described in chapter 10. The Office of Financial Education itself had a small but productive team led first by Camille Busette and then by Janneke Ratcliffe.

11. All these resources remain available for use on the CFPB website at consumerfinance. gov. As of December 2016, "Ask CFPB" had garnered over thirteen million unique visitors.

12. As the FLEC examined the potential for duplication of federal education programs, we found that even the same subjects might be discussed from very different angles—for example, the Department of Labor's discussion of saving for retirement focuses on pension plans and individual 401(k) retirement plans, whereas the Social Security Administration's discussion of the same subject focuses on government benefits, eligibility, claiming, and requirements. Materials on the same general issue such as savings can also be customized effectively for different audiences, such as the military or rural populations.

13. I first encountered what we called the "Reality Days" program at the local level, when it was being presented for students at a high school in Columbus. Some students told us that when their parents heard about it, they wondered if similar programs were available for adults. The credit unions have become major backers of "reality fairs" and have helped spread them all over the country.

CHAPTER 9

1. Over decades, the mushrooming of disclosures had led to a sea of paper that people tend to ignore or just throw away. In the internet age, we are all familiar with the exasperation we feel with endless online verbiage that drives us to say "I agree" just to accept all the contract terms, regardless of whether we realistically can digest or understand them.

2. Our streamlining efforts did pay off in some respects. They led to the rule amending the "ability to repay" credit card provisions that addressed eligibility issues for stay-at-home spouses as described in chapter 4. They also led to changes we made in 2014 that lessened the burden for companies of providing annual disclosures of their privacy policies to consumers if the companies limited their sharing of data about consumers, which prompted Congress to take further steps along the same lines. We exempted nonprofits such as Habitat for Humanity from some of our mortgage rules. And we started writing a rule to allow banks to disclose ATM fees on the ATM computer screen rather than affixing a paper sticker to the machine, which led Congress to pass a law in 2013 to the same effect.

3. It was named for Chuck Schumer, the New York representative (and later senator) who sponsored the bill passed to impose these disclosure requirements, which is known as the Fair Credit and Charge Card Disclosure Act of 1988. Although the law was passed in 1988, it did not take effect until twelve years later in 2000.

4. The CARD Act had required every credit card company to submit its cardholder agreement to the Federal Reserve, and we now were assuming that authority, which the Dodd-Frank Act transferred over to the CFPB.

5. Among the criticisms of the Schumer box are that it cannot capture the complexity of terms that are changing over time, such as variable interest rates, and that it does not cover certain features that matter a great deal to consumers, such as the terms of reward programs, which are not required to be presented to consumers in any standardized fashion. See Tim Chen, "The 'Schumer Box' Is Flawed," *Forbes*, October 28, 2010.

6. The Real Estate Settlement Procedures Act (RESPA) had authorized the Department of Housing and Urban Development to produce forms from the

standpoint of the housing industry, and the Truth in Lending Act (TILA) had authorized the Federal Reserve to produce forms from the standpoint of the mortgage lending industry.

7. I only know two people who have ever claimed to have read through the entire stack of closing documents—my local congressman and the head of the Ohio Bankers League—and both said the upshot was that it annoyed everyone involved and wasted a lot of time.

8. Some of the critics mistakenly believed that if anything at all changed between the issuance of the Closing Disclosure and the execution of the loan, the closing date would have to be postponed. This was wrong, so we produced a one-page sheet for mass distribution with the three limited reasons that a closing date would have to be pushed back: (1) any significant increase in the mortgage rate (one-eighth of a percentage point for a fixed-rate loan and one-quarter of a percentage point for an adjustable-rate loan); (2) the addition of a prepayment penalty; or (3) a material change in the loan product (such as from a fixed-rate loan to an adjustable-rate loan). Any other changes could be handled without having to adjust timelines.

9. The opponents of the new rule were not subtle. Although we preferred to refer to it as the "Know Before You Owe" rule, its formal name was the "TILA-RESPA Integrated Disclosure" rule. Some stakeholders shortened that to "TRID" and gleefully pointed out that it was "dirt" spelled backward. For our part, we recognized the extensive investments that the industry was having to make to alter their application process, tolerance rules, disclosure presentations, closing process, and more. These investments paid dividends for consumers and the health of the mortgage market, which benefited everyone.

10. Spiraling student loan debt has now decoupled from the other categories and is clearly the second largest of these markets behind mortgages, at about $1.6 trillion—and climbing. A growing number of legislative proposals have been introduced to try to curb the problem.

11. We also were under a special disability here because Congress had carved out auto dealers from our jurisdiction altogether. Some of the unfortunate consequences of that exemption are explored more fully in chapter 12.

12. The Federal Reserve, contrary to its traditional instincts, had finally determined from consumer testing that one pricing concept for credit cards—known as double-cycle billing—was so inherently complex that no disclosures could make it comprehensible for consumers, and hence the Fed had banned its use.

13. Of course, financial companies are always free to compete in the marketplace by offering simpler products or shorter, clearer disclosures, but it is telling that few do, and these markets have not shifted to a new equilibrium reflecting such an evolution. An interesting comparison can be made here to competition in the airline industry, where one carrier—Southwest—has consciously adopted a strategy of offering simpler and clearer pricing and services with no unpleasant surprises as a way to attract customers, which it has dubbed "transfarency." Its aggressive advertising around this concept clearly reflects its view that customers will be attracted by this approach.

CHAPTER 10

1. The champion of this project, José Quiñonez, chaired our consumer advisory board for a time and later won a genius grant from the MacArthur Foundation for his innovative work.
2. Under Mayor Michael Bloomberg, New York City's consumer chief Jonathan Mintz started an initiative and continued it after he left office to build and extend a nationwide network known as Cities for Financial Empowerment. It is developing municipal efforts to protect and empower consumers, with special emphasis on banking the unbanked, promoting savings, and providing financial education for young people. Within the bureau, Chris Vaeth and then Keo Chea led our outreach efforts to consumer groups, and Dan Smith led our outreach to financial institutions.
3. Given the CFPB's protracted rulemaking process, we ended up holding four field hearings on payday lending—in Birmingham, Nashville, Richmond, and Kansas City—making it our most prevalent topic. The format and strong response were pretty much the same in each location. Zixta Martinez, who led our External Affairs Division, sited the venues, ran the hearings, and managed the format; our media team, headed by Jennifer Howard, helped shape my messaging for the bureau and provided the driving impetus to get all the pieces prepared for each hearing.
4. The military leadership recognized their significant stake in addressing consumer financial protection issues, because of the time and expense involved in recruiting, training, and promoting their large corps of officers. Every officer whose security clearance was jeopardized created a readiness issue, or if the clearance had to be revoked because of financial troubles, then the Pentagon had to incur all the costs of replacing that officer with someone else.
5. One problem for many military homeowners was that the programs put in place to help struggling mortgage borrowers often required them to become delinquent in order to qualify for assistance. This was not an option for active-duty military, as a delinquency would jeopardize their required security clearance.
6. We paid for this joint program in part out of our civil penalty fund, which was possible because educating consumers is a proper use of the fund and we were using the money to support financial coaching for the military and their families.
7. The "Paying for College" project is described more completely in chapter 9.
8. Our work to promote the program centered on recruiting cities and school districts to take a pledge to inform all employees about this option for tackling their student loans, along with other options such as income-based repayment. In our initial efforts, we were joined by the Richmond Public Schools and the City of South Bend, where "Mayor Pete" Buttigieg set an example by pushing the program among city employees.
9. In 2016, we published a bulletin specifying that the only clear way to comply with the law requiring public disclosure of college credit card marketing agreements is to publish these agreements on the college website. As for college banking services agreements, after the bureau leadership changed hands in 2017, the CFPB stopped reporting on them altogether, even though they pose clear costs and risks for students.

10. Our work with law enforcement to protect seniors against financial exploitation got a boost because our first leader, Skip Humphrey, was the former Minnesota attorney general. After Skip left, he was succeeded by Nora Dowd Eisenhower and then Stacy Canan.

11. The sociologist David Caplovitz laid out the financial difficulties and frequent outrages that low-income consumers face, in terms that resound a half-century later. The sales-and-credit system for the low-income consumer, as he documented it, "is not only different from the larger, more formal economy; in some respects it is a deviant system in which practices that violate prevailing moral standards are commonplace." David Caplovitz, *The Poor Pay More* (New York: Free Press 1967): 30.

12. The Community Reinvestment Act of 1977 was intended to encourage depository institutions to help meet the credit needs of low- and moderate-income neighborhoods, but its effects have been limited as it only modestly constrains the banks to provide such support. Our financial empowerment work was led by Cliff Rosenthal, who had worked with community development financial institutions nationwide, and then by Daniel Dodd-Ramirez, who had done community and social services work in Savannah, Georgia. Asset building and other means to strengthen the financial futures of families and communities are well canvassed in *What It's Worth*, a set of articles that the Federal Reserve Bank of San Francisco and the Corporation for Enterprise Development published jointly in 2015.

13. The FDIC has made a dent in the problem by addressing it in their annual reports and pressing more banks to offer "Safe Bank Accounts." In some other countries— the Scandinavian countries, Canada, Australia, and New Zealand—the entire population is banked. Worldwide, the unbanked population is declining fast, as more than a billion people have become banked over the past decade. See World Bank, "The Global Findex Database: Measuring Financial Inclusion and the Fintech Revolution," 2017. Another more amorphous problem that the FDIC has identified is the "underbanked," who have bank accounts but rely on many alternative sources for financial services. These lines are being blurred with the rise of the "fintech" providers, which are finding new and innovative ways to deliver financial services, including those provided by banks and credit unions. Prepaid accounts and prepaid cards, which are now widely available and are a functional substitute for bank accounts in many respects, are discussed in chapter 14.

14. In line with our general orientation to simplify consumer disclosures, we strongly emphasized plain language in all our consumer-facing materials. We sought to ensure that our information would be more readily comprehensible by keeping it within most recommended guidelines by producing it at an eighth-grade reading level. Our teams won several ClearMark awards from the Center for Plain Language, including top honors for our "Planning for Retirement" tool and one of our "Know Before You Owe" mortgage disclosure forms. Translation of our materials was important as a matter of public access and we translated as much as we could, as fast as we could, especially into Spanish, which is the second-most widely used language by US consumers.

15. These tools and resources are described much more fully in chapter 8. Sometimes our profile was raised in ways we could not control. In November 2015, for example,

a political action committee that did not have to disclose its donors stated that it was spending at least $500,000 on a television ad campaign. The ads inaccurately portrayed the CFPB as a kind of Communist bureaucracy intent on interfering with consumer choice and denying people loans.

CHAPTER 11

1. One issue where we drew criticism was data collection, a point of special concern for Senator Mike Crapo of Idaho, who at times was the ranking member (and later the chair) of the Senate Banking Committee. He and others questioned our efforts to collect and organize data on consumer finance markets based on concerns about privacy and the security of the data. Once we showed them that we typically worked with anonymized data about consumers as a group, rather than personal information that identified individuals, and after an audit concluded that our data security processes were satisfactory, their concerns were largely allayed.

2. See, for example, Christopher Lewis Peterson and Steven A. Graves, "Predatory Lending and the Military: The Law and Geography of 'Payday' Loans in Military Towns," *Ohio State Law Journal* 66 (2005): 653.

3. The first part of Ari's story was told in chapter 1, up to the point where his father found himself stymied. The wide-ranging results of the CFPB's intervention in response to the consumer complaint filed by Ari's father are related here as the rest of the story.

4. In 2016, an article in a military magazine noted that servicemembers, veterans, and their families often are vulnerable "to predatory financial practices" and described the crucial protection that the CFPB's Office of Servicemember Affairs is providing as it "watches their backs." See Christina Wood, "Easy Targets No More," *Military Officer*, December 2016.

5. On Capitol Hill, the financial lobbyists seemed to realize that to oppose protections for servicemembers and their families is largely futile. But under the radar, a fierce battle raged to limit the scope of the new rules, especially the potential effects on credit cards, which by some measures can exceed rates of 36% depending on how one calculates fees and charges as distinct from the interest rates themselves. The trust between the Pentagon and our team was strong enough to hold the line against the opposition.

6. Sometimes exposing bad practices was enough to clean them up. For example, many borrowers have co-signers on their student loans, perhaps a parent or grandparent. If the co-signer dies, we found that some companies considered that a default and called in the loans. That was not against the law, but it was certainly an unappealing practice. When we issued a report describing their callous treatment of borrowers who had just lost loved ones, all the companies denied it. We knew the truth, having investigated the facts, but once we called them out for this practice, they stopped it immediately.

7. Rodney's story was told in chapter 1, up until the point where he discovered that he was a frustrated victim of fraud, unable to see a clear path ahead with his education and his career goals.

8. This was partly a phenomenon created by the "90-10" rule, which requires for-profit colleges to derive at least 10% of their revenue from alternative sources other than federal financial aid sources. Oddly, however, educational benefits earned by military service are defined as an alternative source rather than a federal financial aid source—making this revenue an especially valuable component of the financial plans for any for-profit college. Our efforts to get Congress to change this definition were unavailing.

9. This domino effect of mounting student loan debt on housing, household formation, business startups, and retirement savings is discussed in chapter 1. Since the CFPB first raised the issue in 2013, it has received further attention from economists at the Federal Reserve. See Zachary Bleemer, Meta Brown, Donghoon Lee, and Wilbert van der Klaauw, "Debt, Jobs, or Housing: What's Keeping Millennials at Home?," Federal Reserve Bank of New York Staff Report No. 700, March 2015; Brent W. Ambrose, Larry Cordell, and Shuwei Ma, "The Impact of Student Loan Debt on Small Business Formation," Federal Reserve Bank of Philadelphia Working Paper No. 15-26, July 2015.

10. "Safe harbors" are an interesting regulatory approach. They do not mandate conduct, but they provide assurances that if companies follow the terms outlined, they will have a "safe harbor" from being pursued by the regulator and often also gain immunity from private lawsuits. That creates strong incentives to comply. A major point of contention in our ability-to-repay mortgage underwriting rule was when lenders that followed its terms by making a "qualified mortgage" would obtain a "safe harbor" from being sued (or instead would obtain only a "rebuttable presumption" of compliance if they were sued). Although mortgage lenders could not point to a single lawsuit brought in the first three years after the rule took effect, they continued to insist that the "rebuttable presumption" provided inadequate assurances to incentivize them to offer such loans. Regarding the FCC, the initial idea for the "Know Before You Owe" initiative on cable and phone bills was pushed by Previn Warren at the CFPB, and when it later bore fruit, Evan White coordinated the partnership to make it happen.

11. A study of the effects of consumers receiving email communications about the availability of their credit score concluded that this intervention significantly reduced late payments and increased their credit scores. It also seemed to improve the accuracy of consumer perceptions about their credit scores. See Tatiana Homonoff, Rourke O'Brien, and Abigail Sussman, "Does Knowing Your FICO Score Change Financial Behavior? Evidence from a Field Experiment with Student Loan Borrowers," NBER Working Paper No. 26048, July 2019.

12. Current developments seem to be producing an extended moment of the kind described by the Austrian economist Joseph Schumpeter, where new technologies are creating unprecedented waves of creative destruction. Various moats and walls that previously protected stodgy rent seekers in our economy are being breached or entirely overcome. But in the financial marketplace, many providers may well manage to withstand the siege. One especially impressive innovation, for example, was achieved by the Clearing House, a consortium of larger banks that invested heavily to develop a faster payments system after devoting several years of work to the project. The result is a real-time payments network that accords with a set of

principles the CFPB formulated to ensure that any updated system would embody consumer-friendly safeguards and protections.

13. The leader of Project Catalyst was Dan Quan, who was largely responsible for forging relationships we built with the fintech community. Most companies seem focused on doing things right and were seeking more clarity about how to apply existing rules to products and services with novel features. Whether their initial dedication to "doing the right thing" will survive as the companies grow and evolve to confront the pressures of the competitive market is less clear and certainly is not dependable in each case.

CHAPTER 12

1. The issue of auto lending discrimination and how it arises was first raised in chapter 1, and our fair lending responsibilities, including our auto lending case against Ally Bank, were discussed in chapter 6.

2. In addition to prohibiting discrimination in offering credit, the Equal Credit Opportunity Act's regulations also have an affirmative provision that authorizes creditors to offer special purpose credit programs as a proactive way to extend *more* credit to protected classes of persons who are otherwise likely to be refused credit or to receive it on less favorable terms than other consumers. 12 C.F.R. 1002.8. This provision has promise as one way to help augment access to credit, and it has been utilized by nonprofit organizations and some lenders. We made halting efforts to encourage companies to consider how they could make use of special purpose credit programs to expand credit to disadvantaged groups.

3. The Supreme Court case was *Texas Dept. of Housing & Community Affairs v. Inclusive Communities Project, Inc.*, 135 S. Ct. 2507 (2015). I was especially surprised by the ruling, since after clerking for Justice White, I had served as one of Justice Kennedy's first law clerks and later personally argued seven cases before the court. After the case was argued, as we strategized its likely effects, I told our team there was no chance the court would uphold our position, but it turned out I was wrong.

4. The industry is grounded on the fundamental definition of the concept of "credit." In evaluating whether consumers are "creditworthy," in the sense of being willing and able to repay money lent to them, the industry's data typically encompasses only funds fronted to consumers and later repaid by them (such as mortgages, credit card debt, auto loans, and the like). It does not typically account for other ongoing financial obligations that may feel very similar to consumers (rent, utilities, insurance) and thus may be just as indicative of whether they are good credit risks. Nonetheless, because defaults on these other obligations do tend to get reported as uncollected debt, credit reporting can lead to one-sided treatment of these other categories, focusing only on negative rather than positive credit history. As the companies are expanding the data they collect, including court judgments, traditional lines are becoming blurred and these basic concepts are being reconsidered and updated, which should be largely but not entirely beneficial for consumers.

5. For many years, the courts struggled to evolve from a position of no liability for such physical injuries to consumers, to liability based on negligence, to liability without

fault. California Supreme Court Justice Traynor was instrumental in championing these advances in the law. See Roger J. Traynor, "The Ways and Meanings of Defective Products and Strict Liability," *Tennessee Law Review* 32 (1965): 363. But rousing the public often requires exposing abuses, as was done by pioneering consumer lawyer Ralph Nader in his book, *Unsafe at Any Speed*, and in his advocacy for the recall of the Ford Pinto due to demonstrated dangers of fire from the location of its fuel tank, which at the time was the largest recall (1.5 million vehicles) ordered by the National Highway Traffic Safety Administration in US automotive history.

6. Two months after New York reached this resolution, the Ohio attorney general and thirty of his colleagues wrapped up a separate investigation of the credit reporting companies with an agreed order that imposed more controls on data furnishers, new protections for consumers who dispute their information, and limits on direct-to-consumer marketing. Their enforcement work provided leverage that helped us make further advances (and helped ensure these measures were being carried out properly) through the steady pressure of our supervisory oversight.

7. The open credit score initiative and its effects on consumers were discussed more fully in chapter 11. Part of the impetus for the three largest credit reporting companies to move in this direction came from enforcement actions we brought against them for deceiving customers in marketing credit scores and, with respect to Equifax and TransUnion, for using deceptive marketing to lure consumers into making costly recurring payments to get their credit scores. This was done through "negative option" marketing—free trial periods with automatic enrollment in subscription services if the service is not canceled in time—whose terms were not adequately disclosed to consumers. The combined cost of these violations to the companies was over $20 million.

8. The Fair Debt Collection Practices Act (FDCPA), like many consumer financial laws, represents an attempt to specify and codify some of the conduct that has been judged unfair or deceptive based on many years of experience. Yet it only covers third-party debt collectors, not creditors seeking to collect on their own accounts. And since it was enacted forty years ago, before debt sales were much of a phenomenon, the courts have struggled in resolving whether and how the law applies to debt buyers. Although there is much reason to treat contracted debt collection and collection on purchased debt in the same way—as collecting debts originated by another—the courts have not consistently arrived at that interpretation. In *Henson v. Santander Consumer USA, Inc.*, 137 S. Ct. 1718 (2017), for example, the court held that when a financial company purchases defaulted auto loans from the original lender and attempts to collect on them, it is not a debt collector under the FDCPA.

9. We did not always prevail in these enforcement actions. We pressed several cases with aggressive legal theories against law firms that we believed had filed masses of debt collection cases without meaningful attorney involvement, and in some cases the courts rejected our claims on the ground that we had not presented clear violations of the law.

10. These tools to help people know how to assert their rights against debt collectors were initially devised by Chris Lipsett.

11. The original case decided by a New York federal trial court is *Foti v. NCO Fin. Syst., Inc.*, 424 F. Supp. 2d 643 (S.D.N.Y. 2006). A different approach was taken by

a Minnesota federal trial court in *Zortman v. J.C. Christensen & Assocs., Inc.*, 870 F. Supp. 2d 694 (D. Minn. 2012), and other decisions have also been mixed, leaving debt collectors uncertain how to proceed with any confidence in this situation, and providing impetus for a clear rule to address it.

12. Investigative reporting by newspapers is declining as staffing dwindles and revenues are under challenge from electronic and digital media. Consumer reporting on local television covers some stories, but public exposure of more intricate financial and political scandals remains a key mechanism of effective oversight. We often generated leads for investigations and enforcement actions from facts dug up by enterprising reporters. In other instances, though, merely "breaking the story" might be enough to clean up bad practices that might besmirch a company's reputation with its current and potential customers. As a famed banking expert wrote, "Great firms, with a reputation which they have received from the past, and which they wish to transmit to the future, cannot be guilty of small frauds. They live by a *continuity* of trade, which detected frauds would spoil." Walter Bagehot, "Introductory," in *Lombard Street* (London: Henry S. King and Company 1873). The Wells Fargo scandal represents a distinct challenge to the statement made in this passage.

13. The Supreme Court's line of cases imposing constitutional limits on punitive damages indicates that a penalty award that exceeds compensatory damages by a ratio of 4:1 is close to the constitutional line, and a ratio of 10:1 is presumptively invalid, unless "a particularly egregious act has resulted in only a small amount of economic damages." See *Pacific Mut. Life Ins. Co. v. Haslip*, 499 U.S. 1 (1991); *BMW of North America, Inc. v. Gore*, 517 U.S. 559, 582 (1996); *State Farm Mut. Auto. Ins. Co. v Campbell*, 538 U.S. 408, 425 (2003). But the court upheld a punitive damage award of 526:1 in another case because it involved "a larger pattern of fraud, trickery, and deceit." *TXO Production Corp. v. Alliance Resources Corp.*, 509 U.S. 443, 462 (1993).

14. Although Mike Feuer's capable team would have managed to get a good resolution of the case even on their own, it would have taken much longer and the bank likely would have resisted them at every turn. We had seen a variety of municipal lawsuits against the banks, such as for reverse redlining, get tied up in procedural motions for years or be dismissed for lack of standing, as happened with cities like Baltimore, Cleveland, Chicago, and Miami. Here again, our ability to team up by bringing together different levels and kinds of government authority to pursue a single joint enterprise was powerful, and it was something the CFPB had become very much accustomed to doing over our first five years.

CHAPTER 13

1. These hearings stemmed from the negotiations that occurred on the day of my confirmation vote, when I agreed to certain conditions in discussions with some of the senators. Although they had not been required in the Dodd-Frank Act, nothing prevented the subcommittees from inviting me to testify or me from accepting their invitation, which I had pledged to do. Our chief financial officer, Steve Agostini, accompanied me to these hearings, where we showed that our spending levels

were comfortably within our budget cap and that the details of our spending were reasonable.

2. The bureau unionized in May 2013 by a strong vote of those eligible for membership. As often happens, this created a partner for us to work with to resolve thorny issues about office space and our performance management system. Resolution of those issues also reflected great work by our Office of Minority and Women Inclusion, headed by Stuart Ishimaru, former acting chair of the Equal Employment Opportunity Commission.

3. The controversy over the building renovations was blunted after our inspector general investigated the facts and found the costs of the project to be reasonable. See Federal Reserve IG Report, 2015-FMIC-C-012, "CFPB Headquarters Construction Costs Appear Reasonable and Controls Are Designed Appropriately," July 31, 2015. The inspector general's oversight was always a valuable source of improvements for us. In less than six years, our internal audit team showed our accountability by implementing a total of 122 recommendations concerning all aspects of our operations. This culture of continuous improvement was instilled and embraced by each of our chief operating officers: first Catherine West, then Victor Prince, and finally Sartaj Alag. Our technological independence was key to this progress, and it happened because of persistent work by our chief information officers: successively, Chris Willey, Matthew Burton, Ashwin Vasan, and Jerry Horton. Ashwin also served as one of my special advisers.

4. The structure of the CFPB and its main areas of focus were also well settled by this point, as we laid out in two articles that provided an overview of the workings of the bureau, where I was assisted by Karuna Patel and Morgan Harper. See "Foreword: Consumer Protection in the Financial Marketplace," *Harvard Law and Policy Review* 9 (2015): 307; "Protecting Consumers in the Financial Marketplace: Keynote Address," *University of Chicago Legal Forum* 1 (2013). See also Kelly T. Cochran, "The CFPB at Five Years: Beyond the Numbers," *North Carolina Banking Institute* 21 (2017): 55.

5. Congress typically permits administrative agencies to file enforcement actions either as lawsuits in the courts or as agency actions. Agency actions are heard in the first instance by factfinders known as administrative law judges, whose rulings can then be appealed to the head of the agency. The law sets up processes to create a strict division of functions within the agency to avoid conflicts in handling such matters, and as with court cases, the outcome is ultimately subject to judicial determination if the parties decide to appeal these matters further to a court, as PHH did. The agency's choice of where to file an enforcement action has various pros and cons and gives rise to some strategic considerations. In the bureau's first several years, we rarely had a contested matter that we did not file initially as a court case.

6. The Real Estate Settlement Procedures Act (RESPA) became law in 1974, but both federal and state officials had found it difficult to enforce. Some of the alleged kickback agreements simply rearrange market share, and it is often unclear whether they raise prices or otherwise hurt consumers. A strong reading of the law is that it was intended to prevent any of these kinds of market distortions, but an alternative reading would be that companies like PHH can only be held liable if they are proved to have charged above-market prices for the services they provide.

7. The two main precedents on the constitutional issue, which the court of appeals tried to distinguish, are *Humphrey's Executor v. United States*, 295 U.S. 602 (1935) (involving a member of the Federal Trade Commission), and *Morrison v. Olson*, 487 U.S. 654 (1988) (involving the now-defunct independent counsel). Ironically, the court barely touched on the legal point that produced the $100 million difference in damage awards and had prompted so much attention. Yet the court did reject our judgment that lucrative market share is a "thing of value," holding that PHH could not be held liable under RESPA unless it was proved to have charged above-market prices for the reinsurance services provided by its subsidiary. The Dodd-Frank Act contains a severability clause, which narrowed the scope of the ruling to invalidate only the specific part of the statute being challenged (the removal clause) rather than striking down the entire agency.

8. The vigorous fights that unfolded over each of these rules are recounted more fully in chapter 14.

9. Although the statutes governing independent agency heads may have different wording, they all grant a term of specified length and they all restrict the president's grounds for removing the agency head from office. In the Dodd-Frank Act, the CFPB director is nominated by the president and confirmed by the Senate to serve a term of five years, and is subject to removal by the president only for "inefficiency, neglect of duty, or malfeasance in office," all of which sets a high bar for removal. 12 U.S.C. 5491(c)(3).

10. In this unexpected and unusual situation, our lawyers were very careful in determining what was permissible. Meredith Fuchs, who had served as chief of staff and then as general counsel, had left the bureau by this point, and Mary McLeod had joined us as our new general counsel after more than thirty years of distinguished service at the State Department. Although the circumstances were difficult, the ethics advice they gave me represented the best interests of the bureau and needed to be followed meticulously.

11. As it turned out, many lawsuits were filed in the first years of the Trump administration seeking to enjoin different presidential actions, and many orders were issued granting injunctions against him. But none of these cases had yet transpired, and none involved instances where a court overturned the president's determination to remove someone from office.

12. One sign of the Trump administration's posture on the issue was that the Justice Department switched sides in the case, filing a brief at this stage attacking the constitutionality of the CFPB, whereas the Obama Justice Department had previously defended its constitutionality.

13. The head of the National Economic Council had also served as the point of contact between the White House and the CFPB during the Obama administration when we were working with the Department of Education on student loan debt, with the Department of Defense to protect servicemembers, and with HUD and the Department of Treasury on mortgage market reforms.

14. The constitutionality of the bureau's structure clearly overshadowed any close attention to the statutory issues about improper kickbacks that were the original nub of the case. The case had become widely celebrated at this point, with eleven organizations filing amicus briefs in favor of PHH (including the US Chamber of Commerce and the

American Bankers Association) and seven organizations filing amicus briefs in favor of the CFPB. In January 2018, the full court of appeals decided the case as something of an anticlimax; the court upheld the constitutionality of the CFPB by a vote of seven to three, with seven separate opinions running to a grand total of 250 pages. See *PHH Corp. v. CFPB*, 881 F.3d 75 (D.C. Cir. 2018) (en banc). Notably, all three dissenters on that issue had been members of the original panel that first decided the case, which proved to be a terribly unlucky draw for the bureau. PHH prevailed on the RESPA claims, and no party sought further review, though three of the judges would have found PHH liable based on their reading of the statute, which in some respects mirrored our own interpretations. The constitutional issues remain pending in other cases involving the bureau and seem destined to be determined ultimately by the Supreme Court.

15. Both our legislative team and our legal team were stretched to the breaking point during this period, even though they had been used to consistent pressure from oversight demands from the beginning. We all came to admire their patience and professionalism in the face of constant adversity.

CHAPTER 14

1. A source of substantial harm for many consumers is that banks may reorder transactions, leading to the stacking of multiple overdraft fees in a single day. For example, if a customer (in chronological order) pays for a coffee, for groceries, for gas, and for rent, all in the same day, and the rent payment overdraws the account, the bank might reorder these transactions by processing the rent payment first, causing each of the other three payments to incur overdrafts as well, producing four separate charges. This practice was the target of class action lawsuits that secured some redress and changes in practices. The Federal Reserve also had recently adopted rules to address some overdraft practices, but during my tenure the CFPB researched and considered these issues with a view to possible further regulatory action.

2. The parallel products for deposit accounts, which do not allow overdrafts, are the kinds of safe bank accounts that the Federal Deposit Insurance Corporation and CFPB have promoted, discussed in chapter 10. Under rules adopted by the Federal Reserve prior to the creation of the CFPB, consumers have the choice whether to opt in or opt out of overdraft services on their standard deposit accounts, though opinions vary about the effectiveness of this "choice" mechanism to inform and protect consumers, and how banks may distort it by the ways they implement it. The CFPB sued TCF Bank for allegedly obscuring the fees they charged for overdrafts and making consent to overdraft services seem mandatory, a case that was ultimately resolved jointly with the Office of the Comptroller of the Currency by an order that TCF Bank must pay $25 million in consumer restitution and a $5 million penalty, adopt various conduct provisions, and take steps to remedy harm to consumers from closed accounts and credit reporting issues. We also levied a $10 million penalty against Santander Bank for signing up people for overdraft services without their consent, misleading them into thinking these services were free, and engaging in other deceptive practices. We built on this work by developing "Know Before You Owe" overdraft disclosure prototypes to improve the model form that the banks and credit unions provide to consumers who are deciding whether to opt in for overdraft coverage.

3. These disclosures were an extension of our "Know Before You Owe" project, and our thorough consumer testing of the forms yielded many improvements. We developed both a short-form disclosure to be displayed at the point of sale (with key information so people could comparison shop up front among accounts and related fees) and a long-form disclosure that would be included inside the packaging (with a comprehensive list of fees and other account information).

4. The Congressional Review Act was originally part of the Contract with America and was enacted in 1996. It created a mechanism for overturning federal regulations, which only requires a simple majority vote in both the House and the Senate, as well as presidential approval, though disapproval must occur within specified deadlines. Although the statute had been on the books for two decades, it had only been invoked one time to disapprove a regulation before it came into vogue during the Trump administration.

5. Since the Federal Arbitration Act was passed in 1925, over almost a century of arbitration jurisprudence, the courts have been on quite an odyssey. The earliest decisions reflected a jealous hostility to arbitration as infringing on the power and jurisdiction of the courts. Over time, as the courts found their dockets increasingly clogged, this softened into a posture of neutrality. But for the last few decades, the courts have adopted a stance favoring arbitration as a preferred means of resolving disputes, even as compared to judicial resolution.

6. Group litigation was known in the English common law for centuries and was recognized in the federal courts in the nineteenth-century equity rules. But the foundations of class actions were reformed and solidified when Rule 23 of the Federal Rules of Civil Procedure was overhauled in 1966. Although Congress and the Supreme Court have tightened many components of class actions in recent years, there is no real chance that class actions will be abolished because they enable courts to manage cases where a perpetrator's actions have identical consequences for a mass of victims—cases that are especially prevalent in consumer-facing industries like retail, drugs, autos, insurance, and financial services. And in state courts, it appears that every state except Virginia recognizes class action claims, though some states pose much higher hurdles than others.

7. The practical effect of this change in the law for mortgage loans was less sweeping than it may seem; few mortgage lenders were using arbitration clauses because Fannie Mae and Freddie Mac did not allow them to be included in loans that they purchased. The percentages of customers who were subject to arbitration clauses was much higher in some other markets, such as payday loans and prepaid accounts.

8. The nationwide consumer survey that our team completed was by far the most detailed ever performed on this subject, and even the opponents of the rule relied on its results to argue their case rather than presenting their own alternative data. The final study covered seven markets (credit cards, auto loans, deposits, payday loans, prepaid accounts, student loans, and wireless) where arbitrations occurred.

9. The FSOC was created by the Dodd-Frank Act to identify risks to the financial stability of the United States, promote market discipline, and respond to emerging risks. Its ten voting members consist of the major financial regulators, including the CFPB, and I served on it for almost six years. Uniquely among the other agencies, the CFPB's regulations are subject to disapproval by a two-thirds majority vote of the FSOC if they "would put the safety or soundness of the United States banking system or the stability

of the financial system of the United States at risk." That sets an extraordinarily high bar and thus any scenario in which this would occur is quite implausible.

10. See Kayla Tausche, "Trump Wants to Sack Consumer Protection Chief but Is Afraid of Turning Him into Hero for the Left," CNBC, November 3, 2017. The fact unknown to the reporter of this story was that the White House had gone so far as to place a call to me at the time.

11. This also was the company we hit with a $5 million penalty for destroying documents and otherwise interfering with the bureau's examination process.

12. The colorful facts of our case against the Hydra group are discussed more fully in chapter 6.

13. The same point could be made about the bureau's ability-to-repay mortgage rule. Obviously, if no reforms had taken place in response to that rule, mortgage lending would have plummeted. That could have occurred for various reasons, among them that the new rule banned "no doc" loans and loans underwritten only for a temporary teaser rate rather than over the full life of the loan. If lenders had refused to document the loans they made, or to underwrite them accurately, then their business would have dropped off accordingly, but of course they all made these adjustments. The dire consequences we posited for the industry in the wake of our payday lending rule were based on presuming they made *no* improvements in their lending practices, but there is little chance that would be the lasting outcome.

14. See, for example, Mike Calhoun, "Think There's No Good Alternative to Payday Loans? Think Again," *Washington Post,* June 29, 2016.

15. Although many colleagues took time away from other work to help complete the payday rule, the task would never have gotten done without above-and-beyond efforts by Brian Shearer and Kent Markus.

16. The most recent examples of states with ballot measures are South Dakota, where 76% of the voters approved capping interest rates at 36% in 2016, and Colorado, where 77% of the voters approved the same 36% rate cap in 2018. Before these measures passed, South Dakota's loan rates averaged 652%, whereas Colorado's was 129%. The measures caused almost all payday lenders to leave each state.

CHAPTER 15

1. The Dodd-Frank Act states that the deputy director shall "be appointed by the Director" and shall "serve as acting Director in the absence or unavailability of the Director." 12 U.S.C. 5491(b)(5). Under standard principles of statutory construction, the Dodd-Frank Act, which is both the later and the more specific statute, should prevail over the Vacancies Act, which more generally serves as a default statute that allows the president to install an interim leader in the case of a vacancy where no other process is provided by law. The Justice Department, however, has read the Vacancies Act—perhaps aggressively on behalf of the executive branch— to apply in all situations, regardless of what the agency's governing statute says.

2. See *English v. Trump*, 279 F. Supp. 3d 307 (D.D.C. 2018) (ruling that presidential appointment of the acting CFPB director is a permissible alternative that can supplant the deputy director serving temporarily in that role).

3. See Kevin McCoy, "Mick Mulvaney: Payday Lending Campaign Contributions Pose No Conflicts of Interest," *USA Today*, December 4, 2017. As for the effect of such contributions, Mulvaney was quoted as saying in a speech to the American Bankers Association: "We had a hierarchy in my office in Congress. If you're a lobbyist who never gave us money, I didn't talk to you. If you're a lobbyist who gave us money, I might talk to you." See Diana Hembree, "Mulvaney Is on the Hot Seat for His Stunning 'Pay to Play' Remarks," *Forbes*, April 26, 2018.

4. The largest single resolution in a CFPB enforcement action came against Ocwen Financial Corporation in 2013 for systemic misconduct at every stage of the mortgage servicing process. Ocwen was ordered to provide $2 billion in principal reduction to borrowers who were underwater on their mortgages. The action was taken jointly with the attorneys general of forty-nine states and the District of Columbia.

5. See *Cuomo v. Clearing House Ass'n, L.L.C.*, 557 U.S. 519 (2009).

6. The precise scope of federal preemption of state law under the National Bank Act remains uncertain, though the Dodd-Frank Act may have curbed it further. For a good discussion of these issues, see Adam J. Levitin, "Federalism and Preemption," in *Consumer Finance: Markets and Regulation* (Aspen: Aspen Law and Business 2018). When the CFPB deals with other parts of the federal government, it still runs up against awkward preemption issues that can impede its work, such as the Department of Education's aggressive interference on student loan issues. The department is required to cooperate with the CFPB, but Secretary DeVos terminated the Memorandum of Understanding that had established the framework for such cooperation.

7. See Mike Sorohan, "Mulvaney: Regulation by Enforcement Is 'Done,'" MBA Newslink, October 16, 2018 ("The Bureau is not going anywhere," Mulvaney added. "There is no appetite on Capitol Hill for getting rid of the Bureau. We are here. And as long as we are here, we are going to play an important role in government.").

CHAPTER 16

1. Among the founders, Alexander Hamilton was the leading champion of an energetic executive branch of the government. As he wrote: "Energy in the executive is a leading character in the definition of good government. . . . A feeble executive implies a feeble execution of the government. A feeble execution is but another phrase for a bad execution; and a government ill executed, whatever it may be in theory, must be, in practice, a bad government." Alexander Hamilton, "Federalist No. 70," in *The Federalist Papers* ed. Clinton Rossiter (New York: New American Library, 1961): 423.

2. In a recent Harris poll, 68% of Americans defined themselves as "middle class," while 32% envisioned a time when the middle class would disappear completely, and 24% felt uncertain about its future. The salience of rising economic inequality, and increasing comparisons to the top 1%, are also changing our perceptions of what it means to be part of the middle class. See Emmie Martin, "Nearly 70% of

Americans Consider Themselves Middle-Class—Here's How Many Actually Are," CNBC, September 26, 2018; Melody Hahm, "One-Third of Americans Believe the Middle Class Will Disappear Entirely," Yahoo Finance, September 26, 2018.

3. These principles reflect basic tensions in American life, and the justice of the cause espoused by consumer advocates, who are fighting for honesty, safety, and fair and free competition, is indisputably clear. Although at times the public's concerns are submerged by a flood of corporate power, they always seem to rise again with new movements for reform—whether it be a Square Deal, a New Deal, a Fair Deal, a Great Society, or a New Covenant. The foundations of our democracy are strengthened when people's voices can unite loudly enough to be heard, understood, and followed.

INDEX

For the benefit of digital users, indexed terms that span two pages (e.g., 52–53) may, on occasion, appear on only one of those pages.

31192021970130